I looked up at the trail and there was an NVA walking along. I told Looney. . . "Gooks!"

He told me I was seeing things. I looked again and there were five more men following the first one I saw. The lead man saw us and started to run. I didn't say anything to Looney. I just grabbed both claymore firing devices and squeezed. In a blink of the eye the trail disappeared in a gray-black cloud of exploding C-4 as the claymores spewed their deadly shower of steel balls into the enemy. The rest of the men fired their claymores and more explosions ripped the air. I dropped the clickers, picked up my rifle, and started firing at the bodies on the trail. Over all of the racket I heard Looney saying, "Contact, I say again, the team is in contact, over."

LRRP TEAM LEADER

John Burford

BALLANTINE BOOKS • NEW YORK

A Presidio Press Book
Published by The Random House Publishing Group
Copyright © 1994 by John Burford

Published in the United States of America by Presidio Press, an imprint of The Random House Publishing Group, a division of Random House, Inc., New York, and simultaneously in Canada by Random House of Canada Limited, Toronto.

Presidio Press is a trademark of Random House, Inc.

www.ballantinebooks.com

ISBN 978-0-8041-1051-8

Printed in the United States of America

First Edition: June 1994

THIS BOOK IS DEDICATED TO:

Dr. Patricia E. Davis, English Professor
Kennesaw State College
You rekindled my self-confidence and helped me start
writing again, but more than that, you challenged me.
Every day before I worked on the book,
I would look at the note you wrote to me,
"Let me know when you get it published." Well, here it is.

A VERY SPECIAL THANK YOU TO:

Marsha Burford
Thank you for helping me out during a hard time, and for
the countless hours you spent correcting my terrible
spelling.

Don and Jeannie Harris
Your hours of editing were a great help, and your
encouragement meant a lot to me.

John Looney
For all of the help and tons of encouragement.

Gary Linderer and Kenn Miller
The path is never smooth for the people who go first.
Thank you both for blazing the trail.

PREFACE

In the years after I came home, I lived my life in a way that I thought was normal. When anyone asked me if Vietnam bothered me, I would laugh and tell them no, but I knew something was wrong. There was something missing, and I felt like I had a big hole in me. I had gone through two wives and one girlfriend in the last twenty years, and life was anything but normal.

One day in 1985, I came back to my office to find a note on my desk telling me that *Soldier of Fortune* magazine had called and left me John Looney's phone number. Months earlier, I had made a donation to one of the many causes supported by the magazine, and I made the donation in the name of all the men who served in Company F, 58th Infantry (LRRP), in 1968. I did it hoping someone from the unit would see it and contact me. Don Lynch had started his effort to get the company together, and my name got to him. He called John Looney, and John called *SOF* to get my phone number. The magazine wouldn't give John my number, but they took the time to call my office and pass on John's phone number. I will always be indebted to them for that act of kindness.

I called John, and we decided to meet. I was taking a business trip to Washington, D.C., and I told him that I would swing over to Wheeling Friday afternoon to meet him at his house. I left Atlanta on a Monday morning and started working my way up to Washington. On Thursday, I had a nagging feeling, and I was looking for any good reason to call the trip off and go home. I wanted to see John, yet a large part of me was holding back. I called John Friday morning to let him know I was still coming up, and I could tell by the conversation that John was having the same feelings. I didn't make a special effort to set a time that I would be in Wheeling, and John didn't say that he could get off early and set a time for me to meet him.

It was almost 8:00 P.M. when I pulled up to a gas station to call John and let him know I was in Wheeling. John came over to get me, and we went straight to his house. When we got to the house, John's wife, Gail, came into the room, said "hello" and left. I couldn't help but admire how perceptive she was; she knew we needed to be alone at that time, and she made sure it was that way. We sat on the couch in John's living room and talked. By the third "do you remember," the wall came tumbling down, and it hit both of us like a bright light.

The reason we had felt so much apprehension at meeting was peer rejection. We needed approval for our actions; we needed someone to tell us we did a good job, and all of the wives, girlfriends, family, or counselors in the world couldn't do that. The only person who could give us that approval was a man who had been there with us. I don't mean a person who had been in Vietnam, or even in the same type unit in Vietnam. I mean a man who had stood by your side, who had served with you, and who could say the magic word—you were a good team leader, or radioman, or point man. After John told me he thought I was a good team leader, and I told him he was the best radioman I had served with in the seven years I had been in the army, a wave of relief swept over both of us. The real healing process had started.

I had planned to drop in to visit for an hour or so, and then head back towards Georgia that same night. We quit talking at 4:00 A.M. and went to bed. We got up the next morning at 7:00 A.M. and talked until 4:30 Saturday afternoon. When we wound down, Gail popped back up, and the three of us visited for an hour before I had to leave. The drive home was great, and I set about planning how to see Chambers and Don Harris. John told me that Don Lynch was working on a plan for a reunion of the company in 1986 at Fort Campbell, Kentucky.

June 1986, in the Holiday Inn, Clarksville, there was a

small gathering of Eagles. I stood by the door and watched as the men came into the lobby. The men who hadn't met face-to-face before would come in slowly, and I could understand what they felt. I guess it was best summed up by Command Sergeant Major Burnell. He got to fly over to Fort Campbell with the XVIII Airborne Corps commander and parachute in. Later that afternoon, the Corps commander told Burnell to go to his reunion, and had a couple of his men bring Burnell over in a jeep. Burnell and his escort came into the lobby of the Holiday Inn, and he was mobbed by a double handful of lurps. He was hugged, mugged, and given a beer, and when he turned around and told the young soldiers that brought him over that they could go back to their barracks, he was home now, I knew we had made it.

We have a get-together every year, when we can, and I go as often as I am able. I have seen some wonderful things happen to me and to some of the others. There is a small core of us who have drawn close, and we know that with each meeting, we will pull more of our friends together. Today, the saying "Lurps don't leave Lurps behind" is as strong as it ever was under fire.

If you are a Vietnam veteran, go find your buddies—it can be done—meet with them. Remember, they have your ticket home in their hands.

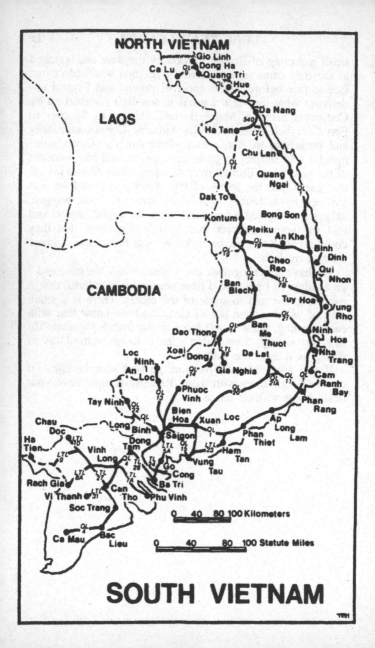

NORTH VIETNAM

Gio Linh
Ca Lu • • Dong Ha
QL • Quang Tri
9 • Hue
QL

LAOS

• Da Nang
540
Ha Tang LTL
QL
14 Chu Lan•

Quang
Ngai
QL

Dak To•

Kontum• Bong Son•

Pleiku
QL • An Khe
19
Binh
Cheo Dinh
Reo
CAMBODIA Qui
Ban LTL Nhon
7B
Biech•

Tuy Hoa•
QL Vung
Ban 21 Rho
Dao Thong• Me
QL Thuot Ninh•
14 Hoa
Xoai Da Lat Nha
Loc • Dong• Trang
Ninh LTL
An 78
Loc• • Gia Nghia Cam
QL Ranh
14 QL QL QL Bay
•Phuoc 20 21A 11
Vinh Phan
Rang
Tay Ninh QL • Loc Ap
22 Bien Xuan• Long
Chau Hoa QL Lam
Doc Long • Saigon 1 Phan
Ha • QL Binh LTL QL Thiet
Tien 10 Dong 5A 15 Ham
LTL Vinh Tam Tan
9 Long QL LTL
Rach • TL 23
Gia LTL Go Vung
8A TL Cong• Tau
LTL Ba Tri
27 Can •
Vi Thanh• Tho •Phu Vinh
LTL
37
Soc Trang•

0 40 80 100 Kilometers

0 40 80 100 Statute Miles
Ca Mau• •Bac
Lieu

SOUTH VIETNAM

TRH

CHAPTER 1

I always jump when my name is called on a PA system, and this time was no different. I don't think I will ever get used to being paged. I finished my conversation with George Reed, we shook hands, and I walked up to the show office. I told the girl behind the desk that I was John Burford. She said she had an important message for me, and handed me a slip of paper. I took it, said thanks, and went out to the hallway. Written on the paper was—It's Friday, call C. D. Burford at work NOW!!—I headed for the pay phones lining the wall to call my brother. He wanted to know why I hadn't called earlier in the week. I said I was sorry but I had gotten busy and the time just got away from me. I told him I had everything under control and I'd be leaving the show in about two hours. He wanted to be sure I could get to Newark, so I ran it down for him again. I'd take the bus to La Guardia Airport, catch the airport shuttle over to the Newark Airport, and call him when I got to Newark so he could come and pick me up. We said good-bye, and I hurried back to the floor of the show to see a few more friends before I left.

I was excited. I hadn't seen my brother and his family in five years, and this show had worked out just right. When I heard Butch Lahmann, the owner of American Specialty, was having a truck accessory and 4X4 trade show in New York City, I knew I could take some time to visit with my brother. I'd been looking forward to getting to his house all week, and to make sure I had the time to visit after the show, I booked a Saturday afternoon flight back to Georgia.

I had been a "manufacturer's representative" for six years, and trade shows were always a busy time. I went

1

back to the hospitality room to see who was still around before I headed back to the booth. I had three booths to visit before I could leave the show, but I worked the eight southern states, and I didn't expect to see very many of my customers up here. What I needed to do was get in touch with more people who made 4X4 accessories, and this was the best time to do it. The two hours till closing time went by quickly, but I managed to see the people I needed to see. When the show closed, I went to the hospitality room, got my suitbag, and headed out for the bus to La Guardia Airport.

We got to La Guardia after an hour of traffic and bumps. Now I know that every time they fill a pothole in any part of America, the hole is sent to New York City. After I quit bouncing, I got my bags and set out to find the shuttle bus for the Newark airport. I quickly found out that the only difference between the ride to La Guardia and the ride to Newark was that it took longer to get to Newark.

I settled down in my seat and gazed out the window at the traffic and the skyline of the city. Slowly I let my mind take a walk through the hallways of my memory. It was 1980, and I had been home eleven years, yet the images were still sharp and clear. All of the faces came back to me, so young and so brave. We were children, but war is for children. Immortal, bold, bulletproof, fearless children; we were all of that, and then some. We laughed in the face of Mister Death every time we met him, yet with each meeting, a small part of us died; we came home old men. To this day, I still hold one little bit of truth close to my heart—it is better to kill than to die.

I was still mentally in Vietnam when the shuttle bus finally got to Newark. I got my bags and called my brother to pick me up at the airport. He drove us to the house, and was I in for a surprise—the three little boys weren't little anymore. David showed me to my room and helped me hang up my suits. Then he asked if I had brought the books and photo albums. I assured him I had brought all the photos and books about Vietnam that I owned, and I asked him if he had gotten the beer he'd promised. He took me downstairs, opened the refrigerator with a flourish, and showed me twenty-four beers, neatly stacked, ice-cold, and waiting. I knew I'd have to keep my end of the deal and tell him and the kids about the time I had spent in Vietnam.

My sister-in-law, Debbie, fixed a great meal, and after dinner, David and the boys headed to the living room while I went upstairs for my photo albums and books. When I got back downstairs, the coffee table was cleared, and a beer was waiting. I knew this would be a difficult job for me. I still hadn't come to grips with the war, and I wasn't sure I knew how to tell the story or how to clean it up to make it suitable for the kids. I laid out the photo albums, my 101st Airborne 1968 yearbook, and took a long pull on my beer.

Then I told my brother I was going to tell the story the way it happened, and if I slipped into the language of the time, then the boys might hear some new words. Also, I wanted to remind him that I had killed a few people over there, and told him that if he saw a problem with that, he needed to let me know. He told me they wanted to hear it like it was, and I could tell the story any way I wanted.

I told him I thought I'd tell them a little bit about the unit, our mission, equipment, and some of the people. Then I'd throw it open to questions. I thought that by answering questions it would be easier for me to keep the story rolling, and get to the points that were of interest to them.

I won't spend any time on the history of the war or how it got started. The Good Lord knows there are enough books on that time in history. Besides, in twenty or thirty years, all of the thinking about the war will have changed, and the history will change with it. A hundred years from now, no one will care about what happened, or why. I only hope that somewhere down the line, the men who had to fight the war get a better shake in life than they do now.

Another point I want to make is the fact that I am going to tell the story straight. We're family, and I don't see a need to embellish the story. Besides, the truth is stranger than fiction. Every man did the best he could, and that was all I asked of my men. I was well trained, and I did my job. When it was time to come home, I did. I put my pants on one leg at a time, just like every other man in the world, but I may have been luckier than most. I always say that I used up all of my good luck just staying alive.

I was sent to Bien Hoa in early July 1968, and reported to the 101st replacement unit. I'll never forget standing in front of that orderly room. I was a sergeant, so when the temporary hooch assignments were made, I was sent to the NCO barracks, right behind the orderly room. I got my bag and followed the path around to the hooch. I was walking toward the door of my hooch when a sergeant came out of the hooch beside mine. I looked at him, and he looked familiar. I glanced at his name tag to see if I could catch his name. He said, "Hey, Burford, what are you doing here?"

I looked back up, and sure enough, it was Jack D. Giboney. Jack and I had been privates together in A Company, 1\506, in 1962. I told him I was just coming in country and was here for SERTS (Screaming Eagle Replacement Training School). He told me to drop my bag and go have a beer with him. We talked for a long time, and he told me I needed to be in the 101st's long-range reconnaissance patrol company. He had served with them before being assigned as an instructor to the SERTS program. Jack had some wild tales, and he had trained with the Aussies' Special Air Service in 1967. I told him the idea sounded good to me, and I would love to go to the LRRPs. Jack said he would fix it right up.

The next morning, I finished in-processing and was sent to the SERTS area to draw weapons and field gear. SERTS was a five-day training program where division combat vets trained the new guys in the tricks of the trade and got them ready to join their combat units. During SERTS, we got up at 0400 hours for PT and spent the rest of the day in classes. We were taught ambush, grenade throwing, walking point, and other combat skills. It also was a good time to get the new men used to the heat and to help them accept the fact that they were in Vietnam.

The first morning of SERTS started with PT and a three-mile run. By 0730 hours, we were seated in the classroom waiting for the instructor. My name was called, and I reported to the NCO in charge, who was standing at the rear of the room. I was pulled out of SERTS and sent to a special five-day school that trained the division's E-4s and E-5s in small-unit leadership. All of the men in the class had at least six months of combat time, and they would be taking over squads and platoons when they were sent back up north to their units. I was the first new guy to attend that school instead of SERTS.

The leadership course was good, and the instructors took a no-bull approach to training. Most of our work was on adjusting artillery, calling in helicopters, directing air strikes, map reading, and ambushing. The men helped me and worked with me in every way. I know I picked up some good ideas from them. We did most of our training at Bien Hoa Air Base, and we trained outside the berm, a twelve-foot-high earthen levee that went completely around the air base.

This was War Zone D, and there were VC everywhere. The first time I got shot at was on the third day of the school. We were on the berm, learning to adjust artillery fire. They had me and another sergeant up on the berm, spotting the rounds, while the rest of the class was at the bottom of the berm, calling in the corrections. I heard a noise that sounded like someone's snapping his fingers over my head. The sergeant with me dove off the berm, but I just stood there, wondering why he did that. A long furrow appeared in the dirt next to my foot, and some of the dirt hit my leg. The lieutenant who was giving the class was hollering for me to get down. I looked at the mark in the dirt next to my foot and understood why the other sergeant had jumped. I made a graceless dive off the berm and landed at his feet. He asked me if I was hit, and I told him no. Then he asked me why I took so long to get down, and I told him I didn't realize anyone was shooting.

The last night of school was a night patrol out to set up an ambush in the Michelin rubber plantation. The Bien Hoa Air Base was in the middle of the plantation, and the engineers had bulldozed and leveled every tree for miles around to stop the VC from setting up mortars within range of the base. We were to go out eight hundred meters and set up the ambush. The ground was plowed, and trees were lying everywhere. It took four hours just to get to the ambush site. The VC never did come by, but they sent their best friend, the Vietnamese mosquito. By daybreak, the score was mosquito: ten, Burford: zero, but I did learn a great lesson; one bottle of bug juice wasn't enough.

The next day I went back to the SERTS area and got my orders to Company F, Airborne, 58th Infantry (LRRP), which was attached to the 101st Airborne Division. I was assigned to the company in July 1968. The 101st was stationed at Camp Eagle, between Hue and Phu Bai, in the northern part of South Vietnam. Company F was a long-range reconnaissance patrol unit, hence the designation LRRP used with the company name. Every infantry division in Vietnam had a LRRP company, and there were two LRRP companies with over two hundred men each assigned to the Field Force headquarters down south. The unit was supposed to have four officers, twenty-five noncommissioned officers (NCOs) and eighty-six enlisted men, but we were never up to full strength.

Our primary mission was long-range reconnaissance patrols, and that's what made our company and our mission different. In most cases, when a regular army unit pulled a reconnaissance patrol, it was for a few hours, and the patrol worked the local area. Our company pulled patrols up to six days long, and sometimes it would be ten or more miles to the closest friendly troops. All of our missions were deep in hostile territory, and we normally had a six-man team or smaller. Our secondary missions were small ambushes, bomb-damage assessment, and when needed, downed-pilot rescue. The small size of our teams and the fact that we operated in the NVA's backyard made our mission much easier. The enemy never booby-trapped his secure areas, so we could work the trails and not have to worry about booby traps or enemy security. The NVA were used to dealing with large American units crashing around in the jungle, and telling the world they were coming with a two-hour artillery bombardment. We just slipped in, did our job, and slipped out. The NVA hated us, and there were standing rewards offered for LRRP teams. We heard there was a fifteen-thousand-dollar reward for a team leader and a ten-thousand-dollar reward for any other team member. This sure did make the team members mad because they all knew they were worth more than a team leader. But we were glad someone thought we were worth something, even if it was the North Vietnamese Army.

The standard team had a team leader, assistant team leader, senior radio operator, second radio operator, senior scout, and scout. At times, we combined teams to come up with a twelve-man team for an ambush or a superhot operation area. Once, I had four lurps and one combat photographer out on a four-day mission. The photographer was glad to get out of the woods at the end of that mission. I have a few of the pictures he took, and he was a darn good photographer, but I was glad I never had to find out if he'd have made a good lurp. On another mission, we were short men, so the platoon medic said he would go as a filler. Since he was a conscientious objector, I told him he couldn't go. When he asked why, I told him there would only be four of us, and if we got hit, I would need every man to have a rifle. He looked at me, smiled, and told me he was in Nam, so what difference did it make? We got him a rifle and showed him how to use it. He did fine on the mission, and went on more missions after I left.

We were called "lurps," and it was a nickname for us. We used that word to describe any number of functions like lurp over to the PX instead of walk over to the PX. If a team was in the field, they were lurping. Our freeze-dried meals were lurp rations, and if you lurped something, that meant to borrow it. You didn't sneak up on someone, you lurped up on him. I still use the word occasionally, and I get some strange looks.

We had some special equipment, but nothing superexotic. Special units were allowed to wear camouflage uniforms, and ours were either a tiger-stripe pattern or a random leaf pattern that we called flower powers. We wore the flower powers most of the time because the VC and the NVA had tiger-stripe uniforms, too. It made the chopper pilots very nervous to land and pick up a group of men with no helmets, no U.S. rucksacks, carrying nonstandard weapons, and wearing tiger stripes.

I carried a regular-issue M-16 rifle that I called my Georgia long rifle. Most of the men had the short version of the M-16 called a CAR-15. I liked the long version and believed it was more accurate than the shorty. The supposed difference in accuracy didn't make any difference since most of our shoot-outs were done within twenty meters or less. There were a few twelve-gauge riot guns around, and two M-79 grenade launchers with their stocks cut down to a pistol grip so they'd fit in the rucksack. We had other weapons such as Sten guns with silencers and AK-47s. The 5th Special Forces had Forward Operations Base (FOB) 1 at Phu Bai, which was C & C Group North (Command and Control Group North—CCN). They controlled the Special Observation Group or SOG teams, and we'd visit with them to bum special equipment. Four of our men were going to transfer to the SOG detachment, but changed their minds after seeing all of the pictures of the unit's MIAs that lined the wall. Outside the air force, SOG had the most MIAs during the war.

All of our men carried extra medical gear, including one can of albumin blood expanders. We had to be our own medics, and we had more first-aid training than regular troops. During Recondo School, every man had to draw blood from another man so we would know how to start the albumin. The team leader carried the morphine shots, a bottle of dextroamphetamine tablets, and an army field-suture kit. We could handle just about any medical problem if we had the time.

We used a South Vietnamese–issue rucksack on a cut-down U.S. Army pack frame, and it was big enough to carry our meals and sleeping cover and such. We didn't need the large army-issue rucksack because we didn't have to live out of it for weeks on end, the way the line doggies did. The load-bearing equipment, LBE for short, was standard issue, and we just hung more junk on it. We turned in our steel helmets and flak jackets when we got to the company; we didn't need that equipment in the LRRP.

The food was great, and we could trade one of our LRRP meals for four of the regular C rations. The lurp meals were freeze-dried, and we had nine different meals.

The army did a good job with the lurps—meals like beef stew, beef and rice, pork and scalloped potatoes, chili, chicken stew, and others. We had sweets with every meal: orange-flavored cornflake bars, fruitcake bars, fudge, and tropical chocolate disks. And to drink, we had cocoa beverage powder or coffee. I liked the orange-flavored cornflake bar; it was good in the morning with a packet of cocoa beverage powder.

It was the people that made the unit, and we had plenty of good people, and a few bad ones. Right after I got in country, the company commander, Captain Sheperd, stepped on a land mine and lost part of his foot. The major problem with that was the land mine was planted at the entrance to his tent. There was a real stink raised about that, and later the army's CID (Criminal Investigation Division) spent a few days with us. Every member of the company was judged crazy after the army psychological profiles were drawn up.

The company got a new commander, Capt. Ken Eklund, a West Pointer on his second tour in Vietnam, and he had asked to be our CO, which was a surprise in light of our bad name after the Sheperd incident. Eklund was a fair man, and once we had his trust and he knew we could function in the field, he let us do our job with no hassles. Most of us felt we could depend on him if we got into deep trouble. He even let me pick some of the areas I patrolled and do all of the planning. More than once, he put his ass on the line for us in both the field and at headquarters. We all knew his primary job was to get the company working or to disband the unit and scatter the men across the division.

It always struck me as funny that no matter how large or small a unit was, we only really got to know the people we worked with, and in Vietnam, it wasn't any different. In the LRRP, life revolved around your platoon and your team. I was in the 2d Platoon, and I can't recall much of anything about the 1st Platoon; it was as if we were in two different worlds. As time wore on and the manpower shrunk, we shifted some men, but still, there were plenty of good men that I never got to go to the field with.

R. C. Burnell was my platoon sergeant and, at times, my acting first sergeant. I liked that man, and if bull hockey were bucks, he would have been rich. We use to go to the club for a drink and he would get mad at the REMFs (the rear echelon guys) because they didn't show enough respect for brave fighting men. The first thing he'd do is pull down the electric light line and bite it in two, then he'd eat the light bulb. In just a matter of seconds, we'd have a large section of the club for lurps only. He was on his second tour in Vietnam, and he would be in the army as long as they would have him.

I was a sergeant (E-5) when I came in country, so they gave me to S.Sgt. (E-6) Philip Byron. I was his assistant team leader on Team 9. Byron was on his second tour in Vietnam. His first tour was with the 1st Cavalry Division in 1965 and 1966. He had fought in the battle of the Ia Drang Valley and had seen plenty of combat. He was a good teacher, and I learned a lot from him. I never saw him panic, and I picked that up from him. I figured any man that had been through all he had would know when it was time to panic. There were a few times when I thought *this* was the right time, but he stayed cool. When I got my team, and we got in trouble, I would think about him and keep my cool.

Sp5. Bruce Proctor was the company medic, but he spent so much time as the operations man that most of us forgot his real job. He was a first-class belly man on the helicopter, and you could count on him to get you in or out. I would bet that Proctor had more bullets fired at him than any other man in the unit. On every hot extraction, the enemy spent most of their effort on trying to knock the helicopter down. I guess the gooks liked to watch the chopper hit the ground.

Sp4. Don Lynch was the company driver. A good kid who would do anything to help us live better. He ended up going out with some teams when we were low on men. He could lurp better than he could drive.

The radio-relay men were our link with the tactical operations center (TOC), and we had some of the best. They were always on duty when a team was in the field. There were many missions when the radio-relay team was put on a hilltop with a small security guard, and they spent six days on around-the-clock radio watch. The radio men had to keep the handset to their ears on the night watch because if a team got in trouble at night, they almost always had to whisper or signal by keying the handset. The relay team was under real pressure during a fire mission. If they made a mistake relaying just one number, the wrong people could die. In the heat of combat, the excitement level was the same, whether men were dealing lead or relaying radio messages. The man on the spot had to be in control.

Most of the men on the teams were really kids, eighteen to twenty-one years old. At twenty-five, I was an old man, but I had an attitude that worked well with the men, and we got along fine. We used a lot of machismo to ward off fear and keep some grasp on basic sanity. We had nicknames, I was Honest John, Larry Chambers was Killer Man, Don Harris was G. T., John Looney was Joe Don, and Meszaros was Mezoo. Our team was called the "Death Makers," a name that came from the Airborne tattoo on my leg. I had business cards printed for the whole company, with space to put your name on the front and anything you wanted on the back. We even had the Doctor Death Maker kit, with special fuses and booby-trap devices for field use. You need to remember that, to pull these long range patrol missions, the army was sending a few men out into the jungle for six days, with no friendly troops anywhere near, so we needed all the hype we could scrape up to keep going back out.

We didn't take officers on missions. A LRRP team was made up of a sergeant E-5 with five other men, grade E-4 or below. Most of the men had less than a year and a half in the army. I was lucky, I'd been in seven years. I'd been to all types of schools and had years of small-unit leadership, map reading, demolitions, patrolling, and related subjects. The time and training paid off in the field, and my teams pulled some great missions. From mid-September until the end of December 1968, we were so short on NCOs that teams were being lead by E-5s with less than two years active duty, and they had to learn how to lead through on-the-job training. Yet in spite of everything, they pulled good missions and brought home the bacon. The LRRP company had one of the highest kill rates and the lowest casualty rate in the 101st Airborne Division.

There was one thing about being a lurp that still haunts me to this day—it was an awesome power trip for a young man. We had all this power in our hands. Once the team was on the ground, the team leader was it; he was in charge, he called the shots, and he had, at his call, all the support and firepower the army could muster. The responsibility of being a team leader was a heavy load, and it rested on some young shoulders. We weren't going out on a holiday trip. The missions were real; there were people out there who wanted to kill you. One mistake, one moment of panic, and six people would cease to exist. Everybody depended on their teammates, and there wasn't any room for a jerk.

In an infantry company, it took an officer to call an air strike, and an officer or ranking NCO to direct artillery fire. Lurp's, rank E-5 and E-4, had that responsibility on a team mission. If a team was in contact, the team leader made the decision to stay on the ground and continue the mission or to have the team extracted. The CO knew the team leader was the man on the spot, and backed him. All of this power was at our fingertips in the form of the radio, and if we needed help, we just keyed the handset. We had a special deal with the army. We knew we couldn't get reinforcements if we got into contact with an enemy force, but they would bust their butts to get artillery, gunships, or air strikes to us. After that, it was up to us to save ourselves.

On one mission, we had the battleship *New Jersey* fire in support of a team. Twice, we had teams come back from heavy contact to find the 17th Cav's commander waiting to welcome them back. Once, when I got back from an overflight, the company commander sent me over to the artillery battalion that was firing support for us. What a trip; the Huey flew me over to the firebase, and the artillery battalion commander met me at the pad. He took me in to meet all of the people in the fire direction control center, and he waited while I coordinated the fire for the coming mission with the fire-control chief. We went from the FDC to the firing battery, and I met the battery commander. The battery commander took me to meet all of the firing crews, and I got to tell them how much we appreciated the good fire support. I was treated like a VIP, and I loved it.

There was a dark side to being a lurp. It just wasn't natural for men to go out on missions of the kind we did, and we had to use a lot of psychological mumbo jumbo to keep going back. Some of the things we lost were the social and moral taboos against killing. They were stripped away from us by the need to survive. Killing became all right; it was good, and for doing it well, we were looked up to by our peers and praised by our superiors. If we got into trouble ("contact"), the solution was to inflict the maximum amount of destruction on our antagonizers and kill them. Swift violence and killing became the solutions of choice. Once the moral and social taboos were stripped away, they couldn't be glued back on. I think of it like a fine china plate; if you break it, you can glue it back together, but it's never again the same. To this day, if I get pushed back into a corner, a calm feeling comes over me as I accept the fact that I am going to do whatever is needed to whoever is bothering me. I now go out of my way to steer clear of trouble.

There was another problem many of the guys had. When our tour in Vietnam was up, we each came back home to being a nobody, and that played with our heads. When I left Vietnam, I was a respected and valuable member of a fighting team. I came home to being just another shipping clerk at Lockheed. Once we had tasted the power, felt the pride and the sense of belonging, we were never the same again. I guess the men I really felt sorry for were the black medics. In any unit, the medic was respected. In a combat unit, the medic was respected, looked up to, and taken care of. We called them "Doc," and there was a bond between the medics and the men they served. They would come home, and within hours, they would go from being called Doc to being called field nigger. They deserved better than that, but they didn't get it.

There was one solid rule in the company. We couldn't allow a personality clash on a team. If there was a problem, all we had to do was go to Sergeant Burnell and state our case. It could be the team leader or a team member, rank made no difference. We were too dependent on each other to allow bad feelings to linger. If a man on my team went to Burnell and said he didn't want to go out with me, he would be put on a new team that same day. No one would think or say anything about it. Likewise, I could refuse to take with me a man I didn't want to have in the field. We were all volunteers, and that carried all the way through the operation.

"Now, that's all of the background storytelling I am going to do. The floor will be open to any and all questions as soon as I go to the kitchen to get another beer."

CHAPTER 2

I came back into the room, sat down, and popped the top on my beer.

"Okay, who has the first question?"

Everyone was quiet for a minute, then my brother decided to start it off.

"John, what were the living conditions like back at Camp Eagle when you weren't out on a mission?"

I sat quietly for a minute and gathered my thoughts. A hundred pictures ran through my mind and I tried to put them into some kind of order. Then an idea struck me, and I reached over and picked up my photo album. Here was a way to answer the questions, and the pictures would get things in the proper order. The pictures were taken in both the old company area and the new company area that we moved into during September 1968. With the photos, they could see for themselves how we lived. I also had my 101st Airborne, first-year pictorial review. This was a yearbook that the division NCO club had put together for the troops. Every trooper who was with the division from December 1967 to December 1968 was mailed one. With my pictures and the yearbook, I knew I could get the story right.

The first picture I came to was the one of my tent in the old company area.

When Camp Eagle was built, it was laid out in the middle of the burial ground for the city of Hue. Our area was near the main PX, on the perimeter wire that made up the outer defense line for the camp. The perimeter wire was a double-apron barbed-wire fence, with three rolls of concertina wire stacked on it. We built two sandbag bunkers near

15

the wire to give us weapons' fire coverage of the wire line. In case of attack, our men were to get to the bunkers and stop the enemy in the wire. We had the bunkers manned every night with machine-gun crews on alert. Bunker guard was one of those rear-area details we all hated.

The engineers had come in with their bulldozers and dug holes in the ground, about four feet deep and sloped at the end so we could get in and out easily. Our GP (general-purpose) tents were put up over the holes, and the walls were rolled up to ground level. We then built sandbag walls about two feet high around each tent. The tent would only hold fourteen men because the sloped end took up some of the room. We set our folding cots along the dirt wall on each side of the hole and left an aisle down the center. Everyone slept with his head near the dirt wall and his feet toward the aisle. The tent was set up to give us some protection from the blast of a 122mm rocket or a mortar round hitting near the tent. If a missile should hit the tent, being in the hole made it easier to find all the pieces to send home. Our tent was on a hillside, with one end open, so we closed it with a blast wall made of sandbags.

We had a real problem when it rained. The holes would fill up with water, in just a few minutes. There was a drain hole in the sandbag wall, but it would always clog, and in no time at all, we would be floating. We got pallets from the PX to line the bottom of the hole and keep us up out of the mud. My home was two pallets placed end to end, with my cot on top of them. We all had mosquito nets on a wooden frame over the cots, and we hung our LBE from the bars. The rest of our equipment was kept under the cot, with our rucksack, waterproof bag, and rifle at one end, and water jug, and cases of soda or beer at the other. I bought a footlocker made from wood the Vietnamese scrounged from our empty artillery ammo boxes. It wasn't much, but it worked, and I could lock it. The footlocker was near the head of my bunk.

When we went on a mission, we always put everything on the cot, in case of rain. There were times when all the men in the tent would be out on missions, and the radio-relay men would forget to check the drain. We'd come back to wet cots and damp gear. We could tell how much rain fell while we were gone by the high-water marks on the legs of our cots.

We always kept a few cases of beer and a case of soda on hand because we never knew when the PX would run out. Once, there was a strike by the overworked longshoremen's union back in the States. We ran completely out of beer and were down to Orange Crush for soda. After the strike ended, it still took another twenty days for new supplies to reach Camp Eagle. To this day, I still can't look an Orange Crush in the face.

There was never any ice, so we learned to drink it all—beer, soda, Kool-Aid, and water—hot. In September, the Seabees built an ice plant for Camp Eagle, and each company was allowed one fifty-pound block every three days. Someone lurped an old chest-type cooler, which we put in a clubhouse we'd built down by our helipad. To stock the club with beer and soda, we pooled our money and sold a few captured AK-47s to the REMFs. Then we sold the drinks back to ourselves and used the profit to keep the club stocked. The first stop after a mission was the club, and the first drink was always free for the returning lurps.

The old company area lacked any type of latrine. There was a two-hole outhouse by the aviation unit that we were attached to, and a lime pit down by the leech pond. To clean up, we had an open-air shower, which was little more than a wooden rack holding a canvas bag with a screw-on shower head. The shower was a gift from the Australian SAS (Special Air Service, i.e., commando) troopers who trained some of the men in the early LRRP units. (A select few men had gone to the jungle warfare school in Malaysia that was run by the SAS.) When it was time to shower, we took our five-gallon water jug over to the water trailer, came back and filled the canvas bag, then got under the shower head. A little water to soap up, followed by a quick rinse, had to get the job done. I had a small plastic basin from the PX for my daily shave and wash time, and I kept it with our five-gallon water jug under my cot.

We washed our uniforms by hand until the Seabees built a laundry at Camp Eagle. After that, we just used the QM laundry and sent our wash off once a week. There never was much laundry to do since we didn't use underwear, and when we were on a mission, we didn't change uniforms. Sometimes our whole week's laundry was six pair of dirty socks and one ripe flower-power uniform.

The PX was good, and we could get snacks, beer, soda, books, and most of the items we could want in the middle of a war. The stock came in cycles; one time all they'd have was Coke, then the next time it would be Pepsi. We could get radios and tape recorders, and we could order all types of gifts from a PX mail-order catalog. There was also a barber shop with ten chairs. With only one type of haircut offered, the line moved fast. We had a couple of open-air movies around Eagle, and there were movies every night. We could go to the movie close to our new company area, and during the movie, we could watch the NVA probe the Marine outpost. We'd see red tracers out, green tracers in, and most times the firefights were better than the flick.

A bunch of us went to see *The Good, the Bad, and the Ugly*. I loved that movie, and Ken Munoz had the sound-track album. I got the psychological warfare guys to make a tape of the main movie theme and the tune "Ecstasy of Gold." When my team was on a mission in an area we called the Game Preserve and had made contact with an NVA force, the psywar chopper flew over and played the music, followed by a Vietnamese telling the NVA to give up or be killed in the night by the lurps. I don't know how the gooks felt about the music, but it scared the heck out of me.

Both Hue and Phu Bai were off-limits to the 101st, so there was no such thing as going to town, but we were allowed to go to the beach as a treat. My team was sent to the beach in December, and we had to go by truck. The 17th Cav used to lend us a chopper to fly to the beach, but on the last trip, the Old Man talked the pilot into letting him fly the Huey. Captain Eklund had a few hours of flight time, but when he took off, the ship had a mechanical failure and crashed three feet from the takeoff point. The helicopter had seventy-six hours of flight time, and it was totaled. Bits and pieces of the helicopter were scattered everywhere. One large section of the main rotor blade hit the team debriefing tent and tore half the tent away. We had two police calls through the company area to find all of the parts. There was an official hearing about the crash, and two warrant officers had to explain why a nonrated individual was in the command seat of the Huey. Which was why, when *we* got to go to the beach, my team had to go by truck.

The trip was one-and-a-half hours long, and we had to go through the city of Hue to get to the beach. Before we left, the Old Man got the truck driver, Don Lynch, and me together and told us that we were to go straight to the beach. Lynch was not to take us to Hue; we were to come straight back from the beach, and we were to be in the company area by 2000 hours. Since we would be on the road, we had to carry our weapons and a basic load of ammunition.

The team had a good supply of beer and whiskey, and I know the heads had some smoke. We were off to have some well-earned fun. A ferry run by the navy took us over to the beach area, and we arrived without incident. We swam, played ball, drank, ate, drank, and drank some more. By two in the afternoon, a few individuals decided it was time to liberate Hue. Lynch stood fast, saying he wouldn't drive us to Hue, so to save him from the wrath of mad lurps and the wrath of the Old Man, I drove the truck. I was in charge; I was drunk. They were my men, and I felt they deserved to see Hue. We took the ferry to the mainland and hit the town in a rush. I had run out of beer, so I stopped and got a few hot beers from a roadside vendor. Those who wanted to get laid, got laid, and those who wanted to get drunker, got drunker. To avoid the MPs, we drove the truck up and down the side streets of Hue. It's hard to hide a two-and-a-half-ton army truck anywhere, but on the side streets of Hue, you could hide anything.

It was near 1700 hours, and the MPs were closing in on us, so we decided to get out of Hue. We headed back to the beach to get the men who had stayed behind with Don. When we got to the ferry, the navy guy took us over to the beach, and then he started to leave. I stopped him and asked where the heck he was going. He told me the ferry quit running at 1700 hours, and he was taking the ferry back to the berth. I told him he was wrong, he was going to wait for me to get the rest of my men. We had to be at Camp Eagle by 2000 hours. He started to give me some lip, so I loaded my M-16 and told him he could either wait or die. I left Miller and Chambers to tell him war stories while I went back to get the rest of the men.

Lynch was hopping mad when we pulled up, but when I fell out of the truck and couldn't get up, he decided to cool off and drive back to Camp Eagle. We stopped at the ferry, loaded up Miller and Chambers, and crossed safely back to the mainland. The sailor wished us a safe trip and said he enjoyed Miller's war stories. On the way out of town, I had to have one more beer, and I was griping so loud that Lynch stopped at a roadside stand to shut me up. I got down off the truck and fell face first into the rice paddy that was behind the stand. I got up, and everyone was laughing at me, so I wheeled around to say something to Looney, and fell backward into the same spot. The men got down and helped me back into the back of the truck. I was covered with paddy muck, so they made me sit at the very back of the truck. They did get me a last hot beer, and when I started to talk about seeing gooks everywhere, they took my M-16 away from me. I don't remember the rest of the trip back to Camp Eagle. I woke up the next morning outside my hooch, still covered with paddy mud. Even my toes had a hangover.

Late in August, the Seabees were starting to build our new company area. They had moved us to a new defensive position on the far side of Camp Eagle, and we now faced the mountains. Nui Khe stood out on the horizon, and we knew it was a stronghold for the NVA. We had new hooches that were above ground. They had screens and plywood floors but we still had to use the GP tents for the roof. They sure beat sleeping in the holes, and when it rained, we didn't float. The Seabees built us a big eight-hole latrine, with a separate shower that had water heaters, and a place to brush our teeth and wash up. When we were lucky, and the operations people remembered to light the water heaters, we could get a hot shower when we came back from the field. The new latrines made for a new problem. Each hole had a quarter of a fifty-five gallon drum under it to catch the waste. To keep everything sanitary, we had a daily waste-burning detail—people on the detail would pull out the cutoff drums, add fuel oil to the waste, light it, and stir it until it was burned to ash. That was the theory, but it failed in practice—the waste wouldn't burn up, or no one would stay around to stir it, or something; it just didn't work. After about a month, the mess was out of hand, and the Old Man told Sergeant Burnell to get a detail to clean up the latrines. My team was on stand-down, so we got the shaft. I had the men dig a big hole down by the wire, and we dumped all 110 gallons of human waste, burnt paper, and fuel oil in the hole and covered it up. The hole was too small and the ground too wet; the mess stayed there, and the dirt we covered it with never packed down. You could go down to the hole weeks later and hit the ground with a shovel, and the ground would roll with a wavelike motion. A million years from now, someone will find that pit, study its contents, and try to tell about life in the twentieth century.

The new company area was next to the NCO club and in front of the main helicopter fuel depot. It didn't take us long to find out we didn't have a choice location for quiet living. The division engineers came in and placed big eight-foot-by-eight-foot white panels through our area to guide the choppers into the refuel area. The NVA used the panels to aim the 122mm rockets they fired from Nui Khe at the fuel dump, and we caught all of the short rounds. The rockets got to be a real pain after the famous bombing halt of 1968. Before the bombing halt, I can remember one rocket attack that hit our side of Camp Eagle.

It was my first rocket attack. Byron and I were going up to the aviation unit for supper. We had our mess kits and were just walking along down by the leech pond, getting ready to turn up the path to the mess hall. A loud rushing noise went right over our heads. When there was a second similar noise right behind it, I looked over to Byron to ask what that noise was. Byron wasn't standing next to me, so

I looked around for him. I heard a voice say, "Get down, you idiot, rockets!" I looked down, and there was Byron in a small depression in the ground next to the trail. Before I could move, the first rocket hit the chopper staging area. Before the second explosion, I was down with Byron, in a tiny hole that couldn't hold one of us. The third and fourth rounds went over and hit the aviation company mess hall. Two men in the mess tent were killed, and the mess hall had to be closed.

After we moved to the new company area, and the bombing halt had been in effect for a month, it started to rain rockets. The time I remember the best was when we had just gotten back from a mission, and I was taking a shower. I didn't hear the warning siren, and none of the clowns came down to warn me. I was all soaped up when the first rocket hit outside the wire. I unassed the shower and headed up the hill, and all I had on was a smile and shower shoes. The men were looking out the door of the bomb shelter and cheering me on. The second rocket hit inside the wire, between our company and the 501st Signal battalion. My speed doubled as the shower shoes flew off my feet. I ran up the dirt hill and dove into the shelter. Everyone was laughing their asses off at my burst of speed and cut-up feet. The other three rockets hit in the refuel area but did little damage. I was mad at the guys for not letting me know the rockets were on the way. We could see the flashes on Nui Khe when the gooks fired the rockets, long before the radar picked them up and sounded the warning.

When we weren't out on missions, we had details to pull. Burning the waste was one detail, but we were also building the defense works for our sector of the line. We had to build two firing bunkers, the TOC (tactical operations center), sandbag the hooches, sandbag the rocket shelters, and build the ammo bunker. All of this construction required thousands of sandbags, but we found a way to get the bags filled. Outside of Camp Eagle was the sandpit, and every day we'd send a truck out to get sandbags filled. We furnished the bags, and the Vietnamese would fill and load them on the truck for a penny each. We got the money from the club fund, so the cost was shared by all. The sandpit was the social highlight of the area—the heads could score a dew bag (a heavy OD plastic bag used to protect the marijuana from the dew) of good smoke, and the desperate members of the unit could find an ugly mamma-san.

One of our great works of sandbag art was the ammo bunker. We worked for weeks digging a hole in the bricklike ground, covering it with a layer of PSP steel, four-by-four planks, and six layers of sandbags. This bunker could withstand a hit with a 122mm rocket any day, but we failed to take into consideration Larry Chambers, who destroyed our bunker in seven seconds.

We were not the best housekeepers when it came to ammo bunkers, and we had a lot of special items in the bunker. We mixed all types of explosives with blasting caps and white phosphorus grenades, CS tear gas grenades, claymore mines, and regular ammo. Before the trouble with the 501st Signal Battalion began, each man kept his ammunition with him, and we would have it all stacked neatly by our bunk. The CO made us put all of our ammo in the bunker after we declared war on the REMFs of the 501st Signal. The bunker was a mess, with ammo stacked everywhere, and all of the explosives and grenades were unpacked. Chambers was on bunker guard one night, and he went to draw some M-16 ammo; as he pulled the bandolier out of the pile of ammo he heard a pop. He had pulled the pin on a trip flare, and as it started to burn, it set the other ammo on fire. Chambers ran up the hill, yelled, "Fire in the hole," and dove into the rocket shelter. The explosion went off about the time Chambers hit the bunker floor. My team and Sergeant Smith's team were on a mission, so the company area was almost empty, and no one got hurt. There was ammo everywhere, and the guys left in the company area spent the next day picking up live ammo all over the place. There was a big investigation to see if it had been sabotage, and a lot of questions were asked. I was glad I had been on a mission, and when I got back Captain Eklund took me down to look at the crater. It was a sight—the wood, the metal, and all the sandbags were gone.

The army had a tradition for military payday, then the first day of the month. Vietnam wasn't any different. If we were on stand-down from a mission, there would be a formation with roll call, and the pay line was formed. I had most of my money going home through allotments, but I still got seventy-five bucks a month for my own expenses. We were paid in MPC (military payment certificates) because the government didn't want a lot of American dollars floating around. So the military was paid in scrip, paper money in all of the regular denominations from the nickel up. Of course, we used it to do business with the Vietnamese even though that is one of the things it was supposed to prevent. Every three months or so, the military would change the MPC. They would lock down all bases for a day, and everyone would have to trade in their old MPC for the new issue. The Vietnamese would come to the wire and try to get the GIs to take their old MPC and trade it for new. By noon, the word would have spread to all of the Vietnamese, and the area would be covered with people trying to trade MPC. We couldn't help them because the unit monitored the amount we traded, and you could only go through the line once. By 1700 hours, the exchange would be over, and most of the Vietnamese would be left with a load of worthless paper.

Another military tradition was mail call. First Sergeant Walker had a picture on his desk of a burned-out army truck. He had taken the picture just outside the main gate to Camp Eagle. The truck was a mail truck coming from Phu Bai, and a gook hit it with an RPG as it neared Camp Eagle. The rocket hit the driver's door and blew the driver's leg off. He got out, but the truck burned to a crisp. The mail and packages were all destroyed. I think he kept the picture to remind the guys who didn't get mail that sometimes things happened to the mail that couldn't be helped, and maybe their letters just got waylaid. A C-130 (four-engine air force cargo plane) full of mail went down flying north from Saigon. Nevertheless, the army did get an *A+* for always trying to get the mail through. We could send letters home for free. All we had to do was put our return address in one corner and write *free* in the corner where the stamp should be.

The care packages from home were always a great treat,

and Mom sent me a couple of batches of chocolate chip cookies while I was gone. It took fifteen days for a letter to do a turnaround, so there was always a lag in communications with home. But it was great to come off a mission and get some letters. We had some men who didn't get any mail, and we had a few who got enough for everyone. We would get packages from churches, with Kool-Aid, socks, writing paper, and a note. My grandfather went to a small church in Marietta, and the congregation sent me a Claxton fruitcake. I never saw a man who wouldn't share his care package with his teammates.

We had an inspector general inspection in October, and most of the operational teams worked their butts off to get on a mission so we could miss the inspection. Like every other unit in the army, we didn't have enough of the things we were supposed to have, and we had too many of the things we weren't. A truck was loaded with the no-no items and sent on a lurp mission to Phu Bai. The Old Man and the top NCOs had to worry about the inspection; it was their job; the teams could have cared less. What were they going to do if we failed, send us to Vietnam?

There was one time when I saw some of the bravest men in the army quake in their boots. At 0730 hours one morning, the medics swarmed over us with lightning speed and announced that it was time for update shots. Panic gripped the company because we were facing nine shots, given with needles, in the hands of OJT (on-the-job trained) medics. The company commander had anticipated our reaction and had all escape routes covered. Never was a sadder lot of lurps lined up anywhere then were there that day. I looked on in disbelief as I saw lurps limp away from the medics after getting nine shots in the arms.

To keep things from getting dull, we had our share of stupid accidents. One day I had to go to the 17th Cav's aid tent because I had been running a fever of 103 degrees for two days. In Vietnam, we had to have a 104-degree temperature for three days before they would think about malaria. The Cav's medics checked me over and decided I had a bug, so they started an IV in my arm to keep me from dehydrating. I was lying on a cot, with the IV in my arm, when the first explosion went off. There were four more in rapid succession. Someone yelled, "Incoming!" and a medic threw me into the bunker attached to the tent. We sat in the bunker for a few minutes, but there weren't any more explosions. A man rushed into the tent and yelled for a medic to get down to the officers' latrine because the colonel had been hit. I thought this is it; the gooks are attacking. I felt like crap, and I was six hundred meters from my gun.

But the all clear was sounded, so we got ready to come out of the bunker. I looked down, and my IV bag had filled up with my blood. The medics took me back to the cot and put the IV bag back on the stand. The colonel came into the tent to get his hand patched up, saw my IV bag, and thought I was getting blood. He came over and ask me where I had been hit. I told him what happened, and he laughed while they worked on him. A half an hour later, a medic sat down with me and told me what all of the racket was about. A helicopter mechanic had set off the 40mm grenade launcher that was mounted in the nose of the gunship he was working on. Most of the rounds had gone off in the revetment, but one had hit the officers' latrine and nailed the colonel.

I stopped the story at that point, and got up to get a beer and take a whiz. When I got back, I sat down and opened my beer. My brother asked about the dope and racial problems he had heard about in the army units in Vietnam. I took a long drink of beer and thought about that question for a minute. I wanted to give him an answer that made good sense. I was in Vietnam in 1968, and the problem was just starting at that time. My answer would be slanted toward our unit.

We just weren't your regular group of people. We didn't have a lot of blacks in the company. There was one black in the 1st Platoon, three blacks in Commo, and two blacks in Supply. We all got along fine; everyone did his job, and we didn't have any problems.

There were people in the company who smoked pot. I

didn't, and the men in the 2d Platoon who did knew my rules about dope—they didn't do it around me; they didn't do it the night before a mission; and they knew I would kill anyone who did it on a mission. We had a special bond because of the way we operated, and there had to be a trust between us. If one of the men wanted to go out behind a grave and smoke a joint at night while we were on stand-down, it wasn't my business to hassle him. I just told the men never to put me in the position where I would have to turn them in. I was a sergeant in the army, and I had a duty.

We did start to have some problems with the army-issue speed. Each team leader had a bottle of one hundred dextroamphetamine tablets, and every man had an emergency escape pack with five tablets. There was a small group of men who started doing a lot of speed. Most of the speed freaks were the older guys who had been with the unit in late 1967 and early 1968, but a few of the new men got to messing with it in September 1968. When we were on a mission, we were always on an adrenaline wave. It started when we were inserted and lasted until we were out. There wasn't a letdown of the adrenaline flow, and we operated at a peak level all of the time. If during a mission the team got in contact, then the body pushed out more adrenaline, and we hit a new high. When we were back in base camp, some of the men tried to simulate that feeling with the dex. We knew there was a problem when the speeders broke into the supply tent and raided the emergency kits. To get things under control, we started to turn in all dex tablets to the first sergeant so he could lock them in the company safe.

The real drug problem was in the noncombat units. There was little to do after duty time, and dope was the escape. The Viet Cong made sure there were plenty of drugs around for the American troops. The enemy had, in fact, turned dope into a major weapon, and they scored a great success with it. Combat soldiers in 1968 didn't put up with dopers in the field, and after 1968, I don't know what happened.

The racial problems were in the same vein. The combat units had a different outlook, and up to 1968, I don't think there was a lot of trouble in the fighting units. The action of combat crossed color lines, and the team spirit won out. The NVA were equal-opportunity butt kickers; they didn't care about color.

Noncombat units had the problems, and the boredom of the situation only added heat. The noncombat units got a large share of blacks when the army sent out a directive in 1967 to make sure there were fewer blacks assigned to infantry units.

Toward the end of 1968, we started to have problems with the blacks in the 501st Signal Battalion. Our company area was located next to one of their companies. There was a group of blacks who would come over to our hooches, while we were out on missions, and break into our footlockers. They would take money, smokes, and anything of value left behind. The men in our unit were getting mad, and it all came to a boil when six blacks mugged Sergeant Byron one night. He was walking around the company area and caught them outside a team hooch. We loaded up our weapons and were headed over to fire up the 501st when the Old Man and Sergeant Burnell stopped us. The next day, the engineers came in and put up barbed wire around our company area. They told us it was to secure the combat command center because we had all of the division operation plans on file. The 501st Signal got the word that our bunker guards had orders to kill anyone who was in the wire. We used to laugh about the fact that we had more wire between us and the 501st than we had between us and the NVA. It was at this time that the CO made us turn in all ammo to the ammo bunker so it would be harder for us to start a war with the 501st Signal.

I believe the Old Man invented most of the details as a type of motivator to keep us going out on missions. If that was his plan, it worked. All in all, we preferred to stay in the field; that was where we wanted to be, and the time went by faster. We didn't get hassled much in base camp, but the details that had to be pulled were the pits. The way we worked, we got a one-day stand-down after a mission, a day to clean gear and plan a mission. Then six days back out.

CHAPTER 3

"Uncle John, I don't understand how you got out to the jungle to go on a mission."

"Well, Andy, we were taken out to the jungle by helicopter. We called it being inserted. All long-range patrol companies were Airborne qualified, so we could parachute in to an AO, but the area we worked in wasn't very well suited to that method. In Europe, the teams were left behind as the NATO forces pulled back so they could perform their mission. Down south in the Delta, sometimes teams were put in by boat. I liked insertion the way we did it, with good old Huey UH-1D helicopters. We made most of our insertions early in the morning at first light. I think the best way to show you would be by telling you about some insertions; picture this."

It was 0630 hours. We'd finished with the insertion briefing, and the team was at the helipad, waiting for the order to load up. To keep busy, Looney and Meszaros were doing commo checks with the radios, while Harris, Chambers, and Taylor looked over the map. I lit up a smoke, settled back, and mentally went over a list of my equipment. In my rucksack I had two gallons of water, twelve freeze-dried rations, fourteen magazines of M-16 ammo, twelve packs of cocoa beverage powder, two packs of cigarettes, four smoke grenades, one claymore mine, one spare battery for the PRC-25 radio, four pair of socks, jungle sweater, poncho liner, poncho, Ho Chi Minh sandals, light rope, camera, and two pounds of C-4 explosive. On my LBE web gear, I had pouches attached to the belt, which contained seven magazines of M-16 ammo, two quarts of water, four smoke

29

grenades, six frag grenades, two white phosphorous grenades, pen-gun flares, compass, three morphine syrettes, and four camouflage grease sticks. Taped to the LBE harness was my first-aid kit, albumin blood expanders, knife, strobe light, and one red smoke grenade. My SOI (signal operating instructions) radio codes, map, and insect repellent were in the cargo pocket of my pants. With the M-16 added in, our gear weighed over seventy pounds, but after the first hours humping, we didn't even notice the weight. We'd be patrolling for six days in the mountains north of the A Shau Valley.

The CO came out of the TOC and signaled that it was time to go. I crushed out my cigarette, slipped into the shoulder straps of my rucksack, and extended my hand up to Chambers so he could pull me to my feet. We had to help one another up because our gear was so heavy. Harris, Taylor, and Meszaros would move to the right side of the chopper, while Looney and Chambers followed me around to the left.

Over to the left of our chopper was the chase ship, and behind it sat the command-and-control ship. The pilots would go through the start-up procedure and work with the controls while the crew chief and door gunner strapped in. When we'd pass the nose of the ship, Mr. Grant, the pilot, would give me the thumbs-up. I'd smile, pat the nose of the ship, and move around to the side door. Mr. Grant had inserted us many times before, and we had a deal—anywhere he put us in, he would come back and get us out.

The whine of the turbine would pick up, and the rotor blades started a lazy rotation over our heads. Chambers and Looney would step around me and climb into the cargo door of the ship. Over on the 17th Cav's helipad, two Cobra gunships were ready to join us. It was always nice to have heavy company along on a trip like this.

I liked to sit on the floor of the helicopter, with my rucksack propped on the back of the pilot's seat and one foot hooked in the door gunner's seat frame. I'd face to the rear, and I would keep my other foot on the skid of the helicopter. I always took my floppy hat off and stuffed it in my shirt before the rotor blades picked up speed and the rotor wash got stronger.

Sergeant Proctor rode as the belly man most days, and his job was to coordinate between the helicopter crew, the C & C ship, and the team. Proctor would kick me on the leg, and I'd look over and give him the okay nod to let him know we were ready. He'd pass the word to Mr. Grant on the ship's radio that the team was loaded and ready.

Mr. Grant was a great pilot—he'd pull in the pitch, the ship would tremble, get light on its skids, and break away from the ground. Grant would kick that bird around 180 degrees, drop the nose to pick up speed, and we'd climb out across the barbed wire that encircled Camp Eagle. The ground dropped away as we gained speed and altitude, and I could watch the chase ship pull into formation behind us. The C & C Huey and the two Cobras would climb up higher on our flank.

We were heading west toward the mountains, and Camp Eagle faded into the horizon behind us. It was daybreak, and we were starting another long-range patrol. The chopper was up eight thousand feet doing about eighty knots, and Vietnam spread out below us in a quilt of square green patches. It was a strange sight; those squares of green dotted with brown bomb craters filled with water. We passed over the mounds of the burial grounds for the city of Hue, and the old imperial tombs. This ancient land was so filled with history, and from up here the land looked so quiet and beautiful; what a shame there had to be a war here. We'd fly over the open area we called the rocket belt, and then to the green vegetation of the jungle and the foothills of our operational area.

I'd look over at Harris, and he'd be watching me. I'd give him my "What, me worry?" smile and signal Proctor for another cigarette. It took about four cigarettes to make an insertion. The smoke would kill the butterflies that always gathered in my stomach.

The wind and noise of the helicopter made conversation impossible, so I would just daydream and let my mind wander as we flew into the AO. On that particular day, I thought about the team. Normal Credit Two-one was our call sign. Half the men on the team were draftees, but we all had to volunteer to be paratroopers, then volunteer again for the LRRP assignment.

Larry Chambers was my point man. He was a California boy with two years of college, but his head was screwed on tight for a twenty-one-year-old. He had a natural feel for the land that made him a good point man, and he had more balls than brains, which made him a good LRRP. I never asked why he got drafted; I was just glad he did.

John Looney was my primary radioman. Another drafted college kid, he wore glasses and wanted to be a school teacher after he finished college. He was so cool under fire that it was unreal. I often wondered what it would take to get him excited; I knew bullets didn't work.

Don Harris was my assistant team leader. He had four years in the army, and he was a regular who was going to make the army a career. He was a Tennessee hillman who knew the woods and got along with the men. He and I cooked up some missions I'm glad we never pulled, and he shared my love of explosives.

John Meszaros was another draftee. He was twenty, and a good radioman. He didn't know the word *no*, but I am sure there were times when he would ask Chambers if he really had to go on patrol with me.

Mike Taylor had just spent a year in an infantry line company, then extended to be a lurp. He would get upset when I used the enemy trails, and he still had a lot of the line company bull in his head. I knew he'd get right and be a good lurp as soon as he accepted the idea that there were only six of us out there.

I had seven years in the army, but I had a break in my service. I had one year of college, and I knew I'd leave the army when this tour was over. I was twenty-five and married, but I was able to relate well with the men. They trusted me, and I never asked them to do anything I wouldn't do. I always walked slack on the point man, and when the going got hairy, I would take the point.

Sergeant Proctor would always bring me back to reality with the five-minutes-out sign. I'd signal him for a smoke and think about getting myself ready to go to work. When the door gunners broke their M-60 machine guns loose from the retainer lock and pulled a round into the chamber, everyone knew it was time to go. I'd look out to see our LZ (landing zone) as we made the high pass. Like a well-choreographed dance, the insertion routine took form as the chase ship lined up five hundred meters behind our chopper. The C & C bird would bank to the right and start a slow climb, while the two Cobras would make a wide 360-degree turn high above the landing zone so they'd be in position to make a firing run if we came into a hot LZ.

As we started the descent to the landing zone, every muscle in the body tightened up. I'd get that tingle of apprehension that always rode down to the jungle with me, and I'd start to gauge the distance to the ground. At about forty feet up, I'd thumb off the safety on my M-16 and flip it to rock and roll (full automatic). I liked to step out on the skid of the chopper to clear the door for Looney and Chambers, and that also allowed me to look forward to cover the nose of the ship during the landing. Harris would be in the same position on the other side of the ship. Every eye would strain as we tried to look through the bush to see if the NVA were waiting for us. This was the most critical time during an insertion; the helicopter was a sitting duck. For the team, the rules were simple: if one man got on the ground, we all got on the ground—no one is left alone.

Five feet from the ground, I'd jump from the ship and run toward the wood line. Looney and Chambers would be to my left side, and we'd run in a crouch, our weapons ready to spray the jungle at the first sign of trouble. We'd dive into the brush. The secret was to pick your spot as you ran; it cut down on surprise and hard landings. On the other side of the LZ, Harris, Meszaros, and Taylor would be doing the same thing. We could lay down a wall of lead on both sides of the landing zone and cover each other if one group ran into trouble. The chase ship would fly over the insertion slick, which would then follow it up into a high orbit away from the touchdown point. To anyone watching, it would look like two helicopters swooped down, then pulled back up without enough time to drop off troops.

No one would move. We'd lie there in total silence and

listen for telltale sounds, like the rustle of a branch, a twig snapping, or the metallic click of an AK-47 being switched from safe to fire.

I'd wait about twenty minutes, and if the enemy hadn't hit the team, I'd feel that we had been safely inserted. Looney could read me; when he saw me start to fish around in my shirt to find my hat, he'd call Harris on the radio to tell him to join up with us. As soon as they were with us, I'd have Looney call the Old Man on the radio to request he release the gunships. The sooner the helicopter crowd was gone, the safer we were. I loved the sound of the rotor blades beating the air. There wasn't any other sound like it, and you could always tell when help was on the way or friends were leaving.

I used my hat as a sweat rag because it was always easy to reach. I knew I was going to need it that day; the sky was a clear blue, and the temperature would go over one hundred degrees by noon. The armpits of my uniform were dark with sweat, and my eyes stung as the sweat poured down my face. We would eat eight to ten salt tablets a day just to fight off heatstroke. Before the week was up, our uniforms would be crusted with salt.

While I waited for the spirit to move me enough to start the mission, Meszaros would tune his radio to the artillery frequency. I'd listen to him make his radio check, and wait for him to tell me that he had good signal. Looney's radio was tuned to the main TOC (tactical operations center) frequency, and Meszaros was on the artillery network; now help was only a radio call away.

When it was time to start moving, I'd pull myself up to one knee and check the compass heading and map one more time. We would struggle to our feet, and I'd give Chambers the sign to move out. Chambers would take the point, and I'd be three feet behind. Looney, with my radio, would be next in the file. I let Looney do most of the radio work, but I needed it close at hand. Taylor would follow Looney, and Meszaros, with the artillery radio, in the number-five slot. Harris, being the assistant team leader, was behind Meszaros and walked the tail-gunner slot. We stayed close together in a file. It was a good formation that allowed us the best in observation and fire pattern if the need came up. Our special camouflage uniforms helped us blend in with the surrounding jungle, and for the next six days, we were on our own. The radios would be our only link with civilization during that time, and we wanted to keep them apart, yet still close to the team leader or the assistant team leader.

"Now, boys, you need to understand that what I described was a normal insertion, and they weren't all normal. Let me tell you about a few times when things just didn't follow the script."

I had a twelve-man team, and we were going to pull a small ambush on a gook high-speed trail that I had discovered on an earlier mission. This trail was right at the edge of the jungle, and a lot of civilian woodcutters worked that area. The NVA soldiers would come out in the late afternoon and mix in with the woodcutters. That was how they infiltrated their forces into town. The plan was to insert early in the afternoon, before the NVA came out, hide in the wood line, and kill them when they came back the next morning. The only catch to the plan was we had to cross the trail to get to the woods. The trail was too wide to jump across, and if we walked across, we'd leave jungle-boot footprints; so I came up with a classic Burford solution to the problem. I'd wear my Ho Chi Minh sandals, tiger-stripe pants, and NVA khaki shirt on the insertion. As soon as we got on the ground, I'd drop my rucksack and LBE, take my weapon and a pouch of magazines, and go up to recon the trail. I reasoned that the woodcutters would think I was a VC flushed by the choppers and not give me a second thought, and if some NVA were there, the few seconds they lost trying to decide who I was would give me time to grease them. After the recon, I would signal the team to come up and cross the trail. Then I would walk over their footprints to hide the tracks and join them in the woods.

The afternoon of the insertion, I was ready to go. I had my Ho Chis on, and was looking good. We loaded up and headed out to the LZ, a large depression, sixty meters by forty meters, with elephant grass in the bottom. It was about forty meters from the trail, so the location was great. The pilot came in hot and right on the money. Forty feet up, I swung out on the skid, and at five feet from the ground, I jumped into a marshy bog. I sunk up to my knees in muck, and the weight of the rucksack carried me right over on my face. I thought my knees would break off. Looney landed on me and drove me deeper into the muck, and we both were hit by Chambers. Harris, Meszaros, and Jim Schwartz weren't doing any better than we were. Snuffy Smith's team came in on the second ship and joined the mess. Except for me, the team pulled its way to firm ground. I was still in the muck, looking for my sandals. Those assholes sat around the edge of the bog and laughed at me fishing around in that stinking mess. I found the sandals, and the rest of the mission went smoothly, except that no NVA showed up that afternoon.

Another time, not only was the insertion goofed up, the whole mission was jinxed. From insertion to extraction, the whole patrol just went to pieces. The company was to put two teams out near the Laotian border north of Camp Eagle. We were short of men, so the Old Man scraped up the two teams on a pick-and-choose basis. The 2d Platoon's team was Sergeant Brooks, TL; me as ATL; Harris, RTO; Ken Munoz, RTO; and Tony Tercero on point. We had all worked together at one time or another, so there weren't any problems with the team structure. The teams' AOs were close together, so the decision was made to put us in at the same time, and the mission went downhill from there. The team from the 1st Platoon got Sergeant Proctor for belly man, and we got Lieutenant Williams. The lieutenant was new, and this was his first trip as belly man. Brooks and Williams made the overflight while I got the team ready. To make matters worse, we were going in on a late afternoon insertion, and it was a rush job.

Brooks and Williams came back from the overflight, and we did the team briefing around 1430 hours. I checked the map, and the LZ looked okay to me. I could tell that we would be going in on a hillside, but that was the pilot's problem. Late in the afternoon, we loaded into the choppers and took off to make the insertion. Munoz and I were on the right side of the Huey, and Brooks, Harris, and Tercero were on the left side.

The ship came in and made the high pass. Then the pilot swung the ship around and started to land. I could see Williams talking with the crew, and the helicopter stopped in a hover, ten feet above the ground. I looked down. Jagged tree stumps about five feet high stuck up all over the LZ. Time was wasting; the longer we hovered there, the better chance that the mission would be compromised. Lieutenant Williams decided we could jump down without any problem and motioned for Brooks to jump. He signaled for me to come across the ship because he wanted us all to go out on the same side of the slick. I scooted across the floor of the chopper on my ass. Munoz was in front of me, and we both were hurrying, trying to catch up with the rest of the team. Munoz was tall and skinny like me, and when he went out the door he just disappeared. I remember thinking to myself, "Where the heck did he go?" When I got to the door I found out. Lieutenant Williams had forgotten to tell the pilot to compensate for the weight loss. Every time a man jumped out the door, the chopper got lighter and popped up a few feet. I was the last person out of the Huey, and we were about fifteen feet above the ground. I landed on Munoz who was lying in a heap on the ground. The weight of my gear, the distance I fell, and the uneven surface of Munoz's rucksack filled my landing with pain.

I just lay on the ground and cursed as I watched the helicopter fly away. We were lucky the only thing broken was Munoz's radio and the radio's extra long antenna. When the first raindrop hit me, I knew it was going to be one of those really crappy missions. That was the only mission I was ever on when it never stopped raining.

We got off the LZ, and Brooks called the Old Man to release the gunships. We started to move west, and hit a good trail within fifty meters of the landing zone. We turned onto the trail and started to follow it to the top of the hill we had inserted on. We had just gotten to the top, and we were stopped to check the map when the shooting started. It came from the direction where the other team had been inserted. We quickly moved into some thick brush alongside the trail and got down. We had been in the AO less than an hour, and the 1st Platoon's team was in contact. It was getting dark, so we stayed in the brush and listened on the radio while the other team got extracted. This wasn't shaping up to be one of our better trips.

Brooks decided we'd spend the night where we were, so we got our sleeping area ready. Getting a sleeping area ready meant that we would get in a circle, if we could, with everyone's feet close together at the center of the circle. Each man would look at the place his body was to occupy, and move any twigs or brush that could make noise if he rolled on them during the night. We'd take our rucksacks and put them where our heads would be when we lay down. Next, we'd crawl out fifteen feet, put out our claymore mines, and bring the wire back to the firing device by our rucksacks. We'd pick the pee tree so everyone would go to the same place, because once we settled in, anything that was moving outside that circle was shot.

Now it was dinner time, but it was too dark to heat the water for our freeze-dried lurp ration. I just took the tape off the plastic bag, unrolled it, and poured in the cold water. Then I stirred it up, rolled the bag up, taped it shut, and stuck it in my shirt. It took fifteen minutes for the cold water to mix with the food, and I hoped my body heat would warm up my meal. While I waited for dinner to "cook," I got my sleeping cover out of the rucksack. I used a Vietnamese poncho, with half a poncho liner tied inside it. It would keep me warm; at that point, dry was out of the question. After dinner, I took all of the trash from eating and put it back in my rucksack; what came out with us, went back with us. We didn't leave anything in the field. After we ate, we'd set the guard times; one hour on and four hours off. There wasn't anything left to do but lie down to go to sleep. I'd wake up automatically every hour to check the guard. I'd prop up on one elbow and spend a few minutes listening, and then I'd lie back down and go to sleep for another hour.

The next morning, our second radio didn't work when we tried to make the morning sitrep (situation report). The signal kept fading out, so the Old Man had to fly out to get radio contact with us. Our signal was so weak that the CO had to be over our position to make contact, but he wouldn't extract us. Brooks wanted to stay where we were and monitor the trails for the next three days. I wanted to patrol the trails and find the gooks. I felt that sitting in the rain for three days would be bad for our health. Brooks pointed out that there was a fifty-foot ceiling and we had no radio contact; a meeting with the NVA could be even worse for our health. Brooks called that one right. So there we sat for three days in a pouring rain. We looked like prunes, and the wrinkles on my finger tips were bigger than the A Shau valley.

The morning of the fifth day, Tercero began throwing up blood, and he said he had stomach pains. I added to the excitement when I got bitten by a spider and had an allergic reaction. I started to feel faint, and I couldn't breathe. The men watched me thrash around on the ground, fighting to breathe, but there wasn't anything they could do. The reaction was so bad that I showed Harris where to cut my throat to give me a tracheotomy if my throat closed up. The effects of the bite wore off in about a hour, but I was drained and very weak.

Brooks decided it was time to get us out of there, and he had Harris try to make radio contact with the Old Man. Harris had lost the long antenna for his radio on the insertion, and Munoz's was broken. Harris got on the radio, and after a few minutes, he made weak contact with a radio-relay team. He told them we needed extraction and that the team was headed north to the only open area that could be used for an LZ, at the junction of a small stream and the river. Harris walked behind me to help steady me as we moved. We were in our fifth day of steady rain, and the ceiling was still on the deck. We didn't know if the relay had understood any of our message.

As we moved through the jungle, vines snagged our uniforms, and brush rubbed against us. After so many days in the rain, our skin was numb and had no feeling. On the way down to the river, I brushed up against some bushes, and a leech crawled onto my eye. I knew he was there

when he became a big dark blotch on my left eye. Afraid
that the leach would bite my eye for blood, I stopped Harris
and told him to get that leech out of there. The team
stopped, and I lay down on the ground while Harris got a
twig and poked the leach to keep it moving. Harris lit a cigarette and blew the smoke in my eye to see if we could get
the leech to crawl out. After a minute or two, we gave up
and put a drop of GI insect repellent in my eye. Well, the
leech came out, and it felt like he took the eye with him.
The eye turned red, and then it went black. We made the
trip to the LZ a lot slower because I could only use my
right eye.

The clearing by the river wasn't so clear; there were
dead trees and a large drop off at the stream bank. We
stopped in the woods, and the men set up security while
Brooks and I went over the map to see if there was any
way out of our AO. I went out to do a detailed reconnaissance of the landing zone. It was a mess—the clearing was
wedge shaped, and dead trees were everywhere; the creek
bank was about eight feet high, and the creek cut the open
area in two. I was sure a helicopter couldn't land in the
space we had available. Harris got to work on the radio, but
he couldn't make contact because of the lousy weather and
the fact we were in a low area.

A couple of hours later, we heard the beat of rotor blades
coming up the river toward our position. Brooks had the
men pick up the claymores while I went out to the open
area to signal the slick. It was a sight to see, a lone
D-model Huey flying along twenty feet above the river.
The ship looked like it was barely moving, and I guessed
it wasn't going over thirty-five knots. I got out my pen gun
and screwed on a red flare. Without thinking, I fired the
flare toward the ship. As I watched the red ball arc toward
the chopper, I knew I had screwed up big time. My
thoughts were confirmed when I saw the door gunner
swing his M-60 toward me. I dove off the stream bank and
rolled under an overhang, but the gunner never opened fire,
and the ship flew on up the river.

I found out later that the door gunner called Mr. Grant on
the intercom and reported that he had seen a tracer round

come at them on the port side. Mr. Grant and Captain Eklund talked it over and decided it was the team they were searching for. It was quite a risk for the chopper to come back down the river, low and slow, to see if it was us who fired the shot and not a NVA .51-caliber machine-gun team.

I crawled back up the bank and was started back toward the woods when I heard the chopper coming back down the river. I ran back to the woods and got the red, emergency flash panel out of my pack. This time when the ship was in sight, I fired the flare parallel to the line of flight and quickly flashed the panel. The chopper slowly turned and started coming my direction. I felt a little funny when I realized that both door gunners had their M-60 machine guns pointed right at me and the Old Man was covering me with his M-16. Mr. Grant pulled right up to me and stopped in a hover; there just wasn't enough room between the tree line and the creek to allow the slick to land.

At my signal, the rest of the team ran out of the woods, Munoz bringing along my rucksack. Proctor kicked out the rope ladder so we could climb up and get in the chopper. Harris and I held the bottom of the ladder while the rest of the men got set for the climb. Munoz went up the ladder first, and then Tercero started up. Tercero got caught by a wait-a-minute vine that was wrapped around his chest while Mr. Grand accidentally let the ship drift over the creek, so Tercero was being pulled off the ladder. As the ship drifted to the left, Harris and I had to let go of the ladder. The ship sunk lower, and the tail boom knocked me to the ground. Harris jumped off the creek bank as the tail rotor blades flashed over his head. Brooks ran to the nose of the ship and frantically signaled Grant. Grant quickly got the slick back up and over the bank while Brooks got the vine off Tercero. Harris climbed back up to help me hold the ladder while Tercero climbed into the helicopter. Brooks went up next and got into the chopper without any problem. Harris followed Brooks up, and I was last man on the ladder.

The last man on the ladder always has a hard climb because the weight on the ladder tends to make it swing under the ship. With all our gear on, it was a real test to get in the chopper. I had my rifle in one hand and the ladder had swung so far under the ship that my back was parallel to the ground. I started to climb up the ladder, and I had to use the one hand wrapped around the rifle to hold the rung while I reached for the next rung. I had made it a few feet, but I was in trouble. The Old Man looked over and decided to help me get in. He reached down and grabbed my LBE harness to pull me up. When he pulled on my harness my feet came off the rung of the ladder. My head and chest were in the door and the rest of me hung out in space. Eklund shouted to me to get my leg up on the skid but I couldn't get my leg up far enough to get it on the skid. Proctor saw the problem, reached down, got a grip on me, and together, he and the Old Man pulled me up and threw me onto the floor of the helicopter. I was in a heap on the floor of the ship with a loaded M-16 stuck up my nose, but I was glad to be on board until I looked up between Mr. Grant and the copilot.

I had been in flight school with Mr. Grant, and I knew a little bit about helicopters and how they flew. I watched as the low-rotor-speed indicator went into the red. Then the stall-warning Klaxon began beeping, and I wished I was back on the ground. I had a bird's-eye view through the front bubble, and I knew we were in big trouble. Grant kicked the ship around 180 degrees with the tail rotor and slammed the cyclic forward—he had to pick up some air speed or crash. The chopper was overloaded, and the heat of the day cut down on the efficiency of the main rotor blades. We started to move forward and pick up a little speed, but we were headed toward a large dead tree. I tried to close my eyes, but I couldn't; I had to watch this crash. But before we could hit the tree, Grant pushed the cyclic to the right and dove the helicopter off the river bank. The skids *had* to have hit the water before Grant got that chopper flying. He built up the air speed and leveled off at forty feet for the flight home. When we got back to Camp Eagle, Tercero and I got a jeep ride to see the medics while Brooks, Harris, and Munoz got a cup of hot soup.

The next day, I spent a few minutes with Mr. Grant and thanked him for coming out to get us. He told me that they never heard the radio call from us, but the Old Man had asked him to hunt for the team. Two ships had gone out for a couple of hours to try to make radio contact with us. The flight up the river was the last resort. Flying up the river at an altitude of twenty feet and a speed of forty knots made them the world's largest sitting duck. They were the dream of every gook with a gun. There was a big debate over whether risking a chopper with six men aboard was worth the chance to find a five-man LRRP team. We hadn't had radio contact in three days, and they didn't know if we were still alive. In the end, Grant told Eklund he could do one of two things, he could order Grant to fly up the river or he could go back to base and write the MIA reports and letters home for five men. Eklund asked him if he would fly that ship up the river, and Grant told Eklund he would fly it anywhere he was told to fly it. They were within ten minutes of turnaround when they found us.

Sometimes the chopper couldn't land or get close enough to the ground for the team to jump in or use a ladder. If the overflight showed that the LZ had too many trees in the way, then the team had to rappel into the area. It took two choppers for a rappel insertion. The ships would be rigged with 120-foot-long nylon mountain ropes, four in the lead ship and two in the chase. We would tie a twelve-foot length of rope around our waists into a Swiss saddle, then put on our rucksacks and LBEs over the rope saddle and thread a snap link around the knot in the saddle. When the helicopter was five minutes out from the LZ, we would stand up by the doors. The belly man helped each man hook up his rappelling rope, and the rest of the rope would be coiled up by our feet. The ship would come to a hover over the LZ, and we would kick out our rope, climb out on the skids, two men to a side, and lean back against the rope. At the belly man's order, we would bend our legs and spring out to free-rappel down the rope—pretty much the way it's done on a cliff—using the brake hand to control the speed of the descent. As soon as we reached the ground, we'd get off the rope and clear the area. The chase ship would come over, and the last two men would rappel down.

Getting out of a tight LZ was the trick. Some fiend invented the McGuire rig, which was a real test of a lurp's desire to live. If the team needed extraction and the chopper couldn't land or get down close to the use the ladder, you would have to make a McGuire extraction. When the slicks were rigged for McGuire, they carried three ropes per ship, each 120 feet long, with a five-foot loop tied in the end. The slick would fly over the hole in the jungle, and the belly man would toss the ropes out. The first three men grabbed the ropes, sat down on the loop, and linked arms with the man in the middle. The belly man then gave the pilot the "all clear," and the pilot lifted the men straight up until they cleared the trees, then flew off with the lurps hanging under the chopper. The chase ship came in next and repeated the action to pick up the rest of the team. The ride back to the nearest firebase was a real thrill. The helicopter pilot would climb to ten thousand feet to get clear of ground fire, and clip along at seventy knots. Down on the ropes, we had a great view, and the feeling that the rope was slipping out from under our asses.

A McGuire extraction was an extraction of last resort, which meant we were almost always in contact during it and that the gooks were all over us. The pilots were good, but they would be taking rounds, and sometimes they didn't clear the trees. More than one team came back picking leaves and twigs out of their cammies and with scratches aplenty, but they came back. There was one great McGuire extraction in our unit. A team was being pulled out under fire, and the last ship was pulling the men up when John Quick's rope got shot in two. Quick fell twenty or more feet to the ground and was knocked out cold. The belly man called the pilot and told him what happened. The pilot stopped, back the helicopter up, and while the door gunners and the two men left on the ropes laid down a hail of fire, the pilot turned that helicopter into a million-dollar bush-hog—he used the rotor blade to chop the tree branches as he lowered the slick toward the ground. The two men on the ropes hit the ground and got out of the loops so they could run over to get John Quick. The door gunners kept pouring out the fire while the pilot landed the ship. The two men dragged Quick back to the helicopter and piled in. The pilot took it straight back up the hole he had chopped and flew it home. The gooks had the ship under fire the whole time, but no one got hit. As a result of his actions that day, the pilot, Mr. Poley, was awarded the Distinguished Flying Cross.

Sergeant Zoschak's team had one of the truly all-time hairy extractions pulled by a team at night. The team had been compromised the first day of its mission, so the men were pulled out. Later that day, the Old Man decided to put them back into the same AO at night. Well, the gooks were out in force, and the insertion point was on the side of Mount Nui Khe. The insertion ship took fire on the way in, and the gooks were so close they could have helped the team get off the chopper. The team was in contact in a matter of minutes, and Gary Linderer greased a gook within handshake range. Zoschak called for an extraction, and the ship that had just put them in turned around and came back for them. There was no LZ, so the pilot put the ship in a hover while the belly man kicked out the ladder. The team climbed up the ladder to get in the slick, but the fire got so heavy that the ship had to start out before Zoschak could get inside the ship. Zoschak clipped his D ring to the ladder and enjoyed his flight to the firebase, outside the ship. To compound the problem, the gooks had a .51-caliber machine gun firing at the Huey, and the gooks higher up the mountain were firing an 82mm mortar down on the helicopter. The company commander had his pilot turn on his lights and fly over the extraction ship to draw fire. Zo and the team got back, but they were rattled.

CHAPTER 4

"Uncle John, did you ever get lost?"

"Jason, I hate to use the word lost but there were a few times when I did get *confused*. There was one time when Larry Chambers and I got lost on a special reconnaissance mission. Let me explain a few of the problems we faced and tell you about a couple of times when the only thing I was sure of was the fact I was in Southeast Asia."

Most people would be terrified at the thought of being dropped in the middle of the jungle with only a map and compass to help them find their way around, but we did it all the time. When you couple that idea to the fact that we were always eight to ten miles from the nearest friendly troops, you start to get an idea of the stress we operated under. There weren't any signposts or friendly corner cops to ask for directions. Yet, we had to radio in our exact location three times a day. We always started our missions from a known point, the LZ, but after we started to move in the jungle, we had to use a combination of compass headings, pace counts, and our ability to read the terrain. Most of the time, our maps were accurate and up-to-date, so we could use the contour lines on the map to follow the true contour of the ground. It was important that the team know where it was at all times. That could be a matter of life or death.

Before a mission, we drew a tracing-paper map overlay that showed the route we were to take, the preplanned artillery concentrations, and where we planned to spend the night. The overlay was made for the operations section so they'd know where to start looking if the team lost radio contact. The same information was drawn on the plastic envelope that covered our map.

We tried to know our location on the ground to within one hundred meters. If we made contact with an enemy force, we needed to quickly get the gunships on target and adjust our preplotted artillery. A team leader didn't have time during contact to read a map. I made it a rule to check my map every few minutes and to stop regularly to study the terrain to confirm our location. I worked on map reading with every man who went out on a mission with me. Every time we stopped for the night, I had each man look at the map so he would know our location in case we got hit and had to split up for escape and evasion. I always encouraged each man to carry his own map.

I was good with a map, and I was always comfortable being in the jungle. I never did worry about getting so lost that no one would ever find me or that I couldn't find my way out. Yet there were times when we got so turned around we just didn't know where the heck we were.

On one mission, we had a twelve-man team out with an impressive lineup of map reading talent. Staff Sergeant Burnell, Lieutenant Williams, and I were all on the same team. I was running the point section, with Chambers on point, me as the slack man, and Harris as my RTO. Two teams had been used to put the mission together, so all of the jobs got mixed up. Burnell took Looney for his RTO, and Harris, who was my ATL under normal circumstances, got stuck with the third radio.

When we got ready to move out on the second morning of the mission, Sergeant Burnell and Lieutenant Williams got with me to go over the direction I was to keep the point man heading. Sergeant Burnell told me to go to the finger of the hill we were on until I hit the ridgeline, then follow the ridge to the left. I looked at my map, then I looked at Burnell's map—we had two different start points! I told Burnell we weren't where we thought we were, and I pointed out the ridgeline and finger we were on. Lieutenant Williams and Burnell looked around for a few minutes, then told me I was wrong and to get the point moving. I went up to Chambers and told him to go three hundred meters up the finger and turn left at the ridge.

We had been moving for a hour when the word came up for the file to stop and take a five-minute break. I went back to Burnell's location, and he wanted to know why we hadn't hit the ridgeline. He ask me if I was lost, and then he wanted to know what was I doing up on the point. I pulled out my map and showed him where we were. Burnell looked at his map, looked around at the terrain, and gave me a sheepish look. We plotted a new compass azimuth to the ridgeline we were supposed to be on. When we stopped that night, he called me over, and the three of us worked out our position on the map before we called in the last situation report of the day. The mistake Burnell had made was only a couple of hundred meters off, but if we had gotten hit that night or the next morning, when we started to move, it could have been a disaster for us.

Knowing our night position was the most important thing we could do. If the NVA were tracking us, or knew we were in the area, they would try to spook us at night. They'd get on line, and while walking through the brush, they would throw rocks and blow whistles to try and get us to fire and give away our position. If they found us, we needed to get artillery, flares, and the gunships in as fast as possible so the team could break contact and pull escape and evasion. Another trick the NVA liked to pull was to pinpoint our location and quietly surround us at night. Then, in the morning when we started to move out, they would ambush the team. When the NVA got a team like that, they almost always killed everyone before the RTO could even call for help.

There was a mission I was on with Sergeant Byron when the gooks spent five hours one night searching for our team. They walked all around us, but our luck held, and they missed us. The next morning Harris and I went out thirty meters and did a 360-degree recon of our location before Byron would move the team. The idea was to have Harris and me trip any gook ambush early and give Byron time to call in artillery fire. The team would give covering fire so Harris and I could break contact and get back to the team's position.

In September 1968, the 1st Cavalry Division (Airmobile) left Camp Evans and moved to the III Corps area to guard the approaches to Saigon. That meant the 101st now had to cover two division-size AOs, and we were short one brigade. The division's 3d Brigade was based down south in the III Corps area, at Phan Rang. The LRRP company had to run missions from both Camp Eagle and Camp Evans. The extra load put a strain on all of the teams.

The only time I got my team lost in Vietnam was on a mission out of Camp Evans. We were spread so thin trying to cover two AOs that I could scrounge only a five-man team for the mission. I was the TL, Harris was ATL and had the second radio, Taylor was point man, James Evans was RTO, and Thomas Soals, who was just out of the NCO academy, was the scout. We were working our first mission out of Camp Evans, and I had just gotten new maps when we were assigned to patrol near the Da Krong River, on the border between Vietnam and Laos.

Intelligence reported that an NVA battalion had a base camp in the area, and we were to find it. I did the overflight, and the only LZ I could find in the AO was a oneship LZ on a hilltop near the center of the AO. Near the LZ was a junction of two rivers, one of which came out of Laos and joined the Da Krong River, which formed the border between the two countries. The Da Krong then joined the Rao Lao, the main river in the A Shau Valley. I knew this river was a main supply artery from Laos to the A Shau, and I expected to find more NVA than I wanted to. I told Harris to have each man carry an extra claymore and one extra bandolier of rifle ammo. We were going for a six-day trip in an active area, and I wanted to be loaded for bear.

I wasn't real happy with the team makeup; Taylor had just come over to the LRRP from an infantry company, and this was to be his second trip out with me. Evans had never been out with me, and he had a bit of an attitude problem because he hadn't finished NCO academy. This was Sergeant Soals's first trip to the field, and he had only been in country a few weeks.

We came into the LZ on schedule, and the insertion went smoothly for the first three minutes. Then the gunships spotted two sampans on the Da Krong and requested permission to attack. The CO gave them the okay, so the gunships started attacking the two sampans on the river, and the C & C ship flew over to direct the attack. I got as mad as I had ever been; the shooting and flying around would alert the NVA to the fact that something was going on in the area. The large volume of radio traffic between all of the aircraft was on the same radio frequency as the team's. If the NVA had a radio monitor team at the headquarters we were looking for, attracted by all the aircraft radio traffic, they would hear our team make its insertion sitrep and know we were in their territory.

There were other problems: if the enemy hit the team, we'd have trouble getting into the radio net to call for help; the gunships would soon be low on fuel and ammo, and we could get our butts chopped up before more help reached us; the chase ship saw three gooks at the bottom of the hill that we'd inserted on, and when the pilot tried to call the C & C chopper to report the sighting, he couldn't get through. I didn't find out that we had been seen until the next day. I felt the Old Man should have held off attacking the sampans because it jeopardized our mission.

As an extra precaution, I had the team lay dog in the jungle by the LZ for two hours to let all of the excitement die down. I wanted to make sure we were near an LZ in case the NVA came looking for us. We started to move out along our planned route around 0900 hours. There weren't any trails around the LZ, so we were breaking brush every step of the way. We had to go slow and pick our way through the jungle as quietly as possible. We tried not to make any noise because we never knew when we would stumble upon a camp or bunker line. On a trail, we could at least see tracks that would tell us if the enemy was active in the area. The tangle was thick, so Taylor was having trouble keeping on the compass heading. I knew the pace count was off by the time we were five hundred meters off the LZ.

I was pushing the team to make up the time we'd lost at the insertion point. Harris was used to working with me, and he knew I was one of the more aggressive patrollers in the company. I liked to cover the AO, and I believed in moving at least a thousand meters a day if the situation allowed. Our AOs were six thousand meters by two thousand meters, and that's a lot of jungle. You couldn't do a good job of reconning an AO if you only moved five or six hundred meters a day. By 1600 hours, I knew we wouldn't make the first night's stopping point.

Taylor stopped moving and signaled for me to come forward. The team got down, each man covering his area of responsibility, while I moved up to see Taylor. He pointed up; strung in the trees over his head were six strands of blue commo wire. I looked at Taylor and shook my head; that was a bad sign. The NVA used blue wire, and the United States used black wire. The North Vietnamese Army was poor, and they never strung wire and just left it. In I Corps, when you found blue commo wire, you found gooks.

It was late so I decided we'd spend the night near this area. I told Taylor we would backtrack twenty or thirty meters and look for a place to spend the night. He was to check to make sure we didn't leave a trail back to our night location. I got the team turned around, and we started heading back the way we had come. We hadn't moved far when Harris spotted a thick clump of bushes that would give the team good cover—our home for the night—so we cleared our sleeping areas and put out the claymore mines.

I let half the team fix dinner while Harris and I put together the evening sitrep. We were on a flat, tablelike ridge, and there weren't any good terrain features to help me pinpoint our location. I told Harris to call the artillery battery on his radio and have them fire preplotted concentration A-6. He was to ask for one round of white phosphorus, set for a two-hundred-foot air burst. I had looked at the map and felt A-6 was close to our present position. The round should go off to my right front, and then I could get an idea of where I was. The round popped in the right area, so I shot a back azimuth to my location and plotted our position on the map.

I got the men together, and we discussed what we had seen. Then, we checked the map to see what the night's

E & E route would be. I told everyone we were going to request a change of direction from the Old Man during the night's sitrep. I fixed a chicken stew lurp and a canteen cup of chocolate beverage powder, and sat down to plot the new headings we would use in the morning. At 1800 hours, I told Evans to get the TOC on the radio. When we got through to the radio team, I took the handset and gave our night location, using the grape code, and requested permission to follow the wire we had located. I believed we could quickly trace the wire to the battalion base camp we were looking for. The sitrep had to be brief, because the enemy monitored the radio frequencies and could get a radio fix on the team if we didn't practice good radio discipline. After I made the report, we picked guard shifts and settled down to spend a quiet night, with no interruptions.

We woke up, fixed some breakfast, and made the morning sitrep before 0700 hours. We wanted to make some progress, but we ended up in some of the thickest jungle I had ever seen. We never got a glimpse of the sun; all we had was heat, bugs, leeches, and all the wait-a-minute vines in the whole stinking country. We stopped at 1200 hours to make our noon report and take a thirty-minute break. I had two orange-flavored corn flake bars and a Hershey's tropical chocolate disk for lunch, and we all relaxed for a few minutes. After the break, we started moving, and within thirty minutes, Taylor stopped and called me forward. I went to see what was wrong. We were at the edge of a cliff overlooking the river valley. I had been so intent on following the wire that I hadn't noticed that we had been veering off course. I pulled out the map and found out real quick I didn't know where the heck we were. The jungle was so thick I couldn't use artillery or have the Old Man fly out to spot us. I decided it would be best to go down to the river and see if I could figure out where we were. At the river, I could at least use the map to check terrain features, and if worse came to worst, I could at least have a helicopter come out and locate us.

The men weren't real cheered by the news that we were lost, but I felt everyone needed to know what the score was. The blue wire went down the cliff, so we were going

amazon.com

SGvN5Mz4Lx

Purchase Order #: SPL funds Zip Book FY22-23
Order of July 27, 2023

Qty. Item

1   **LRRP Team Leader: A Memoir of Vietnam**
       Burford, John --- Mass Market Paperback
       0804110514
       0804110514 9780804110518

Return or replace your item
Visit Amazon.com/returns

0/GvN5Mz4Lx/-2 of 2-//TCY9-CART-A/second-nominated-day/0/0730-11:30/0730-04:00

B3-
M2

down with it. The footing was terrible, and we were slipping, sliding, and falling all the way down the slope. I knew we had to sound like a herd of cows coming down. It was at least three hundred feet down to the river, and by the time we were halfway there, everyone was exhausted. I stopped the team, and we sat on a small ledge to rest. After a short while, I told Harris I was going to go on down to the river, and if I didn't come back up in fifteen minutes, he was to bring the team on down to the river.

The climb down got harder, and the last ten feet was a vertical drop. I dropped to the sand at the bottom of the cliff and hid behind a wall of vines. I stayed in the vines for a few minutes to listen for any movement. When I peeked out, I could see sand covered with rocks, and the river. To my right, a natural spring flowed from the wall of the cliff and spilled into a pool surrounded by sand. It looked like a picture out of a magazine ad for a tropical paradise. Except there were footprints all around the edge, prints made by bare feet. I thought to myself, well, so much for the tropical paradise. I got down and crawled through the vines to the edge of the pool. The tracks weren't very old, and the sand between the toe prints still had a sharp edge.

I looked up and down the sandspit, but I didn't see or hear anyone. I crawled back along the cliff to the left until I hit the blue commo wire. The wire came down the cliff and disappeared under a pile of rocks. I could see the hump in the ground where the gooks had buried the wire, and the hump headed straight to the river and into Laos. We would have to stay in the river valley long enough for me to plot this find and call in a sitrep.

I knew the team would start down in a few minutes, and the place where they would come down was so steep we couldn't easily climb back up. I decided I had better pull a quick recon of the area before the team got down; one person could work his way up the cliff, but five men under fire would be trapped. I kicked my 16 on to rock and roll, and eased out of the vines. I went one hundred meters in both directions, and I didn't see any signs of the enemy. I moved back to the spot where I had come down and waited for the team. After thirty minutes, I began to worry. I listened for them but didn't hear a thing. I decided to go up and get them, but I quickly found out I couldn't get back up the rock face. I was stuck on the river, and my team was sitting on a ledge halfway up the cliff. I looked at my watch. Over forty minutes had passed since I had climbed down to the river.

I waited five more minutes, and my temper started to boil. I was in a heck of a fix. I knew the sound of a rifle shot would carry a long way, and I didn't know if they would know that was a signal to get them to come down. I thought for a minute and decided that in this valley, with the noise of the river, a human voice wouldn't carry very far. I waited for a minute, and looked around before I shouted up the cliff. "Harris, come here." It worked; in a few minutes, down came my four lost sheep. Evans started to say something about me shouting on a mission, when I cut him off and told him to shut up. I took Harris off to the side and asked him why he hadn't come as I told him to. Harris said he told the team to start down, but Evans said he wouldn't go because I told them I would be back in fifteen minutes. Harris said he didn't know what to do. I told Harris he was the assistant team leader, and I expected him to follow my orders and take over if I wasn't there. We walked back over to the team. I got the men together, and I told them Harris was the ATL, and when he gave an order they would follow it. I also told them if anyone didn't like that, they should speak up now, and I would have them extracted right away. No one said a word; they knew I was mad.

I sent Harris fifty meters downstream, and Taylor fifty meters upstream, and told them to cover the flanks and watch for NVA. I left Evans at the base of the cliff, while Soals and I went out to the river to try and get some idea of where we were. I needed to get a good position fix on the wire. I knew that in a few weeks a Special Observation Group team would go over to the other side of the river and see where the wire led. I wanted to be sure they could find the starting point. It took Soals and me ten minutes to pinpoint our position, but we were sure of the location.

I knew we'd have a hard time getting radio contact from

down in the river valley, and we couldn't get out. I wanted to call in a sitrep for the find, and follow the trail that we had found at the base of the cliff. There was a small hill, about thirty-five feet high, in the curve of the river. The hill was covered with elephant grass and a few dead trees. It was in the middle of the valley, and climbing it would get us up a little higher to help us make radio contact.

We headed over to the hill in team formation, and were pushing through the grass when we hit an ant cluster. Taylor and I stirred them up, and the ants attacked Evans, turning him every way but loose, and he came out of his gear in record time. He stripped down naked, and we had to cover him with bug juice to get the ants off him. The ant bites were everywhere, and he looked like he had a bad case of measles. We shook the ants out of his uniform and enjoyed a good laugh while he got dressed. We moved on up the hill and stopped at the top to make the sitrep. Evans got mad because he had to unpack his rucksack to get the long antenna for the radio. He threw down his extra claymore and told me he wasn't going to carry it anymore. I told him he needed to settle down and cool it for his health.

We got radio contact with the CO, told him our location, and all about the wire and footprints. He told me we had done a good job, and then he set in and started to chew my ass out. We were out of our AO, and we were too close to the Laotian border. I told him we were going to move on to a trail we found by the river and double back into the AO. I also wanted to go to the area where they fired up the sampans to see if we could find any wreckage. He okayed the change in the mission, and *then* he told me the chase ship had seen three gooks watching the LZ when we were inserted. I told him all of the signs we had found pointed to an active base camp in the area and I expected contact anytime.

We moved along the trail for a couple of hours, until it was time to stop for the night. Our wide, sandy area had turned into a narrow rocky passage, just eight feet wide. We had the cliff on one side of us and the river on the other. I looked at the map. The cliff beside us was as steep as Mount Everest and looked to be twice as high. I decided we would stay right on the trail, and had the men put a claymore mine at each end of the trail. I waded out about fifteen feet and placed three claymores on some rocks sticking up in the river. If the gooks came down the river in sampans during the night, we could smoke them if we had to. We fixed dinner. picked guard times, and looked for the smallest rocks to sleep on. We settled down to a long, and very uncomfortable, quiet night.

The next morning we woke up, ate some breakfast, and packed our gear. We moved out, and we hadn't gone fifty meters when the trail we were following disappeared. Taylor stopped and looked back at me; I just shook my head. The cliff had given way to a very steep hillside with thick vegetation and a lot of loose rock. I couldn't see any sign of the trail along the hillside. I walked up to Taylor and looked at the river, then I got down on my hands and knees and looked closer at the water. I could see a ledge under the water and could tell that was the path. The gooks had known the hillside was too steep to walk on, so they followed the ledge. I told Taylor we were going to follow the trail. He had to go slow and use his foot to feel along in front of him. I had the men get close together, so they could grab the man in front if he slipped. With all the gear we had on, one misstep, and a man could drown. I didn't know how deep the river was alongside the ledge, and I couldn't feel the bottom when I tried to check. I told Harris that since he was last man in line, to be very careful, because I would miss him if he drowned.

I was sure we would be safe in the water because we were right at the bank, and viewed from the opposite shore, our uniforms would blend in with the vegetation. We were moving slow, so there would be no wake or waves, and if the NVA on the far side of the river saw us, they wouldn't be able to tell whether we were friend or foe. The only worry I had about us being in the water was with the Asian crocodile, and the many large brands of water snake living in the rivers of Vietnam.

So we slipped into the water. It was waist-deep, and not real cold. A couple of times, it came up to my chest. We had been in the water for a hour when Taylor stopped and pointed toward the middle of the river. Two caymans were swimming upstream, but they didn't seem to be paying any attention to us. I passed the word that no one was to shoot. If they turned toward us, we would toss a couple of grenades and let the concussion do the work. The caymans kept on going, and so did we.

We were in the water for four hours before we could find a place to start up the hill. We had looked everywhere for signs of the sampans the Cobras had fired up, but we never found so much as a scrap of wood. I decided it was time to get up to the top of the hill and see if we could find the base camp. We climbed out of the river, and sat in the bushes for a few minutes to let the water drain out of our boots.

Taylor took the point and started up the hill. I was right behind him, and it was a hard climb up. The brush grew downhill, and it was thick and tangled. Evans was lagging back behind me and wouldn't keep closed up. We had gone a couple of hundred feet up the hill when Taylor saw a bunker. Before I could say "no," he whipped out a grenade, yelled "Bunker" as loud as he could and threw the grenade up the hill. I watched in horror as the grenade arced up the hill, hit the top of the bunker, and bounced back on us. I dove backward into the brush, and the explosion threw my feet over my head. I heard the shrapnel cut through the bush as I made a somersault in full combat gear, hit the ground, and rolled into Evans. I crawled over to Taylor to see if he was hit. He was sitting there in a daze, but he was okay. I told him not to do that again, or he would piss me off. He stammered something about seeing movement in the bunker and told me he would be more careful. We got in some bushes and waited to see if anyone came to check on the explosion. After an hour, we moved on up the hill.

Where we stopped on the crest of the hill, there was a treetop observation platform. The NVA had wrapped vines around the tree to make a crude climbing aid. I ask Harris to climb the tree, but the vines broke under his weight. I wanted to use the platform to help me pinpoint our location. After we decided no one could get up the tree, I told Harris to call the artillery for a WP spotter air burst. We'd been in the river for four hours, and the lack of ground references made me unsure of where we were. Taylor and Evans moved out ten meters to give us security, while Harris called in the fire mission. Sergeant Soals and I stood near the crest of the ridgeline to spot the explosion and mark our place on the map. I pointed to the next ridge and told Soals the WP should pop right over the end of that ridge. Harris finished the fire mission and told the FDC to shoot. In a few seconds, we heard the rushing noise of an incoming round. I pointed to the ridgeline just as the shell exploded in the air above us. The shell casing ripped down through the trees and hit the ground twenty meters away. After Soals and I got up, I told Harris that must have been a short round and I wanted him to have the guns repeat range and fire one more shot. I listened as Harris told the FDC we had lost the round and to repeat range and fire one more WP air burst. When Harris said, "Shoot," Soals and I turned toward the ridge to see where the round would hit. We heard the round coming, and I knew we were in trouble. With a sharp crack, the shell exploded over our heads, and the case slapped into the ground just in front of me.

I took the map and looked at it again, shot new azimuths, and checked the artillery preplots. After a few minutes, I told Harris to get Evans's radio; we needed to call the Old Man. I got on the radio and told the CO about the tree stand and the bunker. I also told him I was so lost I couldn't find my ass with both hands and a search warrant, so I needed an air fix on my location. He said he would be out in thirty minutes and that we needed to be ready to direct the chopper to our position.

When we got an air spot, we used the clock method of direction to guide the Huey over our location. The nose of the ship was twelve o'clock, left was nine o'clock, right was three, and the tail was six. As the chopper flew by, we would tell the pilot to turn our direction by telling him a time. The idea was to get the ship to fly overhead, and when the slick passed directly over you, you'd tell them to mark the position. The CO then could check the map from the air and tell you where you were. The trick was to get spotted as fast as you could because the NVA could see the chopper too, and no one liked to have a chopper hanging around attracting attention.

The CO was right on time, and we made short work of getting spotted. The Old Man gave me the new coordinates for my location. He also told me there was an extra ridgeline that didn't show on the map. I thanked him for the help then sat down to plot our new direction to travel.

After lunch, I got with Taylor and pointed out the new direction I wanted him to go. As we lurped across the ridge, I kept seeing tree stumps scattered around the area, and no two stumps were close together. I didn't understand the meaning of the stumps, so I stopped the men and passed the word to move slow and scan everything. The brush just kept getting thicker, and Taylor was having trouble getting through the wait-a-minute vines. He stopped and asked me if we could go in a different direction to find an easier passage. He wanted to get off the ridgetop and see if the brush thinned out on the sides of the hill. I looked at the map and told Taylor he could move to his right and go down to the bottom of the small valley formed by the ridgelines.

The side of the ridge was steep, and the footing was more than tricky. We were all watching our step as we worked our way down the slope. We had gone down the slope twenty feet when I looked up. My heart stopped as the icy hand of fear gripped me. There they were, a whole line of bunkers facing us from the other ridgeline. Evans bumped into me, and the team stopped. I got the men down, but I couldn't get to Taylor, so he kept walking down the slope. I signaled Harris to stay and cover me as I went down the hill and grabbed Taylor. I quietly pulled him down, leaned forward, and whispered in his ear, "Look across the valley!" As he looked at the line of bunkers stretched along the ridge, Taylor turned very pale. We slowly worked our way back up to the rest of the team. We watched the bunker line and didn't see or hear any movement. After a few minutes, I decided that the bunkers must be empty.

I told Harris, Evans, and Soals to spread out and cover the bunker line. Taylor and I were going to go over to the bunkers to see if there were any signs of the enemy. I told

Harris that if shooting started, they were to lay down a base of fire so Taylor and I could get back across the valley. I also told him that if we were hit and went down, they were to pull back to the top of the ridgeline and get the artillery and gunships working while he called for an extraction.

I got Taylor, and we started back down the slope. I knew in my heart that the bunkers were empty, but I had a hard time getting my ass to believe it. We kicked our 16s to rock and roll and walked down the side of the valley. We'd take a step, then stop to scan the bunker line, then take another step. Our fingers were tensed over the triggers of our rifles and every muscle in our bodies was ready to spring at the first shot. The barrels of the rifles followed our eyes across the bunker line as we worked our way down the slope. It took ten nerve-wracking minutes to reach the small stream at the bottom of the vee. I kept wondering when "they" were going to open fire. I guessed they would let Taylor and me start up their side of the hill in hope that the rest of the unit would follow. I was sure they would want to kill as many of us as they could with the first volley. We stepped over the stream and started up the hill in a low crouch. The smaller the target the better. Right then I wished I was two feet tall. Halfway up the hill, we could tell the bunkers were empty, and a wave of relief swept over us. Now all we had to worry about were booby traps.

We reached the bunker line and carefully checked out the first fighting position. Living hooches had been built over fighting bunkers, and trails ran behind the positions connecting them. I decided to check five hooches in each direction before I called the rest of the team over. I went to the right and Taylor went to the left. We followed the trail along the ridge until we'd each checked five hooches. At each stop, we'd check for visible booby traps and signs of recent habitation. When Taylor and I met back at bunker one, we reviewed what we had seen, and I felt the area was safe. I sent Taylor to signal Harris while I looked for concealed booby traps in the first hooch.

Once I had the team back together, I told them we'd spend the next four hours looking around. After we finished the recon, we'd make our sitrep, and spend the night in the

NVA base camp. My plan for the next day was to probe more of the camp and get it plotted on the map. Harris brought up a good question about the NVA coming home and finding us sleeping in their bed. I told him that this was a large camp, and I doubted if the whole unit would come in tonight. We'd have to watch out for an advance party, but not the main unit.

I broke the men down into search teams, Harris and Soals being one team, Taylor and I being the other. I left Evans to search the two hooches on each side of our new home. We had four hours of good light left, but I didn't want to split up the team too much. I told Harris to go along the east trail until he had either been gone one hour, or ran out of bunkers. Taylor and I would take the west trail. The two search teams left, and Evans started his search of the positions around our night position.

There were bunkers on every finger of the mountain, and the trails that connected them wound around the valley walls. The path split twice while we were following it, and we could see more bunkers on the adjoining ridges. I knew this base camp had to be at least a regimental headquarters. When our time ran out, we headed back to Evans's position. Harris got back shortly after we did, and his eyes were as big as saucers. He reported that the bunker line hooked back to the right and his trail had divided a number of times. Evans found the kitchen area during his search, and led the team down to the spring at the bottom of the vee. There was a stove that had three ovens, and the whole thing was made of baked clay. Soals walked around the top of the stove and fell into a shallow tunnel, which we followed up toward the top of the hill. There we found a large pit covered with brush, a smoke collector pit used to dissipate the cooking smoke so it couldn't easily be seen by an aircraft. The smells in the area told us it had been a while since anyone had been around. We went back up to the hooch that we had chosen to spend the night in, and got ready to eat dinner.

I took a little time to check out the workmanship of the hooch we were in. The roof was woven palm fronds, and it was in good repair. There were woven palm sleeping mats on the floor and woven shades that could be let down when it rained. All of the construction was done without nails, and the fits were great. Under the hooch was a fighting bunker, with a thick log roof and an entranceway from the living area at both ends. The firing slot was open, and the fields of fire were clear. This was no quickly thrown together position. I felt like a burglar in the night, hoping the real owners didn't decide to come home.

Harris and I worked up the sitrep and plotted as much of the base camp on our maps as we could. I called the Old Man and started telling him about our find and that we were laying it out on the map. I also told him that I had decided to stay in the base camp overnight and we were going to resume the search in the morning. He okayed the idea and told me to check in early the next day before we started our search. I couldn't tell him everything, because we didn't want to stay on the air that long, but he knew we had made a major find.

Taylor was sitting at the front of the bunker, and was getting ready to fix his lurp. He took his knife and started to dig a small hole for his C-4 when he hit metal. We all froze as Taylor gently probed the ground with his knife. He moved some dirt, and then he started to dig a trench with the knife. I thought he had gone over the hill when he started to laugh. With a great deal of flurry, he held up a brand-new AK-47, still wrapped in the oilpaper. That brought our first day's weapon find up to seven.

After dinner, we set the guard times and put out our claymore mines. We put them on both sides of the hooch, and two in the front. The hooch was big enough to hold all of us, with room to spare, and we settled down to get some sleep. We all pulled two, one-hour guard shifts during the night. I woke up automatically every hour and would lie there and listen for a few minutes before I went back to sleep.

Late that night, Taylor put his hand on my arm and squeezed until I woke up. I knew it wasn't time for me to go on guard. Taylor leaned over and whispered in my ear, "Sarge, listen." I propped up on one elbow and held my breath while I searched the night with my ears. Then I heard it, a faint sound coming from the far end of the valley. Taylor leaned over again, "Do you hear it?" I nodded, yes. I lay there and listened; I knew the sound, but I couldn't place it. Then it came to me in a rush—someone was chopping wood, somewhere up the valley. I looked at my watch. It was 2300 hours. No one chops wood in the middle of the night. I leaned over to Taylor and whispered, "Chopping?" He nodded. It wasn't regular chopping; whoever it was wasn't cutting down trees; they were signaling someone. The sound stopped; I waited a few minutes, but nothing else was heard. I told Taylor to pass the word to the next guard to wake me if he heard any strange noise, no matter what. The rest of the night passed quietly, but I was glad to see daylight.

We made an early report, and I told the CO I was sure we were being shadowed, I felt the reason the NVA hadn't bothered us was because there weren't enough of them to take us on. I stressed the fact that I believed a major unit was headed back to the base camp and last night's chopping was a signal to that unit. Captain Eklund said the division had decided to insert an infantry company in the area to destroy the camp. We needed to conduct a thorough search of the area by 1200 hours. The incoming CO would need to know how many engineers and how much C-4 to bring in with the company.

I kept the team together for the morning search because I was feeling more and more like we had company close in the area. I wanted us to be able to react to any attack with full firepower. We started to move along the trail to the north, and were plotting the fighting positions on our map as we went. We had moved to the second ridgeline when we made our first major find of the day. Harris looked into a large bunker and found two radio sets and a field phone. We could tell the equipment had been sitting for a while, but it looked like it was serviceable to me. We moved on until we hit a split in the trail. Bunkers lay on both arms of the paths. The trails ran parallel to each other so I let Harris and Soals take the low path, while the rest of us stayed on the original path. We made sure we could maintain visual contact, and kept on mapping. Taylor made the best find of the trip when he came across a rucksack and two pouches full of papers. A quick search told us the backpack belonged to a colonel in the North Vietnamese Army. I felt strange going through his pack. There were letters to him from East Europe, pictures of him in dress whites, and two pictures of his family. He had a wife and two children back home. We found his party card, a battle flag, and a lot of papers in French. The words "MINH b6" were written on the inside flap of the rucksack. A chill ran up my back as I thought it could have just as easily been a gook going through my gear.

By 1200 hours, we had mapped out over one hundred bunkers and brought our weapons-found count up to fifteen. I had Evans call the CO on the TAC frequency, and I described our find. The Old Man told me to move all of the captured equipment to the small clearing we had found on the ridgetop. He was going to fly out and drop down two duffel bags tied onto a rope for us. We were to put all the equipment we had found in the bags, and they would haul it back to Camp Evans. The division G-2 wanted to see the rucksack and its contents. Then the team was to move back to the LZ we had inserted into four days earlier and secure it for the company that was flying out to destroy the complex. The plan called for the company to be inserted by 1500 hours. We were to get on the last ship, and they would bring us back to Camp Evans. Captain Eklund told me that division had not found a unit to send in to relieve us, but he expected everything to be on schedule.

The Huey with the bags showed up at 1230 hours, and we loaded the loot. We were pooped from lugging all of the goodies up the hill, but we had to get moving right away if we were to reach the insertion LZ on time. We stayed on the top of the ridgeline and busted our asses to get to the LZ. Taylor did a good job of keeping on course, and we arrived at the hilltop at 1445 hours. I called the Old Man to let him know we had the landing zone secured. He told me there was going to be a little holdup because the division had not been able to come up with an infantry company to put in the AO, nor had they found any engineers to set the explosives to destroy the bunkers.

Our LZ was the only LZ in the AO, and it was a one-ship landing area. I had the men spread out around the top so we could see all of the sides of the hill. I told Harris that we might not get out that day, but that we would be staying on the hilltop. We settled down for the wait and kept our eyes on the wood line surrounding the bottom of the hill. A little later, Harris called me over to tell me he had seen movement in the woods to his front. I felt that our shadows were trying to see what we were up to, so I told him to keep his eyes peeled and stay down. Evans waved me back over to his area to tell me the CO had called. A company was on the way, but they only had seven choppers so it would take three lifts to get them all on the ground. We had been on the LZ for two hours, and I was getting a little uptight. The NVA could do a lot in two hours, and we knew they were around here somewhere. When Evans said the first lift was fifteen minutes out, I dug a couple of smoke grenades out of my pack and got ready to guide the ships in.

Harris called out that he saw more movement to his front. I was in a real pickle; I didn't want to start a fight, but I needed to know what the gooks were up to. I couldn't let the infantry company come into an ambush, so I decided to do a little recon by fire. If a lot of gooks fired back, I could tell the choppers it was a hot LZ and get the team extracted. I told everyone we'd throw two hand grenades and then fire two M-16 magazines. On the count of three, we pulled pins, flung the grenades down the hillside, and opened fire with our rifles. Nothing happened. I did notice that we threw ten grenades, but there were only six explosions. I had everyone throw one more grenade, and that time only three went off. I made a mental note to draw new grenades for the next trip; Carrying dud grenades around could be fatal.

The beat of rotor blades announced the arrival of the infantry company, so I got Evans to bring his radio down to the helipad. The LZ was small, and on a slope, so I had to guide each chopper into the landing area. Evans got radio contact with the lead ship and told me to pop the smoke. I popped a red smoke, and Evans hollered to me that the pilot had identified the smoke. I stepped to the edge of the

LZ and raised my arms over my head. The pilot would
guide in on me, and I'd lower my arms to give him a plane
of reference and help him set the Huey down. As I stood
there, I couldn't help but think I made one heck of a good
target.

The first ship flared out and settled into the LZ. The
minute the skids hit the ground, the troops in the chopper
jumped off. As it lifted off, the next ship was lining up to
make its approach, and I raised my arms again.

After the fourth chopper unloaded, the company sent its
own pathfinder team to bring in the rest of the lift. I told
Evans to tell the men to get ready to get on the last Huey;
it was ours, and I walked down the hill to meet with the
company commander to brief him on the situation.

The CO and the 1st Platoon leader were huddled over
their map when I arrived. The RTO waved me over, and I
squatted down with them. The captain told me his men had
been in the field thirty-five days and were heading to the
firebase for a break when the call came to divert to this LZ.
The company was out of water, needed rest, and the base
camp had better be worth the effort. I got my map out and
started to brief them. I pointed out the spring at the bottom
of the ridge so they could get fresh water. I also explained
that we had been shadowed ever since we had gotten in the
AO and showed them the missing ridgeline on the map. He
asked me if we were going to stay with the company to act
as guides, and I told him my orders were to take the team
out on the last chopper I gave him my map, which had
most of the bunkers marked, and I reviewed with him the
types of equipment we had located, the blue commo wire
we found, and the signaling we had heard the night before.
He agreed that we'd run across a major find, and he'd have
his hands full destroying all of the bunkers.

When I walked back up the hill to join the men, I noticed that Taylor was laughing, so I asked him what had
happened. He was almost in tears as he told me the story.
It seems a brand-spanking-new lieutenant had spotted them
sitting around a dead tree at the edge of the LZ. Here were
four men sitting on their ass, with no helmets, no rucksacks, and wearing camo uniforms. He ran up the hill, hel-

met pulled down to the bridge of his noise, rifle at high port, and demanded to know what unit they were with. At least Taylor stood up when he said "58 LRRPs." Then, the lieutenant asked what they were doing there. Taylor told him we had been on a recon mission. At that point, the officer looked the men over and asked how long they had been there. Taylor said five days. A funny look came over the lieutenant's face, and in a much nicer tone, he asked how many of us there were. Taylor gave him a deadpan look and told him, "Five, sir." The dude freaked out, spun about on his heels, and marched back down the hill. The poor kid had come up to chew some ass, and found he was in the wrong place.

When Evans got up and put on his radio pack, we knew it was time for us to get to the helipad and catch the last ship. The bird hovered in, and as the grunts climbed off, we climbed on. When that ship broke ground, I heaved a sigh of relief. I had bad feelings about the AO, and I was glad to be heading back to Camp Evans.

When we landed at Camp Evans, Sergeant Burnell was sitting by a pile of equipment, so I went over and asked him what was up. He said to load the gear on the two choppers behind him; we were going back to Eagle. We loaded the equipment, and I ask him what happened to the loot we had sent back. He hemmed and hawed a bit, then told me the G-2 people and the chopper pilots had split it up. All that was left was the colonel's empty backpack, a Russian steel helmet, and an NVA canteen. None of my men wanted the leftovers, so I kept them. Mr. Grant overheard the conversation and offered to return the AK-47, but I told him we had plenty of them.

We got on the Huey for the ride home, and the crew chief gave me a headset. After we got airborne, Grant called me on the intercom to express his appreciation for all the wonderful gifts and countless hours of flying joy we had found for him. He was going to give us the scenic flight home. When Grant laughed, I knew we were in for a ride. The ship made a sickening drop to the right. I turned around to look between the pilot's seats and saw the ground rushing up towards us. At ten feet, Grant leveled the chopper out, and we made the thirty-mile trip to Camp Eagle going eighty knots, a whole ten feet above the ground. One time, we did pull up long enough to clear a farmer sitting on a water buffalo. As we approached Eagle, Grant pulled into a tight climbing turn that pinned us to the floor with G force. Those of us with our eyes open got a super view of the Royal tombs. We roared in over the wire to a soft landing at the company helipad. While the men unloaded the Huey, I walked around to Grant's side of the ship and opened his door. Grant pulled off his helmet gave me a big, silly grin and leaned over to hear what I was saying. I told him, if the next time he came out to extract my team he was met by more accurate ground fire, he should look to see who was doing the shooting. He just laughed and told me to "come again soon."

After supper, I went to the orderly room to see Sergeant Burnell. He wanted to know if I was still mad about the missing souvenirs. I told him there would be plenty more times to get good loot. I sat down and told Burnell that I didn't want Evans going to the field on any team I was leading. We talked for a while, and I made my case as strongly as I could without getting Evans in trouble. Evans was okay but we didn't work well together. The transfer was made that night.

The next afternoon, Sergeant Proctor called me to the orderly room. He told me that the company that had relieved us yesterday had been hit at 1500 hours today and was in a big firefight in the base camp while we were talking. The 1/501st was going in to join the fight, and the company had taken heavy casualties.

"So, you can see, boys, there were a number of ways to get lost. The maps were good, but sometimes whole mountains were missed. When you were in low areas, with no visible terrain features, you just couldn't always tell where you were. Of course, there was good old stupidity always ready to work for you."

One time I got lost through 100 percent pure stupidity, and there were a few hours when I thought Larry Chambers and I were finished. We had inserted a twelve-man team to pull an ambush on a gook high-speed trail I had worked before. We were going to move about three klicks through some very thick jungle to our ambush site. The jungle was impassable without the use of machetes, and we didn't carry or use anything like that. I reported to the Old Man that we were stopped cold and requested a change of ambush site. The CO denied the request, so I told Sergeant Smith, the ATL on the mission, that Chambers and I would scout ahead to see if there wasn't an easier way through there. I got Chambers, and we dropped our rucksacks and all of our LBE. All we would carry was our M-16 rifle, one bandolier of seven magazines, and our compass and map. We were only going out a couple of hundred meters to see if the vegetation thinned out, or if we could find somewhere to pick our way through the bush quietly. I told Smitty we would be gone for thirty minutes, tops. Snuffy Smith and I had worked together a lot, and I could see a trace of disbelief in his eyes.

We had gone about seventy-five meters when the vegetation got so dense we were forced to crawl on our hands and knees. I kept pushing on, but there was no letup in the thickness of the brush. We crawled for over an hour before I realized how much time had passed. In addition, we had become completely disoriented from crawling around. We got to a streambed where we were able to stand up. I got the map out, but the ground around us was flat, so we had no elevations to work with. The streambed didn't show on the map, and we had lost count of the distance we had traveled. Chambers said I should shoot an azimuth so we could locate our position. I asked him what was I supposed to shoot to, and from where. It didn't take a rocket scientist to see we were lost. We had started off following an azimuth to the south, so we would head north to see if we could hit the trail near where we had inserted. I knew there was little chance of hitting the team's location, but I felt we would be close.

We had been gone over two hours, and it was time for the noon sitrep. Smitty called in, gave the team's location, and reported negative activity. The Old Man came back on the radio and wanted to know why the team hadn't moved since our call this morning. Smitty did his best to beat around the bush, but the CO pinned him down when he told Snuffy to get the Six (that is, me) on the radio. Smith still tried to cover for me when he told the Old Man that the jungle was thick and I was doing a little recon. When the captain asked how long I had been gone, Smitty had to tell him. The Old Man came unglued and chewed a big hole in Smitty's ass. He instructed Sergeant Smith to call back in thirty minutes, or if I showed up, to have me call back immediately. The thirty minutes flew by, and Smith had to report us as still missing. The CO made Smitty call in an artillery WP air burst every fifteen minutes hoping we would hear it and be able to guide back on the sound.

Chambers and I were back to crawling, but at least we were heading north. The jungle just got thicker and moving got harder. By now, we had been away from the team for over four hours, and I knew I was in big trouble. We hit a section of bush that thinned out, and we were finally able to get up and walk. We moved about a hundred meters when we hit the open area that surrounded the trail. I took the map, studied the wood line we were in, and the other wood line I could see across the open area. Then, I showed Chambers right where we were on the map and told him all we needed to do was follow the tree line back up to the team. My luck held out, and we walked right up on the team in less than ten minutes.

Smitty told me to call the Old Man "right now," so I called in and got the ass chewing of the year. I had been wrong. I told the captain that the jungle was too thick to move through, and I had gotten lost while doing the recon. I told him that tomorrow I would take the team around to the east and get to the ambush site in time to set up for a morning ambush. Smith asked me if we had heard the artillery fire and used it to find our way back. Chambers told him we never heard the first sound the whole time we were out. Smith made me swear I'd never go on another recon like that when he was around.

CHAPTER 5

"Uncle John, I have a question."

"Okay, Erik, what's your question?"

"You have talked about 'making contact' and 'enemy' units. What was it like when you found the enemy?"

When we found, or bumped into, the enemy, we reported that the team was in contact. Being lurps, we had options during contact that regular infantrymen didn't have—we could move away; we could hide and watch; if the odds were in our favor, we could fight. On LRRP missions, our primary instructions were to break contact and continue the mission if possible. If we couldn't shake the enemy, then we were to pull back to an LZ for extraction. But if things got out of hand and we were being overrun, we would scatter and try to avoid the enemy using escape and evasion procedures. There was always a chance that someone could get away and get back to friendly troops.

The infantryman's options were to fight—make contact and hold it, pile on the force, and destroy the enemy unit. Regular units were taught that at the first sighting of the enemy, or the sound of fire, they were to return fire. When we got men who had been in the regular infantry units, it took us a little time to retrain them so they would be used to the way we operated. The key to a lurp's survival during contact was knowing when to shoot, and better, when not to shoot.

I always believed that if a team on a LRRP mission had to use its guns, then someone had made a mistake. It may have been faulty intelligence (i.e., the G-2 didn't know the enemy was near the LZ, or the estimated strength of the unit in the area could have been wrong). There were times when someone on the team left a sign or made a mistake that allowed the gooks to track the team. I know there were plenty of cases when the team leader made a bad call. It didn't matter what the problem was, once the first shot was fired, the mission was compromised, and in most cases, the team had to be extracted.

When the shooting just couldn't be avoided, we almost always had the element of surprise on our side. I called that element the lurp factor, and it had saved many a man's life. Gary Linderer was a great example of the lurp factor. On his second mission, the team he was with had to walk on a trail due to the thickness of the undergrowth. The team was stopped for a break when an NVA soldier stepped out on the trail right in front of Linderer. While the gook tried to figure out who the heck these guys were, Linderer opened fire and hit the man. Linderer knew he had hit the gook, but the guy managed to get away. Before the team had a chance to search for him, they heard more NVA coming through the bush, and the team had to pull back to call for an extraction.

John Looney had a close call on one of his early missions. The team he was attached to was moving up a streambed and had stopped for a break. Four NVA came walking down the streambed. The LRRP team climbed back up the bank to ambush the gooks, but the gooks got there too soon. Looney's feet were still in the water when the first man came into view. The NVA saw Looney and started to wave to him. He had his hand about halfway up when he realized Looney wasn't a friend. The shooting was over in seconds, and four dead NVA lay in the water. The stream turned red with their blood while the team made a quick check of the bodies. Looney noticed that the lead NVA had a wedding band on, and seeing the ring kind of rattled John. The team had to end the mission because it had been compromised by all the shooting. It's a sure bet John Looney is still alive today because of the lurp factor. In both of those examples, there was no chance to avoid the contact. The teams involved did the right thing, at the right time, but both of the missions were blown.

My most memorable nonfiring contact mission was the last mission I was on with Sergeant Byron. The team was composed of Byron, TL; me, ATL; Harris, point; Looney, RTO; Saenz, RTO; and Chambers, scout. Lawrence Saenz had just transferred to the company from the 501 Signal Battalion. He had been in country for a year, but this was his first trip to the woods. Larry Chambers had just come to the company from the States, and it was his first mission.

We were on a trip to an AO in the Game Preserve, and we had to insert on a one-ship LZ on the top of a hill. The lead ship dropped us off right at first light, so we spread out around the LZ and lay dog for thirty minutes. I was lying behind a log on the far side of the LZ when I heard a shot that was fired a good distance down the hill, so I just kept watching in that direction. Later, Sergeant Byron came over to my position and asked me if I'd seen anything. I told him about the shot from the valley, and he told me he didn't hear any shot fired. He thought I must have imagined it. Right on cue, four more rounds went off down below. I looked at him with one of those grins and shook my head. Byron went to Looney's position and called the Old Man on the radio. He told the CO about the gooks. Byron knew we hadn't been spotted, so he told the CO to go ahead and release the gunships.

The shooter made us change the direction we were going to take. We had planned to come off the hill and go due north down to the valley. Since that was right where the shots had been fired, Byron decided to go east and move down a long finger that ran off the hilltop. When we got to the bottom of the hill, we'd hook back to the valley to see what the shooting was about. We plotted a new azimuth, and Harris started down the finger. We were moving in the standard team formation—Harris on point; Byron at slack; Looney, his RTO, was next; then Chambers; Saenz, the artillery RTO; and me, bringing up the rear as the tail gunner.

It was one of those superhot, clear days, and we were soaked with sweat in just a few minutes. The finger wasn't steep, but the thickness of the jungle made moving difficult. The heat and humidity hung without letup. The first hour of a mission was the hardest: the gear hadn't settled in, and our shoulders hadn't gotten numb from the pressure of the LBE harness and our rucksack straps. Byron stopped the team for a ten-minute break every hour. We'd lie down on the ground and face out toward our individual areas of responsibility. We'd lie quietly and listen to the sounds of the jungle. If Byron felt it was clear, then we could roll over and scoot down against the rucksack. This would take the strain of the pack straps off our shoulders and give the blood a chance to circulate. We'd be halfway sitting up, with our rifle across our laps. For the next few minutes, we could enjoy the finer things of life, like getting a drink of hot water, popping two salt tablets, adding more camouflage stick to replace the paint that had washed away with the sweat, putting on more bug juice, or watching the leeches race each other to see who got to bite us first. No matter how much bug juice we put on, there was always one hardy leech who would fight his way through and get us. We sweated so much that the salt in the sweat would form a white crust on our uniforms. The back and the armpits of the jacket would be stiff with salt. When Byron signaled the break was over, we'd have to help each other get up.

We had been moving for three hours when we hit a high-speed trail. Harris stopped, and Byron signaled for us to get down. Everyone covered his area while Byron looked at the trail. In a few minutes, he called me forward to let me inspect the trail. There were footprints everywhere, some made by bare feet, some with Ho Chi Minh sandals, and a few sneaker prints. The trail was three feet wide and worn down about five inches. It looked like a gook interstate highway there in the middle of nowhere. Byron pulled the team back twenty-five meters from the trail. The team set up a hasty perimeter while Byron and I huddled over the map to plot the location of the find. We decided that the trail ran from the open area five thousand meters east of us, back to the base camp we were looking for there in the Game Preserve.

Our mission was to patrol from the valley, east to the open area, and we knew the Old Man wouldn't let us make a major change of direction. All of our preplotted artillery fire was to the east, so we'd be forced to go that direction. I looked at my watch, saw that it was only 1030 hours, and hatched a brilliant idea. I asked Byron if I could take Looney and Harris and lurp west on the trail through the valley where we'd heard the shooting. This would allow us to find out who had been in the valley when we inserted and see if we could find any signs of the base camp. If we could find good signs, we could justify a later mission to go west. I explained to Byron that we would have radio contact with him, so he could adjust artillery fire for us if we got in trouble. I would only go out one hour then come back, so we'd be doing a side recon and not a change of mission. Byron approved the idea, so I grabbed Harris and Looney, and we got ready to go.

When it was time to move out, Byron pulled me off to the side and told me to be careful and take it slow. I put Harris on point, I walked slack, and Looney, with the radio, was tail gunner. We stayed in the jungle and moved parallel to the trail. As we started to enter the valley, the terrain got rough. The walls of the valley were steep and rocky, and the valley narrowed down. There was a stream in the valley, and it pushed the trail higher up on the valley wall. The stream and the steep sides of the valley forced us to use the trail as we moved deeper into the valley. At one point, it was a twenty-foot vertical drop down to the stream, and the valley wall was straight up beside us. The trail was hard-packed dirt, so we didn't leave any footprints. We moved slowly, our weapons ready, and all of our senses fine tuned. If some shooting had started, we'd have been out of luck; there wasn't any place to go, nor was there an ounce of cover.

The trail started to descend toward the creek, and we came to a place where the trail got wide, and there was a large deep pool. Harris spotted something on the ground, and we went over to investigate. There were some candy papers scattered about the area. I took one of the papers and wiped my finger across it. The powdered sugar wasn't sticky yet so I knew the paper was fresh. Looney found a cigarette butt near a log, took a sniff, and told me it was fresh. That must have been the spot where our shooters had been when we inserted. It looked a lot like an old swimming hole back home. A nice place to kick back and rest. I found myself wishing I could take a swim and act like a kid for a while. Instead, I put away my dreams, and I took a few minutes to plot the place on the map. I felt we could fire some artillery harassment and interdiction fire here the next morning and bump off a few gooks. I had Looney call Byron to let him know we were okay and had found some signs.

We had fifteen minutes left before we needed to start back, so I told Harris that we'd keep on moving west. The stream went into the creek, and we could see the path under the water. This was a neat way to hide a trail. From the air a spotter could see the water but there'd be no sign of a trail. I decided to take the point for the rest of the trip, so I waded into the stream, and we continued our journey. We'd been going up the stream for a few minutes when we came to a downed tree, which blocked the creek, and a lot of brush had piled up behind it. I saw where the NVA using the trail had stepped out of the water to get around the blockage and I headed in that direction. I got to the bank and was about to step out when I froze. The bank was muddy, and the sticks and brush on the bank were covered with wet mud. What caught my eye was the mud still dripping from the sticks where men had just climbed out of the stream ahead of us. I decided it was time to head back. We were right on their ass, and it was no time to start a fight. Before he turned back, I had Looney take two pictures of the muddy bank. When we reached the pool area, we set up a hasty ambush. If the gooks were following us, we could surprise them and pop off a few rounds.

I had Looney call Byron to tell him we were coming back and to tell him what we had found. I gave the gooks ten minutes, and when they didn't show up, I felt it was safe to head for Byron. We moved back down the trail to the team's position, and we were glad to get back together with them. Byron had the team move one hundred meters away from the trail and set up in a defensive circle. We stayed in this area to have lunch and call in the noon sitrep. We were in a great position. If the NVA had followed us back down the trail, we'd have been able to hear them while they searched for us and we could avoid detection.

Looney started trying to call the TOC on the PRC-25, but he couldn't get through. He changed over to the long antenna and tried again, but still couldn't make radio contact. Byron had Looney unscrew the long antenna and moved the radio over near a big tree, then they motioned for me to come over. The plan was simple—I would climb the tree with the commo wire and the long antenna. Then, I'd wrap the bare end of the commo wire around the base of the antenna and drop the wire back down to Looney. He would take the other end of the wire and stick it in the antenna socket. The Rube Goldburg setup worked, and Looney called in the sitrep.

While I held on to the tree and the antenna, I started to itch everywhere. I looked at my hand and saw that it was covered with ants. I couldn't let go of the antenna, nor could I get out of the tree until Looney was finished with his radio transmission. The ants were kicking my ass, and I couldn't holler down to hurry Looney up. Byron finally looked up and motioned for me to come on down. I set a record for getting out of a tree, hitting the ground, and stripping off my uniform. Byron looked at me like I was nuts until he saw my red welts and the ants. Looney and Byron squirted me with bug juice while Harris shook the ants out of my jacket. There I was in the jungle of Vietnam wearing nothing but my boots and hat while I was swatting at the ants. If the NVA had found us, we wouldn't have had to fire a shot, they would have died laughing. But we won the battle of the ants.

I got dressed, and the team started toward the trail. Byron decided to parallel the trail back to the base of the hill where we had inserted. We needed to plot as much of the trail as we could on the map, and monitor enemy movement. It took the rest of the afternoon to work our way back to the point where Byron wanted to spend the night, fifty meters from the trail. We set out claymores and cleared a sleeping area. After we set up, Byron got everyone together and opened the map. We discussed the plan for the next day. We were going to move to the trail the next morning and parallel the trail to the east for the following two days. This would bring us out to the open area for extraction on the fourth day.

There was still plenty of light left, so we were able to fix a hot dinner. We weren't always able to fix a hot meal in the field, but when circumstances allowed, we could rustle up some great food. I took a chicken and rice lurp, two packs of cocoa beverage powder, a fruitcake bar, and a small ball of C-4 explosive out of my pack. I filled a canteen cup with water and lit the ball of C-4. The C-4 burned with a pale blue flame but without smoke or odor. Best of all, a ball no larger than the end of my thumb would bring a canteen cup of water to a rolling boil in less than two minutes. I'd pour most of the hot water into the plastic bag with the chicken and rice, stir, and roll the bag up to soak for a few minutes. Then, I'd add the cocoa to the remaining hot water so it would mix easy, stir it, and add more water. In just a few minutes my dinner was ready—steaming hot chicken and rice, a cup of chocolate milk, and a fruitcake bar for dessert. No finer meal could be had in the whole of Southeast Asia. After dinner, we repacked our waste and picked the guard times. Byron had made the night sitrep, and it was time to settle down for a quiet night.

Byron woke me by placing his hand over my mouth; he leaned over and whispered, "Gooks." My blood turned to ice; those weren't the words I wanted to wake up to. I rolled over very slowly, placed one hand on my rifle, and found the claymore firing device with the other. The gooks were on the trail, and we could hear them talking. I woke Chambers, who was next to me, and whispered to him to hold still and be ready to fire. The NVA had flashlights, and they were shining them around. It sounded like they were breaking down into small search groups, and we could hear them enter the jungle. I took my sleeping cover and quietly stuffed it under the flap of my rucksack. In the silence that surrounded us, I could sense the other men getting ready for the fight. Saenz had his radio tuned to the artillery frequency, and Byron had given him the fire mission instructions during the night briefing. Looney was waiting for the order to call the TOC. I went over the fire drill in my head one more time—Byron, Harris, Chambers, and I would set off our claymores and fire one magazine on full auto. Looney would call the TOC, report contact, and request the gunships, while Saenz called Red Leg for an artillery fire mission with WP and flares. Harris, Byron, Looney, and Saenz would then form up and start toward the LZ while Chambers and I would fire one more magazine and throw one hand grenade each. The team would head for the LZ, where Chambers and I would stop short and quickly set up a claymore ambush while the rest of the team secured the LZ for the extraction. If it worked as smoothly as it sounded, then everything would be okay. The gooks crashed around near us, but never got close enough that we had to fire. For the next hour, we could hear them blow whistles, throw sticks, and talk. Slowly, the commotion moved away from us, and our area got quiet, but no one slept that night.

The next morning, we had a cold breakfast and called in the sitrep. When it was time to start patrolling, Byron sent Harris and me out on a quick 360-degree recon of our overnight camp. We were to see if the gooks had set an ambush for us. We made it around and came back to report that the area was clear. We got in team order and started to move to the trail. When we got near it, we saw plenty of signs of the NVA.

We spent the whole day checking the trail and confirming its location on the map so that division G-2 could pass copies to units working the area. It had been a long day, and we had covered twice as much area as we had planned to. Byron decided to keep the team away from the trail so we could spend a quiet night. We set up our perimeter and got to fix another hot meal. The night passed quietly until some animal decided to catch a bird near us for dinner. The bird escaped right through the team, with the animal in hot pursuit, but that's another story. After our pulses slowed down, most of us went back to sleep.

Day three was a carbon copy of day two. Hour after hour, we measured, paced off, and azimuthed the trail. By the end of the day, most of the trail was on the map. Byron decided to stay close to the trail and monitor the enemy foot traffic that night. By 1600 hours, we had found a good spot—the brush was thick and afforded us great concealment. We moved off the trail and set up our nightly circle. Looney and Chambers were about three feet from the trail. Byron and I were two feet behind them, and Harris and Saenz were just behind us. We were close to the path, but that was the only way we could monitor the enemy movement. Looney and Chambers couldn't set claymores in front of their position, but Byron and I were able to place ours so the blast would fan out over the trail. Harris and Saenz set claymores behind us to cover our butts. Since we were so close to the trail we did not heat our meals. We ate quickly, packed away the waste, and got our sleeping spot ready.

Byron and I had gotten together to make the night sitrep, and I was plotting some artillery H & I fire to hit the valley where the trail went into the stream. I knew we could hit that area with a good barrage of high explosive rounds in the morning and bag a few gooks. Byron had pulled Looney's rucksack toward us so we could use the radio. Looney had put on the long antenna, and we had good radio reception. Byron was talking on the radio while I worked out the coordinates for the artillery fire. Byron was going to relay the fire mission through our TOC. I was looking at the map and telling Byron the coordinates when he grabbed my leg and squeezed. I stopped talking and looked at him. He had the handset buried in his cheek and was looking at the trail. I slowly turned my head to look toward the path, and I saw the shadowy outline of men walking down the trail. I glanced down at Looney and Chambers; they were frozen with their hands on their rifles. My heart stopped beating, and a cold chill ran up my spine. No one moved, no one breathed. It was as if we had turned to stone. Thirteen of the enemy walked past us without so much as a glance in our direction. Looney was so close to them that he could have tripped them with his rifle barrel. There wasn't a one of us who wasn't rattled. Looney's and Chambers' weapons were lying on the ground, and they couldn't pick them up because the movement could have given us away. Byron and I were two feet away from our M-16s, and Harris and Saenz didn't look any better prepared for a fight than the rest of us.

The shadows had been gone for a minute when I was able to get my heart to restart. I looked to Byron, and he nodded toward our weapons. Chambers looked back at me, and I motioned for him to pick up his rifle very slowly and quietly. I leaned back, picked up Byron's M-16, and passed it over to him. Then, I picked up my rifle and rolled over to face down the trail in the direction the NVA had gone. The shock was over, and the team was functioning: Harris, Looney, and I faced the way the enemy had gone; Chambers and Saenz were facing the direction they had come; Byron was on the radio reporting that the team was in contact. Byron told the Old Man what had happened and finished giving the H & I coordinates for the fire mission the next morning. Our luck had held; if Chambers, being a new man, had panicked and fired, or even raised his rifle, the gooks would have been all over us. They had the element of surprise and outnumbered us. We would have been in a world of hurt.

Byron decided that the gooks weren't looking for us, so we would stay where we were and count how many came back in the morning. The team was on 50 percent alert, which meant little or no sleep for any of us. One shift was Byron, Looney, and Harris, and the other shift was me, Chambers, and Saenz. We got to sleep for two hours, stay awake for two hours, then sleep for two more hours. It made for a long night, but no one was in the mood to sleep while on guard. I woke up at 0530 hours, during Byron's guard shift. I lay there for a few minutes, but I knew I couldn't go back to sleep. I sat up and nodded to Byron. It was nautical twilight, the time when it starts to get light, but the sun is still below the horizon. I was just sitting there, reflecting on life and wishing I could smoke a cigarette. Being a chain smoker was the hardest part of being a lurp.

At daybreak, here came the gooks, whistling and talking, their gear clanking. I reached for my rifle and couldn't find it, so I just lay back down. If the shooting started, I could find the gun. The men walked right by us, heading to their base camp. I wondered if the American troops were so noisy around their firebases. That morning sure destroyed, for me, the myth of the NVA being crafty jungle fighters. We, on the other hand, had mastered the quiet, shadow war pioneered by the enemy.

We counted twenty men coming back in, and this time we expected them, so we were neither shocked nor surprised. Byron radioed to report the enemy movement and to remind the TOC to fire the H & I mission at 0730 hours. We felt this was the same group that had fired the shots the morning we inserted, and if they followed the timetable, they would get to the valley at the same time as our artillery rounds. I hoped they would still be bopping along the way they were when they passed us so we could kill at least half of them.

It got light around 0700 hours, and we didn't have any more traffic on the trail. Byron okayed a hot meal, so out came the C-4, and the water was boiling in no time. No one was allowed to make hot coffee in the field; the smell carried too far, so cocoa had to do. I fixed a spaghetti lurp and had an orange-flavored cornflake bar. I washed breakfast down with a cup of hot cocoa. Right on schedule, we heard the rush of artillery rounds going over our heads. Seconds later, we heard the crack of exploding rounds, and we knew that if gooks were in that valley, they were catching it. We had requested air burst for the first volley so we could give them a shower of hot steel.

The CO ordered us to stay at the same location and to keep monitoring the trail. Everyone smiled, we knew we were going to have an easy day. All we had to do was sit around and relax. But by 1100 hours, the heat had beaten us into a limp pile, and the leeches were forming up for the third assault. Our thoughts were on how to escape this self-made trap. Byron had made the noon sitrep and suggested that the team move to a new section of the trail, but the Old Man vetoed the idea because he felt we were safer in a known location. He was worried that the gooks would see us if we tried to find a new place from which to monitor the trail.

That afternoon, the NVA were on schedule, and this time

we were alert, down, and with our weapons ready. Eighteen men walked past us without so much as a glance in our direction. We spent another night on 50 percent alert and were waiting the next morning when the gooks came back. Only six people came back this time. It looked like the NVA were infiltrating troops into Hue. We never saw any signs of porters or supplies being brought back by the returning troops. We made our sitrep, and once more, the Old Man ordered us to stay where we were.

Byron was getting worried about the field time we had spent in one area. After five days in the field, and two days in the same spot, we were getting a little ripe. Even though we took pills to prevent it, mother nature still made her demands, and the gooks had noses too. The sense of smell was one of the best detection weapons we had, and it worked just as well for the other side. During the noon sitrep, the CO told Byron he was going to pull us out at 1600 hours and put in a twelve-man ambush team. We were elated at the idea of getting out of there, but we felt we should get to pull the ambush. The Old Man explained that the ambush wouldn't take place until the next morning. He believed our team was tired since we hadn't had much sleep in four days. The fresh troops would be a safer bet. Also, we weren't enough for so large an ambush. The CO figured that, since he had to add troops, why not pull us. He was right, but that didn't make us any happier. He did tell Byron that one man would have to stay with the new team to help the men find the right spot on the trail. We drew for the short stick to see who got to stay. Harris won.

We started to move toward the open area at 1400 hours. Due to the amount of enemy traffic in the AO, Byron wanted to be sure the LZ was secure. Byron and I were concerned about the insertion. We would have to pop a smoke grenade to guide the ships in, and the gooks might see it. Two Hueys landing to drop off the twelve-man ambush team would make a lot of noise, and the timing was wrong. The ambush team needed to get in by noon to be on the safe side. We felt it would take the team at least an hour to get back to our old location, and they still had to recon the area, pick out their emergency escape route, and set up the ambush before the gooks showed up. The plan was to let the gooks walk through the ambush that night and blast them the next morning when they came back. We felt the gooks would be tired from being up all night and more relaxed as they returned to the safe haven of their territory. With their guard down, they would make an easy target.

The helicopters were on time, and Looney got contact with the lead ship. Byron told him to give them the all clear to land. The pilot called for smoke and Byron tossed out a green smoke, hoping the green smoke would blend in with the jungle so the NVA wouldn't be able to see it. The lead ship flared out, and I guided it to the touchdown. As the Huey settled to the ground, Sgt. Jeff Ignacio led the first six-man element out of the helicopter. As soon as the last man cleared the door, I ducked and waved the chopper off. Ignacio and Byron huddled for a quick conference with Harris. The second ship landed, and the rest of the ambush team unloaded. I held the chopper while Byron finished the short briefing. Our team was loaded, and the pilot kept looking at me with a what's-the-holdup look. Byron finally started over towards the Huey, so I waved to the pilot and sprinted around to the cargo door. Byron and I both piled into the chopper, and away we went. I watched Ignacio's men form up and head into the jungle as our ship climbed away.

Harris told me the story of the ambush the next day. The team headed to where we had spent our time. Harris was point, and everything went smoothly. Ignacio got the men in position and the claymore mines out. He wanted to get the basic ambush set up quickly, and then he could do some recon of the area. Harris was going back to his position after a meeting with Ignacio when he heard the sound of people on the trail. Everyone got down to hide and let the enemy pass on by. It looked like the NVA had heard the noise of the insertion, and they came up the trail looking for the lurps, in full uniform with pith helmets, web gear, and AK-47s. The NVA were walking in a crouch and looking back into the bush. It hit the fan when an NVA soldier and David Blankinship made eye contact. Ignacio's RTO, Coleman, and Blankinship were on the flank, and they started the fight. Claymores went off, rifles fired, and hand grenades were thrown in one mad minute. The NVA pulled back to regroup for a flank attack. Ignacio decided it was time to get the heck out of Dodge and headed back to the extraction point. The artillery he had called crashed into the jungle where the team had been. The gunships were on station in record time, and the extraction slicks were close behind. It was getting near dark, and the extraction came off without a hitch.

Our team was doing its debriefing when the contact call came in. We grabbed our rifles, web gear, and headed to the helipad. We were going to be the reaction force to go in and help extract the team in contact. When the CO sent back word that the team was out safe, we stood down. It was too dark to get out and look for bodies, so we went back to the debriefing. The *thump thump* of rotor blades heralded the return of the team, and we all met them at the helipad. Those guys were surrounded by shouting, laughing, and back-slapping friends, and we were glad to have them home unhurt. The Old Man announced that we would put a force in the next day to search for signs of the enemy.

Sergeant Burnell took twelve men back to the ambush site the next day. We inserted in the open area near the trail and found two bodies lying in the grass, out in the open. We knew by Ignacio's debriefing that they didn't kill anyone near the extraction point so the gooks had carried them out there. The bodies were stripped of all gear and uniforms, and they were dressed in the traditional Vietnamese peasant wear. I stood there a minute, looking at the bodies. They looked like two little kids sleeping in the grass. It struck me how fragile life was, one second warm and alive, and the next cold and dead. We pushed deeper into the jungle and found two more bodies stripped of their equipment. The blood trails were everywhere, but we didn't find the first piece of gear. After a couple of hours looking around, Burnell decided to call it off, and we called the choppers for extraction.

So you can see, when it was a firing contact it was short and brutal. A standard LRRP team couldn't sustain combat for more than a few minutes. We didn't have the firepower, or the manpower, to fight for long. There wasn't a lot of need to carry a large amount of ammo. If the team couldn't break contact in ten minutes, then the men were dead.

In the case of nonfiring contact, a team could shadow an enemy unit for days. Gen. Patrick Burton once told a story about a LRRP team from the 1st Cavalry Division that screened an NVA sapper battalion for four days. The sappers were trying to slip up on the Cav's base camp to launch a surprise attack. The night of the attack, the sappers got the surprise when nine hundred of them charged out of the jungle, and the Cav turned on the spotlights. The quad fifty-caliber machine guns mounted on the backs of six two-and-a-half-ton trucks, parked along the defensive wire, opened up and massacred the sappers. The advance warning given by the lurps and the pinpoint direction provided by the team allowed the 1st Cavalry to do the ambushing.

CHAPTER 6

"Uncle John, did you ever ambush anybody?"

"Yeah, Andy, I pulled my share of ambushes, some good and some bad. Let me tell you about ambushes."

Ambushing wasn't an exact science. It was one of those little jobs in life where more things could go wrong than could go right, and in most cases they did. The army had all types of books on how to ambush. These books covered a wide range of subjects such as: the type of ambush, straight line, X, or L, or whether to use tanks, infantry, or helicopters to do the ambushing. In Recondo School and in SERTS training, we had had classes on pulling ambushes. And we had classes given by members of the company. We put a lot of effort into teaching how to pull off a good ambush. During the day, I sometimes took my team outside the wire at Camp Eagle to a nearby wood line to practice setting up an ambush. Yet, when it came time to pull an ambush, the things that could go wrong were always there to haunt you.

The number of things that could go wrong were staggering. There were times when the gooks didn't show up, and some times when too many showed up. The ambusher sometimes became the ambushee, like what happened to the team I was telling about earlier. There was a story going around about a Marine ambush where a tiger came upon the Marines lying in ambush and dragged a Marine off. The story went that the gooks were just entering the kill zone when the tiger got one of the Marines. He didn't holler or shoot because it would alert the enemy, and the Marine let the tiger drag him off. As soon as the ambush was sprung, the Marine shot the tiger and returned to the ambush. I don't know a lot about tigers or Marines, but I believe that story came right out of Parris Island, South Carolina, and not Da Nang, South Vietnam. I do know you couldn't find a bookie in the world who'd give odds on a successful ambush.

In general, the long-range patrol companies pulled more successful ambushes, with higher body counts, than the infantry units in country. That is a big statement to make, but the logic of the situation backs me up. When an infantry company worked an AO, it would sweep in and tramp around for a day or two. Sometimes the whole battalion would be in the AO, so there would be three or four hundred GIs on the sweep. In Vietnam, the SOP for an infantry unit was to put out small ambushes every night. After three years, the gooks got wise to the program, and the ambushes rarely got results. On the other hand, an LRRP team was inserted into the enemy's secure area and remained there undetected. Sometimes we would wait days before we sprung an ambush, or not hit at all. We'd just watch the trail to see if there were any good targets, and come back later to do the job. Our method of operation gave us an advantage that allowed us to get more kills and, many times, more important targets.

Many of our ambushes were what I called the hasty ambush. These ambushes weren't a planned part of the mission, but the circumstances in play at that time brought them about. The story about John Looney's first kill was a good example of a hasty ambush. The team heard the enemy coming and was moving to hide in the bushes to spring an ambush when the enemy saw them, and they had to open fire. I liked to do a hasty ambush when the team was being extracted. This was a habit I picked up from Sergeant Byron. When we got to the LZ, I would drop off one man to watch the path we made getting to the LZ. The rest of the team would move on to the pickup point and set up a defensive position while I contacted the extraction ship. The man left behind was to give us early warning, and to let us know if the gooks had trailed us back to the landing zone. He would stay there until he heard the chopper coming in to land, and then he would run to catch up with us for the extraction.

One time when the hasty ambush worked well for us was during a mission outside Firebase Birmingham. The team was getting close to the pickup, and Kenn Miller got dropped off as the trail watcher. Everything was going smoothly, and our extraction ship was on the way in. The team had just gotten up and was starting to move toward the LZ when Miller started shooting. I told the team to head for the ship; I'd wait for Miller. The team was halfway to the helicopter when Miller broke through the bush. He had a big grin on his face, and he didn't even slow down when he saw me. I was behind him all the way across the LZ, and I landed on top of him when we both dove through the helicopter door. The pilot had us up and out of there in half a heartbeat. Once we had cleared the area, Miller told me that three gooks had walked right up to him. They were so busy following our trail, they never saw the man who shot them. Kenn said he didn't take the time to check the bodies, but he did give them eighteen bars of the twenty-round twist, which was our slang way of saying he shot them.

There was another time when a poor decision on the part of a team leader during a mission turned into a disaster for the unit. The team leader decided to pull an ambush, but it was the wrong time and the wrong place. A poorly planned and executed ambush cost the team four men killed and seven more wounded. The reaction force that had to go in to rescue them had thirteen men wounded. November 20 was a black day for Company F of the 58th LRRPs.

There is one ambush in particular that always comes to mind when I think of Vietnam. We all called it "the grass ambush," and for good reason. On 30 November, Sergeant Proctor called me to the orderly room to give me the warning order for a mission. I was going to be the team leader of a twelve-man team, and we were going to patrol over to the trail where Byron and I had counted all of the NVA a few months earlier. On this trip, we were going to set up an ambush and see if we couldn't help even out the score for 20 November.

I went back to the hooch and found Sergeant Smith. He and I had worked together before, and we didn't have any problems with the command structure. I knew I could always count on Snuffy Smith, even though I tested his sense of humor at times. Snuffy was glad to pitch in with me for the mission, so we went out and started to round up our men. As word spread we were flooded with volunteers who wanted to go with us. It was nice to have the pick of the unit, but we owed it to our own team members to let them go if they wanted to. We were going to be put in on 1 December, so the planning was going to be rushed.

I didn't have time to practice setting up a twelve-man ambush, or to take the combined team outside the wire to let them work together. And I didn't get to spend much time worrying about it because there was a lot of work we needed to do to get ready for this mission. Snuffy and I drew up an expanded equipment list for the mission, and all of the increase in equipment was in the form of firepower. We added extra claymores, hand grenades, rifle ammo, and for good luck, two M-79 grenade launchers. I vetoed the idea of M-60 machine guns. We were going to be lurping for two days to get to the trail, and I felt the heavy guns would get in the way. I also knew I wasn't going to bite off more than I could chew. The loss we took on the twentieth was still fresh in everyone's mind, and no one wanted a repeat of that.

Smith, Proctor, Captain Eklund, and I got together and picked the LZ for the insertion. We needed to land at least two days from the target area yet in an easy area to move through. We were trying to smokescreen our intentions. The gooks had good memories, and we had made contact on that trail in September. There was a major base camp up that trail, and I didn't want to tip off our hand with a bad insertion. Just the thought of having an NVA line company tracking my ambush team gave me cold chills. Smith and I were so busy that we let the Old Man and Proctor make the overflight to see if the LZ was usable. This drop-off LZ was in a deep, open vee that cut back into the wood line, and we were going in near the point of the vee. The Old Man flew out, made a high pass of the LZ, and came back and told me it was a good place to go in.

Smith drew the ammo and helped the team members pack their gear, while I drew the overlay and plotted the artillery. Snuffy had the men ready for inspection by 1800 hours and got them gathered up in one of the empty hooches, with all of the equipment laid out. I made a quick walk-through inspection and told Snuffy he was looking good. While the men repacked, Smith and I sat down and got ready for the insertion briefing scheduled for 2000 hours. We had a lot of work to get finished in just a little time. I had to pick the location for the ambush, work out our E & E route, plot a secondary extraction point, and draw a detailed map of our route to the ambush. Smith had his ATL, Kenn Miller, make sure the men got finished with dinner and were in the company briefing room on time. We finished our work right at 2000 hours and rushed down to the meeting.

The briefing room was packed when Smith and I got down there. We had the helicopter pilots for both the slicks and the gunships, the radio-relay team, the TOC team, the LRRP team, and the Cav's G-2 team in one small room. We had a lot of details to cover, so the briefing lasted for over an hour. When I finished talking, the Old Man okayed the plan and asked if there were any questions. No one spoke, so he released everyone except Smith, me, the TOC team and the G-2. We spent another hour reviewing plans and picking apart the details. The Cav's commander didn't want another team getting its butt kicked, and neither did the CO. The meeting broke up at 2130 hours, and Snuffy and I still had to pack our personal equipment. I got to bed at 2400 hours, and we had to get up at 0430 hours to get ready for the insertion.

0430 hit like a bomb, and I didn't want to get up. I sat on the edge of the cot and smoked two cigarettes just to get my eyes open. I got dressed and headed to the latrine to shave and brush my teeth. It'd be the last time I'd get to do that for a few days. The insertion team always got to eat first, and the cooks fixed us a good breakfast. I always wondered if the cooks had a grim sense of humor and were giving us that condemned man's last meal. The rest of the time was spent putting on face paint, checking gear, and trying to kill the butterflies.

We loaded up at 0630 and headed to the west. The LZ

was socked in by heavy ground fog that day so we got to spend an hour touring Vietnam from the air. When the LZ was still socked in on the second try, all of the choppers started to run low on fuel so we got to fly back to Camp Eagle and refuel. Third trip out was the charm, and Mr. Grant headed the ship down to the LZ.

When the Huey got close to the ground I swung out on the skid, and what I saw shocked me so much, I almost fell off the ship. We were landing right on top of the largest high-speed trail I had ever seen in Vietnam. Grant used the trail to line up the ship and straddled it with the helicopter skids. Our plan was for all team members to head for the wood line on the pilot's side of the ship, so we would get everyone together quicker. I was thankful that Snuffy had worked that out while we were doing the planning because the trail threw a kink in the mission. I had no idea if there were trail watchers who had seen us land, or if there was an enemy force in the woods waiting to move toward Hue. If shooting started, we would be better off having all of the men together. I had Looney call the C & C ship to report the trail, and alert the Old Man to the fact that we might be in contact within minutes. While Looney and I were on the radio, Smith got the team into a defensive position. If the enemy probed our location, we would be ready to meet the attack.

The two gunships made a low pass to see if they could spot anyone or draw fire. They reported back that everything looked quiet to them. I kept the gunships on station for thirty minutes while the team moved parallel to the trail toward the west. I had seen where the trail entered the jungle about two hundred meters west of the insertion point, and I wanted a closer look at that area. When we got to the mouth of the trail, I saw a couple of bomb craters on the far side of the path and a horseshoe-shaped clearing that flanked the trail. We pulled back to the wood line, set up a new defensive position, and released the gunships. I decided to stay there for a while and watch the trail to see if there was any enemy traffic.

I told Looney I needed to talk with the Old Man and for him to get radio contact with the TOC. While John worked with the radio, I got with Snuffy and laid out my plan. I would take Looney and Meszaros with me up the trail to look for signs of recent activity. He would put together a quick-reaction force of Chambers, Miller, Saenz, and Schwartz. If my recon element got in contact and couldn't make it back, they would come up the trail and rescue us. If I didn't need the reaction force, then he could use the whole team to cover us when we pulled back. No matter what happened, he was to keep his five men to secure the extraction point. Looney called me over to the radio, and I quickly told the CO we were going to do a short recon to make sure no gooks were around.

I sat down and started to take my boots off. Looney didn't even ask; he just started to follow suit. I looked over to Meszaros and told him to put on his Ho Chi Minhs and drop his gear; we were going on a little trip. Smitty shifted the rest of the men around the perimeter so the reaction team was in the back. This way, if they had to leave, he didn't have to shuffle the men again. We checked to make sure that Looney, Saenz, and Munoz had their radio on the TOC frequency and that the team's fourth radio was tuned to the artillery push. I stood up and put my ammo pouch over my shoulder, while Looney put on his radio pack, and Meszaros shoved four hand grenades in his pants pockets. I looked around. Everything was in order, so we headed out to make our way around the wood line to the trail.

The trail was covered with footprints, and most of them looked fresh. We stopped by the trail and listened to the sounds of the jungle. After a few minutes, I was satisfied that there weren't any gooks around, so I signaled Meszaros to start up the trail. He was on point and moved up the right side of the path. I fell in behind him to walk slack. I walked up the left side of the path, and stayed ten meters behind. Looney brought up the tail-gunner slot, ten meters behind me on the right side of the trail. We were spread out so if the enemy opened fire it'd be harder to hit all of us at once. We moved slowly up the trail, searching for trail-watcher bunkers or tree stands. The feel of gooks was in the air, and the pucker factor was nine. We had covered two hundred meters when Meszaros stopped and slowly got down. I signaled for Looney to stop, and we both got down. Meszaros waved me forward, and I moved up beside him. He pointed to a bunker just in front of him. I asked him if he had seen any movement, and he said no. As he went up to the side of the position and looked in, I covered him. He waved the all clear, so I flagged Looney to come up, and I joined Meszaros at the bunker. There were cigarette butts and a rice-ball wrapper on the floor, and Meszaros told me to sniff. I stuck my head in the bunker, and I knew immediately the gooks had been there.

I told the guys that there wasn't any need to go further up the trail. All of the signs said this was an active trail, and we were near the staging area used by the gooks before they headed out to Hue. Looney called Sergeant Smith and told him we were on our way back. Looney took the lead going back, and Meszaros brought up the rear to cover our butts. As soon as we got back, we put on our boots, and I got with Smith to plot the trail and bunker on our maps. I told Snuffy the place was a gold mine of gooks, and I was going to call the company commander to see if we could stay there and pull our ambush. Looney fired up the PRC-25 and called the TOC. I got on the handset and reported all of the signs we had seen, the trail dimensions, and my best guess of the number of enemy using the trail daily. Then I asked permission to change the location of the ambush. I didn't know the Old Man could say no in so many ways. I signed off and told Snuffy to get ready to move out.

I had Chambers on point, with Meszaros walking his slack, and we were moving to the west. We had come down a small hill, crossed a creek, and were moving into the edge of the wood line. I signaled Chambers to start moving deeper into the jungle. We needed to get on the right heading if we were to come out anywhere near the spot I had picked for the ambush. The jungle got thicker, and thicker, and in ten minutes, Chambers was stopped. I went forward to look the situation over and saw at a glance we were in big trouble. The jungle was such a dense tangle, we couldn't see two feet in front of us. I walked back to Smitty's position and told him to hold the team there, Chambers and I were going to go forward to see how far the mess went.

I went back to Chambers and told him to drop his rucksack, get one bandolier of ammo, and follow me. We headed out, and within minutes, we were crawling on our hands and knees in thick vines. I had planned to go out a hundred meters just to see if we could get through, and now we were lost. I had become disoriented and lost track of time. It took over four hours for us to find our way back to the team, and there were times when I wasn't sure we'd get back. Smith was mad; the Old Man was mad; everybody was mad. I got on the radio, and the CO chewed my butt for five minutes and then told me he was glad we were okay. I explained to him what I had tried to do and I had gotten lost. I told him I was going to move back toward the trail, spend the night, and plot a new course for us to take the next day.

We moved back toward the trail and found a good spot to spend the night that was near the trail and hidden. After we had settled in, I had Smitty get together a four-man trail-watch team. There was a clump of woods right by the trail, and I wanted him to go down there and set up an outpost. I made it clear they weren't to engage any enemy force unless they were detected. Smith took Saenz as his RTO, Schwartz, and Miller, and they slipped down to the woods by the trail. The woods were right on the trail, but I felt anyone coming out would have stopped back near the bunker. Snuffy reported back that the team was in position and the trail was clear. I told him to stay alert and call if there was any trouble.

We still had a couple of hours of light left, so I told the men to fix a hot dinner. Looney was lying beside me, monitoring the radio while I worked with the map. I needed to find a way over to the other trail that wouldn't be so hard to follow. Looney sat up and had a funny look on his face. I looked over and asked what the problem was. He told me that Saenz was whispering on the radio and he couldn't understand what he was saying. I said, "Well, talk to him and find out."

Looney looked up from the handset and said, "Gooks, lots of gooks!"

I used hand signs to signal the men "contact," and everyone reached for weapons. Well, so much for hot dinner, I thought. Looney told me there were twenty-five gooks standing on the trail right beside the woods. I could see the mission going up in smoke if one of them decided to step into the woods to relieve himself before they went to town. Saenz reported eight had weapons and they seemed to be getting ready to move on. I told Munoz to do a commo check with the artillery fire direction control, and tell them we might need a fire mission and to go on standby. The TOC had been monitoring the conversation, and now the Old Man was on the radio wanting to know if we were in contact. I had Looney tell him no and to wait one minute; I needed to contact the outpost. Smith came on the radio and told me in a whisper that Miller thought they could kill all of the gooks in no time. I told him no way; we didn't know if they were waiting for more people. I asked the CO to come on the artillery frequency because I needed to keep the TOC radio open for the OP. Smith wasn't in a good position down there, and I wanted him to be able to get through at any time.

Munoz told me the Old Man was on the way out with two Cobras. The thought flashed through my mind that the gooks might hear the choppers and jump into the woods with Smith to hide. Miller would have his hands full then! Saenz called and told Looney the gooks were moving east toward Hue. A wave of relief swept over me. I wanted some distance between the outpost and the gooks when the gunships arrived. I looked at the map and tried to figure out where the gooks would be in a few minutes when the guns were on station. I worked up a full eight-digit coordinate and called it to the Cobras. The Old Man broke in to chew me out for giving it as coordinates and not the grape code, but I felt that since the gunships would have to fire right over the men in the outpost, I wanted the pilots to be sure of the target.

The afternoon air was filled with the beat of rotor blades and the staccato rip of 7.62mm miniguns as the Cobras flashed by. Saenz called and told Looney they were being hit by the choppers, and to check fire. Looney called the pilots and told them to break off the attack. The pilots said they had hit where I told them to. Then, Saenz called back, and meekly told us it was the hot brass from the miniguns that had hit them. The gunships reported they hadn't seen anyone, so I sent them home. I told everyone to lay dog for thirty minutes to see what the gooks were going to do. In all of the excitement, no one from the outpost thought to tell me that only twenty gooks had gone east toward Hue. Five NVA with AK-47s went back west toward the trail-watcher's bunker. These men were an escort for the supply team that was going to Hue, and they would wait back up the trail for the bearers to return in the morning.

At 1800 hours, I called Snuffy on the radio and asked if he had all the excitement he needed for the day. I got a big "yes" on that point, so I told him to bring the outpost back to our location for the night. When Smitty's men got back, everyone ganged around to hear their story, and it took me a few minutes to get the team settled down. I reminded all the men that there were gooks around and we were on 50 percent alert. I asked Snuffy if he would like to ambush the gooks when they came back in from their shopping trip. He smiled and asked me what I had on my mind. I told him we could call the CO and get the ambush approved. Then, we would move down to the trail later, set up the ambush, and pop them in the morning. He liked the idea, so I got Looney to call the TOC.

It took a little time, but I was able to convince the company commander that we could move down to the trail in the dark and set up our ambush. I figured the food gathering party would come back to rendezvous with their guides before daylight. There had been a good moon the night before, so I knew we would be able to see the gooks when they came back. We had practiced setting up ambushes, so all of the men had a good idea of what to do. I told him that if the people didn't return, we would pick up and move to the area where we originally planned to pull the ambush. We worked out a few details on the radio, and the Old Man told me that I could try to hit the gooks in the morning.

I called the team together and gave them the good news. While they finished eating, Snuffy and I worked out the ambush plan. I showed Smith the open area that I wanted to use near the trail. One end was anchored on the wood line that he had watched the trail from, and the other end would be near the stream running through the area. We broke the team down into six two-man cells, and started to place them on the map. I was worried about the rear of the ambush. We would be leaving our rucksacks in that area and moving nearly two hundred meters toward the trail. I asked Snuffy if he would mind being the rear cover. He wasn't too happy about that, because he knew he would miss the action, but he could see the need for two good men to cover our butts.

The plan came together quickly, and I made the rest of the cell assignments. Miller, and Saenz as his RTO, would anchor the left flank in the wood line. I would be in the center of the site, with Looney as my RTO. Evans would anchor the left flank near the stream, with Munoz on the radio. Smith was rear guard, with McCain as RTO. Chambers and Schwartz would be between me and Miller, and Meszaros and Kines would be between me and Evans. Chambers, Meszaros, and I were to do the body check after the ambush. I got the two flank cells together and told them I wanted a WP grenade hooked to the electrical firing line of their last claymore, and placed about twenty-five feet further out on the trail. This grenade would go off when the claymores were fired and help seal the ambush. We reviewed the setup procedures and the order: not to fire until I started firing. I knew Evans would tell us when the gooks started to enter the kill zone, and all of the radios would pick up the news.

I had everyone check their equipment and set out the items they would carry to the ambush site. Miller and I made up the two WP trail closers, and I gave mine to Evans. I had broken the cells down to try and put good friends together so they could help each other stay awake. We would move down to the trail after midnight to set up the ambush, and we would be on 100 percent alert the rest of the time. I told the men to get some sleep now; Smith and I needed to work out the radio plan, and we would pull guard. I didn't feel like trying to sleep. I was keyed up, and I knew there would be some action tomorrow. I broke out the bottle of dex tablets, and Smith and I took one. We spent the next two hours working on the plan and deciding when his RTO would switch to the artillery frequency. This was the first time I had a lot of time to think about going into combat. Always before, it was a quick setup or a flash contact. Now, I had at least seven more hours to stew over it. Everything was going through my head: was the plan good? would the gooks show up? would everyone do their job? and what had I forgotten? It didn't take me long to decide it was easier to stumble into a gunfight than to plan one.

At 0030 hours, I started to wake the men up. I got everyone together and reviewed the plan, went over assignments, and gave them the password. Smith and I passed out three dex tablets to each man, one for now, and the others to take later if they needed them to stay awake. I made sure all of the RTOs knew I expected a commo check every hour, on the hour, starting with Saenz and going back to McCain. The moon was hidden by some clouds, but we had enough light to see by. I had Looney call the radio relay and tell them we were moving into our ambush position. Everyone secured their gear, and we got in a file, ready to move out.

I took the point, with Looney walking my slack. I wanted to keep the cells together so it would be easy to split up and get into our positions. We started down a slope and moved seventy-five meters to the spring that would be the rear marker for the ambush. The spring ran through the area, parallel to the trail, and was a good point of reference. We stopped in the bushes by the spring for a short break while I checked the compass. I was on the right heading, and we started up a gentle rise toward the trail. After about fifty meters, the ground leveled off, and I could see the trail thirty-five meters away. We stopped and got down. I wanted to lay dog here for a few minutes and listen to the night. We waited a little while, and I decided it was time to do it. I took Looney forward to a low clump of bushes and told him that was our spot. I sent him forward to set up our claymores while I went back to get Miller and Chambers.

I took the two right flank cells around and spotted them in their ambush positions. I had to know exactly where they were, and I didn't want to have to move around after the setup. I went back and got Meszaros and Evans and took them to the left flank. I came back to Smith and told him to set up his four claymores for as wide a kill zone as he could. This would be his position, at the rear of the ambush site.

It took thirty minutes to get everything set up. After all of the radio men had checked in, we were set. I stood up and took one last look. The claymores were out, hidden in the grass, with their firing wires covered. The cover for the men looked okay, and since I felt we would be hitting the gooks at first light, we were well hidden. There wasn't much more I could do; it was up to the gooks from here on in. I got down, laid out four magazines for my M-16, and checked the claymore firing devices. This was going to be a long night. Looney passed on the word that no one could move; it was now a free-fire zone.

The 0200 radio check went smoothly, and I knew things were working well. At the 0300 radio check, Looney told me he couldn't get contact with Munoz. I told John to keep trying; they could be having radio trouble. After twenty minutes, I told Looney to stop trying, and I asked him how the radio sounded at the 0200 check in. He told me it was five by five. He also reminded me that we had put a new battery in every radio last night after the briefing. The 0400 hour check came, and still no Munoz on the air. Snuffy called me and asked what was I going to do, and I said "Nothing." I wasn't going to walk up there and see what the problem was. Too many people had been shot while moving around at night on an ambush. I told Looney they would probably wake up around 0600, or when the shooting started. We couldn't get contact with Munoz at either the 0500 or 0600 check.

I was on my third dex by 0600 and they were getting to me. I told Looney I was seeing things, and he told me to cool it; nothing was moving. I was a little steamed about Evans and Munoz. They were on the flank that the gooks would be approaching from, and I guessed they were asleep. I was mentally kicking myself in the ass for putting them out there. I had better men, but I let the buddy plan get in the way. The best I could hope for was the gooks' not seeing them when they came back. I guess I should have added, *if* they came back. It was starting to get light, and the NVA should have been there already. The light gave me a whole new set of problems.

I had set the ambush up in the dark and had counted on the dark to help hide us. With every new bit of daylight, we lost cover. It didn't take me long to see we had our bare butts hung out. The Old Man called Looney and told him he had sent the gunships out. I was mad; I hadn't asked for gunships, and I didn't want them flying around our location. After a few minutes, I told Looney I thought the gooks weren't coming back, and to call the Old Man to get the gunships stopped. I could hear the distant beat of the rotor blades, and we weren't going to need them. I looked up at the trail and there was an NVA walking along. I told Looney, "Gooks!"

He told me I was seeing things. I looked again, and there were five more men following the first one I saw. The lead man saw us and started to run. I didn't say anything to Looney. I just grabbed both claymore firing devices and squeezed. In a blink of the eye the trail disappeared in a gray-black cloud of exploding C-4 as the claymores spewed their deadly shower of steel balls into the enemy. The rest of the men fired their claymores and more explosions ripped the air. I dropped the clickers, picked up my rifle, and started firing at the bodies on the trail. Over all of the racket, I heard Looney saying, "Contact, I say again, the team is in contact. Over."

Looney grabbed my arm and hollered that Miller was taking fire from outside the ambush zone. I looked over, and sure enough, there were green tracers coming from the distant wood line. I could tell it was heavy fire, so there had to be a lot of troops on the left flank. It didn't take long to see that there was an escort waiting for the group I had shot up. Looney told me the gunships were on station and wanted a target. I told John to take out that wood line fast. While he was talking to the pilots, I had Mosraros's cell shift fire to the wood line. Chambers, Schwartz, and I kept firing at the trail. I had seen a man jump into one of the bomb craters on the far side of the trail, and I wanted to keep him out of the fight. By that time, the gunships were lined up and making their first pass on the NVA in the wood line. I told Looney to call Smith and tell him to stay put: we had gooks everywhere. I also told him to have McCain go to the artillery frequency and alert the gunners that we would need a fire mission. I was still shooting when Looney told me that Munoz had made field repairs on his radio and was asking what was going on.

After the third gun run on the wood line, the green tracers stopped, and I had Looney shift the Cobras to make a run parallel to the trail. John knew how to direct those gunships, and they made a hot run down the trail. They called back that they were low on ammo so they pulled off to conserve their rounds in case we needed more help. I called for a cease fire, and the team quit firing. I ejected the empty magazine from my M-16 and reloaded it with the fourth magazine I had laid out. I couldn't believe I had fired three magazines of ammunition. The air was full of cordite from all the firing, and it stung my eyes and nose. The silence was unreal: it was so thick you could feel it. I decided to see if the man in the bomb crater was alive, so I called out in my broken Vietnamese, *"Chao ong, chieu hoi, chieu hoi."* I was asking him to give up. I was up on my knees, holding my rifle in my left hand. The Vietnamese man came out of that bomb crater like Jesse Owens out of the gate. He ran up the side of the crater and hit the flat of the trail at high speed. I was shocked at seeing him and the speed that he was making. I brought the M-16 to my shoulder and fired four rounds at him. He never even slowed down, and he ran past Miller so fast that neither Miller nor Saenz got off a shot. I just knelt there, looking in the direction he went. Then I looked at Looney with a funny look on my face and said, "Did you see that?"

Looney was laughing, and said, "Looks like you missed to me, Sarge."

I held my rifle out in front of me and looked down the barrel. I told John the barrel must be bent, or the sight was broken. I didn't have a lot of time to worry about it because there were too many things that needed to be done. I sent Kines back to join up with Snuffy, and told Looney to call him to let him know he was getting the extra man. I had Looney tell Snuffy to move to a position where he could cover our back and see the area where we left the rucksacks. Next, I told Schwartz to go over to the left flank and tell Miller to move out to the west and set up a blocking force. Saenz, Schwartz, and Miller, with his M-79, would screen the hot flank. Looney got on the radio to Evans and told him to watch for stragglers who might try to attack the right flank. While Looney took care of the shifting of the men, I got Chambers and Meszaros to go with me to check the bodies. Checking the bodies wasn't one of the fun things lurps got to do, but we needed to make sure they were dead. The worst part was searching them. We had to do a strip search to look for documents and their ID cards. I assigned that job to Chambers and Meszaros.

I got up and started toward the trail; Chambers fell in behind me, and Meszaros was to my right. The first body we came to was that of a young boy who might have been fifteen at best. He was facedown on the trail, with his arms spread out by his head. In the dirt beside him was a loaded RPG launcher. The rocket propelled grenade that was fired by the launcher could destroy a light tank or armored personnel carrier. It sure wasn't a kid's toy. I looked at him for a minute, then I looked at the rest of the trail. To my right was a woman's body, and to the left was the body of a man. In the bomb crater, there was another woman's body. I told Meszaros to check the woman to the right, and Chambers to check the boy. I would go to the left and check the man.

I turned and started walking up the trail, and I had taken three steps when a rifle shot rang out behind me. I spun around with my weapon ready, and I was leveled down on Chambers. He had a funny look on his face, and I could tell he was shook. I asked him what he was doing firing his gun right behind me. He told me that the kid wasn't dead; and after I had passed the kid's body, the boy had started to pick up the RPG and shoot me in the back. He said all he could do was put his rifle behind the boy's ear and give him a brain tumor. I looked at the boy's hands, and now one hand gripped the handle of the RPG. I would have been a dead duck. If the round had traveled far enough to arm, the explosion would have scattered me over half of Vietnam, and could have killed Chambers, too. If the round didn't arm, then I would have had a hole 3.5 inches in diameter through me, and the backblast from the round being fired would have hurt or killed Chambers. I thanked him and gave him a LRRP patch and a pin. I told him to search the body and pin the patch on it so the NVA would know we had been to visit. I turned around and walked up to the next body. The man was on his back, so I knelt down and checked him to see if he was dead. After I checked, I threw his rifle over toward Looney's position. I left him and moved to the bomb crater to check the woman. I pinned a LRRP patch on the woman, and told Chambers to search all of the bodies, while I checked with Miller.

Before I could get started toward Miller's position, Looney called me over to him, so I went back to see what he wanted. He told me the Cav's Air Rifle Platoon had tried to insert into an opening to the west of us and they had been shot out. We had heard shooting, and I was wondering what was going on. They took two KIA and four WIA, and that told me there were plenty of NVA around. I had Looney call Saenz to see if he had monitored the radio report, then I went back to meet with Snuffy to see what he thought about the situation. I told him I believed we needed to get extracted real soon, and he agreed. I asked him to move up to the rucksacks and secure that area.

On my way back to the trail, Looney flagged me again. He said Lieutenant Jackson, our XO, wanted to talk to me on the radio, right now. I took the handset and called the lieutenant. He asked me if I could see his helicopter east of my position. I looked over, and there was an LOH-6 hovering three hundred yards to my right. I confirmed seeing him and asked what he needed. He told me that he had landed near the trail to look at a bag of rice. When he got out of the chopper, a girl had come out of the woods and fired an AK-47 at him. He made it back to the ship, and they took off. He had the gunships fire up the woods, and I was to move over there now to check out the rice and the woods. I started to remind him that I only had twelve men and our hands were full, but I let it slide. I told him we would get an element over there ASAP.

I had no choice but to get Chambers and Meszaros to stop the search and go with Looney and me. I told John to call Munoz and let them know we were coming; I didn't need to get shot by my own men. We moved out in a file, with Chambers on point. We got to Evans's position, and I noticed that they had a large area of matted-down grass in their location. We had moved about one hundred meters when we hit a large stream bed with a heavy wood line around it. I could tell this was where the gooks had hidden last night when the Cobras were looking for them. We walked fifty more meters when Looney grabbed me and stopped the team. We got down, and Looney told me he was monitoring Lieutenant Jackson's radio and he was talking with the Cav's Air Rifles. The Cav's men were at the rice bag and had captured the girl. They were setting up a defensive perimeter to wait for a helicopter to come in to pick up the POW. We were less than sixty meters from these clowns, and no one had even told us they were on the ground. If Looney hadn't heard the radio message, we would have walked into their defense line, and gotten fired up by their men. I had Looney call the Air Rifles and tell them that after they got the POW out to move three hundred meters west on the trail to link up with us. I turned our group around, and we went back to the ambush site.

I dropped Meszaros off with Evans, and told them that the porters seemed to be better armed than we thought they were. I wanted three men to cover the right flank just in case the Air Rifle Platoon pushed the gooks into my area. I had Looney get on the radio to alert Smith to watch out for the porters; they were armed and might be driven his way. I knew that I had some NVA on the west flank because they had fired at us, and hit the Air Rifles hard. Now, I had the porters on the east flank who were armed and willing to fight. I wasn't having one of my better days. And the dex was wearing off. I looked at my watch, and it was

0945 hours; I had been up for twenty-nine hours. I told Chambers and Looney to go back to Sergeant Smith's position to get their rucksacks and bring them back to the ambush site. We would be extracting from there.

I went over to Miller's location to check with him. He hadn't seen any movement to his front, and he felt we were clear. I had him take Saenz and Schwartz, and recon further up the trail. I was going to have our extraction ships come into the ambush area to pick us up, and I didn't want them getting a hot welcome. Miller knew there were NVA out there, and he asked how far I wanted him to go. I told him to go out about one hundred meters, and if they got hit, he was to break contact and *di-di* back. Miller gave me that you've-got-to-be-nuts look, got his men, and started out.

When I got back to my position, Looney was there, and he had brought my rucksack back for me. I thanked him and dug out another dex tablet. The only thing we could do now was wait for the Air Rifles to get to us. I told Chambers to forget about finishing the body search; the Cav's men could do that. He seemed relieved at not having to do the strip search. I moved us to a spot that had some shade, and we sat down to wait. Munoz called on the radio to tell me the Air Rifles were at his location, and I told him to come back to our position with the Cav's men.

Meszaros, Evans, and Munoz came walking down the trail, followed by the men of the Air Rifle Platoon. I walked over to meet them, and sent my men back to Snuffy Smith's position to get their rucksacks. The platoon sergeant and I went back to the shady spot and got out the map. We reviewed the situation while I pointed out the area where the enemy fire had come from and showed him how the trail ran to the west. I told him I had a recon element out to the west, and I had not heard from them. He told me to call the men back and he would set up a defensive perimeter with his men. They were going to stay and destroy the RPG and the rice after we were pulled out. I had Looney get on the radio, call Miller, and tell him to return to our position.

I told the Air Rifle platoon sergeant that I needed to look at something and I'd be back in a few minutes. I looked over to Looney, and told him to get his radio on and come with me. We walked up to the trail and headed east toward the position Evans and Munoz were in during the ambush. I knew they were asleep, and I was going to go back and see if I could prove it. I had asked them earlier what had happened. Evans told me that the radio wasn't working and they didn't see the gooks go past their position. After the shooting started, their radio got repaired real fast, and I was taking John back with me now to check the visibility from their position.

We had stretched our luck to the limits on that ambush. The early choppers had spooked the gooks, and the porters had hidden in the woods while the command group had speeded up and walked into our ambush. If they all had hidden, then when I called off the ambush, as I started to do, they could have caught us in between the returning group and the unit that was waiting for them to return. We would have been outnumbered, surrounded, and shot up in a heartbeat. If the command group that came by Evans' position had seen them sacked out, they could have killed them, and come down the flank of the ambush. We could have lost four to six men before we could have stopped them. I was upset, and I didn't like being lied to.

When we got to the position they were in during the ambush, I had Looney lie down with his radio beside him. First, I had him call Munoz on the radio and get a short count. I asked him how the transmission was, and he said clear with no problem. I had him call Snuffy and do the same thing, and he gave me the same answer. Next, I walked over to the trail and looked back at John. I couldn't believe the gooks hadn't seen Evans and Munoz. I asked Looney if he could see me. He told me he could see me from midshin up, so I moved to another position. His answer was the same. I could see he didn't feel at ease doing the spotting, but he knew Evans and Munoz could have gotten him killed by their carelessness. On the way back to the team, he asked me what I was going to do. I told him I didn't know, but he could sure bet I was going to see the Old Man about it.

When we returned to the team, Miller was back, and I could tell he was excited about something so I went over to see what was up. Miller told me that they had found the gook I had shot at. He was dead, and they found him sitting up by a tree. He had been hit three times in the side, and it looked like the gunships had hit him twice in the chest. Miller said the chest wounds had exit holes right into the tree. I didn't feel real glad I had hit that man. I guess I had hoped he had made his getaway. He was the enemy, but he had spirit and a zest for life. I had to admire that, and I hoped I could make that good an accounting for myself. I asked Miller and Saenz why they didn't fire when the man ran past them. They both said they were so surprised at the speed that he had built up when he ran by them that they didn't think to fire.

There weren't any ships available, so we got to sit around and wait for our extraction until 1330 hours. I was beat; the lack of sleep and the stress of the ambush had drained me. When the ships got in, we loaded up and headed for home. I got back to my hooch, sat down on the bunk, and fell asleep. I understand they tried to wake me up for the debriefings, but they never got me up. I woke up at 0530 hours the next day, with the worst dex withdrawal hangover I had ever gotten.

I went to see the CO after breakfast to review the ambush and the problems that had cropped up. He told me that the Cav's men had found more documents on the bodies and wanted to know why we didn't find them. I explained to him that the problem with Lieutenant Jackson calling me away and that we didn't finish the search because the Cav's men were there. I discussed the problem that had come up with Evans and Munoz. I wanted to court-martial them. I believed that they had been asleep, and I described the circumstances in detail.

The Old Man said that since I couldn't prove they were sleeping, I should forget it. I went back to the hooch, and Looney came over to ask what the Old Man had said. He told me that all of the men had talked about what had happened, and the word was out that Evans and Munoz couldn't be trusted. I had a meeting with Sergeant Smith, their team leader, and told him to be careful to cover his butt.

CHAPTER 7

"Uncle John, did you ever do anything besides go out to the jungle and fight?"

"Jason, we had some recreational time, even in the middle of a war."

I told you about the teams' getting to go to the beach outside of Hue and the movies that were set up around Camp Eagle. The army understood that all of the men needed a little time off. Everyone in Vietnam was entitled to one six-day R & R outside Vietnam during his tour. There were R & R centers in every major country around the Pacific basin, but the favorite spots for the single men were Thailand, Hong Kong, and Australia. The married men would try to get to Hawaii, and have their wives meet them there. The army had in-country R & R centers for shorter time spans, and those were used to reward men for doing their job exceptionally well.

Back in the base camps and on the firebases, we did what we could to entertain ourselves. The big USO shows came around as much as possible, but they were still few and far between. We found that sometimes a few quiet hours to read our mail and write letters was the best form of entertainment. I read a lot of books and the newspapers that many of the guys got from home. Some sporting goods were issued to each company supply room. We had a horse-shoe pit near the helipad, and many games of football were played on the helipad. We even had an archery set for a while, but after a freak accident, it disappeared. One of the lurps using the set felt a little like William Tell and ended up putting a blunt arrow through Frank Souza's hand. You never saw so many lurps trying to convince the medics that the NVA were using bows and arrows to conserve ammo.

The main NCO club was behind the company area, and we spent a few hours up there, bending the elbow. In the company area, there was always a game of hearts going on, and there never was a shortage of players. A good card game could eat up some hours. We had our own little club down by the helipad, and we left our rank at the door. The beer was always cold, and we would sit around and drink with the team, or carry a few back to the hooch for the guys playing cards. We spent countless hours just sitting around talking. All of the E-5s lived in the same hooch as their team, and that helped in the bonding process that made the team work well in the field. I don't remember what we talked about, but we did it for hours on end. If there is anything I miss about the war, it is the closeness we developed. I have never found that with any other person since I came home.

Camp Eagle was a forward combat base, so we didn't have all of the comforts that many REMFs enjoyed down south. There weren't any hooch girls. And, like I told you, Hue was off-limits. I understand that later in 1969 there were some Red Cross girls at Eagle, and they knew some of the lurps in our company. The last American girl I saw when I got in country was the stewardess on the Northwest Orient aircraft that brought me to Vietnam; the first American girl I saw at the end of my tour was the stewardess on the Northwest Orient aircraft that took me to California. They were all pretty girls, too.

The army tried to make things better by putting a lot of effort into the major holidays. Thanksgiving had to be the best example of that effort. The mood and spirit in F Company at Thanksgiving time were at a low point. On 20 November, the company took the first casualties we'd had since early June. The fact that four of the men were killed, and that five of the seven that had been wounded were hit so bad they would never really come back to the company, put us all in the dumps. There wasn't a man in the company who didn't lose a friend. We were pulling missions on top of missions. I had come back in from a mission on the twenty-first, gone back out on a new patrol the twenty-fourth, and we returned from that mission on the twenty-seventh.

Thanksgiving day was the twenty-eighth, and the company was on stand-down for the day. The cooks started to work early on a traditional Thanksgiving dinner for the troops. Breakfast was a quick affair—we got eggs, cereal, toast, SOS, and the boot. Everyone understood why they gave us the rush; it was quite a feat to turn out the whole nine yards of a Thanksgiving dinner on field stoves. But the crowd scene was almost like home, a bunch of hungry kids hanging around waiting for the big dinner. They got a football game going down on the helipad, to work up an appetite. I had gotten the warning order for a mission that would insert on Friday, so I spent Thanksgiving morning working on the details of the trip.

At dinnertime, what was left of the company got together at the mess hall. One of the chaplains came by and talked about the brotherhood of men and all that we had to be thankful for, then it was dinnertime. The cooks had really put on the dog. There were tablecloths, and the tables were set with little menus at each seat; there were small paper cups of salted nuts, hard candy, and shrimp cocktails. The dining tent had Thanksgiving decorations, and the center of the table was lined with fresh pies. We had a complete turkey dinner with all of the trimmings that were allowed by the army, and then some. The cooks had really put their hearts into the meal, and we rewarded them by attacking the dinner like a pack of hungry wolves. There isn't a cook in the world who doesn't love watching people enjoy the fruits of his or her work. There was more than one misty eye at the table when we sat down—some for the friends who were missing the meal, some for the homes we were all missing.

After dinner, a combat photographer came by and borrowed Blankinship and Tercero. He needed a picture of two combat soldiers eating some C rations on Thanksgiving. We had to search the company area to find a can of turkey loaf. They took the turkey loaf down to the open area below the helipad, opened the can, and took a picture, while the rest of the men in the company stood on the bank and jeered.

I went back to my hooch, got my LBE and M-16, and went down to the helipad to get aboard the waiting helicopter to make the overflight for the next day's mission. It struck me as kind of funny; two hours earlier we had been talking about the brotherhood of man and peace on earth. Now, I was going out to find those brothers of mine so I could go out the next day and kill them. I couldn't help but wonder if the world would ever grow up.

We did other things to relax. When First Sergeant Walker got his orders to go home, we had a cookout and beer bust. The cooks pulled a little of that old cook magic, and steaks, hotdogs, and spare hamburger meat appeared. We borrowed wire racks from the mess hall and got some charcoal from the Vietnamese. Before dinnertime, we dug a pit, fired up the charcoal, and iced down a load of beer. That afternoon, we had a home-style cookout. We had music, food, booze, and the best friends in the world; who needed anything more.

The night before I left to come home, we pulled one of the best hoaxes ever perpetrated on new guys. The company was still in the dumps. We had pulled some good missions, and killed fifteen of the enemy in the previous twenty-six days, but the pressure of pulling missions on top of missions was taking its toll. We never did let the war kill our sense of humor, but I do believe it did warp it just a little. This was the snipe hunt to end all snipe hunts. The few replacements we had gotten during the past months had come from other units within the division. We did get a cherry once in a while, but they came in ones or twos. On 16 December, here came six shiny new cherry privates. All of the new guys were put in my hooch because there were only five men left in the hooch, and I was leaving the next day.

I didn't pay much attention to the youngsters, and they avoided me because I was a sergeant. I was busy wrapping up all of the loose ends and getting ready to go home. Just before dinner, Chambers and Meszaros came over to see the new guys and introduce themselves. I was half listening when one of the new guys made a fatal statement. This rather mouthy kid told Chambers they had to come over to

Vietnam to win the war because we sure couldn't. He went on to add that they would be glad to show us how to do it. All I had to do was look at Chambers and Meszaros, and see how tensed up they were, to know there was trouble in the air. I walked over to my guys and told them they needed to go back to their hooch and get ready for dinner. Both of them gave me a butt-out look, but they could tell I wasn't kidding.

At the mess hall, I could see the word was spreading fast. The men were mad, and they had a right to be, but the new guys didn't realize what they had said. To come into this camp and tell these men they couldn't win the war was tantamount to a declaration of war, and to tell them a bunch of cherry new guys were going to show them how to win it was the Pearl Harbor. I could see this breaking out into a fight, or worse, and the new men were going to have to work into the teams. Trouble now could destroy the process of assimilation and sour the relationships all of the men would need to carry on for the next year.

I went to Looney's hooch after dinner, and it was full of angry young men. The tone settled down when I came in, but I was considered one of the boys, so the talk went on. I got a beer and sat down on a footlocker while the guys hashed it over. I was trying to think of some way to cool the problem down, when an idea flashed into my head. I held up my hand, got the crew quieted down, and then I proposed an idea. The way to handle the situation was to let the new guys make jerks of themselves, and for us to never let them know we had gotten mad at them. We also needed to do it so they would never know we set them up. I got the attention of the men, and they gathered around to hear me out. The idea was to fake a night ambush outside the wire, ask them to go along, and we would go off for a while. Later, we would come back with a story to set the hook, and the next morning we would string them up like a catch of fish.

The cast of characters included me, Chambers, Meszaros, and a bit part for McCain, who slept in my hooch and had bunker guard that night. I told Chambers to wait about forty-five minutes, and then come over to get me. We didn't have a script, so we would have to wing it. Chambers was a ham, so I knew we'd have no problem pulling this one off. I drank the rest of my beer and went back over to my hooch to finish packing.

One of the new men asked if I was going home, and I told him that my time was up. The rest of the men were sitting around, writing letters and trying to relax. There is nothing worse than the first day in a new unit, and when it's a combat unit, it's really bad. I could tell the new men were uptight, and I felt sorry for them. They didn't know anyone, and they didn't know what to do. McCain was getting his gear ready for bunker-guard duty when Chambers and Meszaros came through the door. Chambers said, "Hi," to the new guys and walked over to my bunk. Meszaros asked me if I had finished packing my field gear, and I told him that I hadn't gotten that far yet. I looked at both of them and asked them what they had on their minds.

Chambers looked around the hooch, leaned toward me, and said, "Sarge, why don't you, Meszaros, and I go outside the wire to the ambush trail and bag a couple of gooks tonight?"

I looked at both of them and told them they were out of their minds. There was no way I would go back out with them after the last screwup. I put my finger right in Meszaros's face and told him I was still mad about him almost getting me killed that last time. The new guys had stopped doing anything, and two of them had moved closer to hear the conversation. The fish were nibbling the bait, and now that we had an audience, the ham came out in full force. Meszaros launched into a story about how it hadn't been his fault. He didn't see the last gook who had fallen behind, and he really did think he was getting the last gook in the file. He pointed out that it had all worked out okay. I reminded him that Chambers got the last man in the file, and I was barely able to get the AK-47 his gook dropped so I could shoot the other two gooks in the file. I also went into a story about how the two bunkers on the defensive line had opened up on us, and that we had to wait three extra hours to sneak back in the wire. I looked at him and said, "If that's your idea of working out okay, you're a sick puppy."

Chambers piped in with how they would be more careful this time, and he would make sure things wouldn't get screwed up. Then, he started telling me how cool it would be to nail a couple of gooks my last night in I Corps and add to my body count. I looked down at the floor and pretended to be thinking the deal over. Really, I was choking back the urge to bust out laughing. Chambers asked me if I was getting chicken just because I was short. I said, okay, I'd go, but we would have to be careful. I didn't want to leave I Corps on a stretcher or in a plastic bag.

I told McCain that we would come out by his bunker and use the standard password. I also told him to be sure and let the other guy with him know. He said he would pass the word, and for us to be careful and have good hunting. I told Chambers and Meszaros to get ready; we would leave in twenty minutes.

Chambers spun around to the mouthy new guy who was standing behind him and said, "You want to go, *new guy?*" I thought the kid was going to faint. He turned pale, and stuttered something about hurting his foot during SERTS training so he would be on profile for a few days. The rest of the new guys set a new speed record for getting busy doing something. It got so quiet you could have heard a mouse fart. I told Chambers to forget it; I didn't need to take any new guys to baby-sit.

Chambers and Meszaros left to change uniforms, and McCain went to the bunker. I took off my regular fatigues and put on a set of tiger stripes. I taped the pants legs at midthigh and boot tops, and started to apply the camouflage grease stick to my face. I finished the picture by sitting down and getting my knife and stone out. I whistled a tune while I made a major production of sharpening my blade. In twenty minutes, here came Chambers and Meszaros fully dressed out, and ready to go. The new guys didn't look up, but you could tell they were watching us out of the corner of their eyes. We talked real quiet for a minute, then left out the back door.

The three of us went to the end hooch, where no one

lived, and pulled together some empty footlockers to sit on. It didn't take long for Looney to show up with some beer, and we split our guts laughing about the show. We sent Looney down to check on the new guys. He went in my hooch and asked if anyone had seen Sergeant Burford. No one said a word, so John said that he hoped I hadn't gone with Chambers. One of the new guys asked if we were crazy, and Looney said, no, we just liked to kill. Looney came back to the hooch and reported that word of what we had done was spreading through the company.

In no time at all, there were fifteen men in the hooch. Everyone brought beer, and we told the story again and again. The spirit of the hoax was spreading, and the whole company pitched in to help pull it off. Men kept stopping by my hooch to tell the new guys how crazy Burford, Chambers, and Meszaros were, and how we went out like that all of the time. There were stories about how, even on missions, the three of us would disappear for hours. One of the men told the new guys to keep it quiet because the company commander had warned us not to go out like that again. About 2230 hours, Miller came up with the idea of bringing back weapons from the mission. The word went out through the company, and in fifteen minutes we had ten rifles in the hooch. I decided that was a little overkill, so I picked one AK-47 and an old French rifle to take back as the loot. It was getting late, and everyone started to drift off to their hooches, so the three of us got ready to make our grand return.

We ran back up the company street, and yanked open the door to my hooch. We kind of tumbled in the door, and we were talking in whispers about things like, "Did you see him kick, and he almost got away." Chambers faked a trip and kicked the mouthy new guy's bunk to wake him up, but there wasn't any need for that because those guys were awake. I lit a candle on my footlocker, got my wash basin out, filled it with water, and started to wash up. I asked Meszaros if I had gotten any blood on him. He said, "No," that the spray had missed him. Chambers sat on the bunk he had kicked and said, "Hey, new guy, you ever seen an AK-47?" The man said he had seen one at SERTS. Chambers said, "No, I mean a real AK-47," and dropped the gun on the new guy's chest. The kid let out a gasp and asked Chambers where he got it. Meszaros said that Sergeant Burford had killed the gook who was carrying it. When the kid asked how, Chambers asked me for my knife, which had a rusty spot on the blade. The spot felt sticky. Chambers told the new guy to feel the blade, and when he hit the rust, he asked Chambers what it was. Chambers said, "Blood ... new guy." The kid's hand came off that blade like it was red hot. I stuck my face in the wash basin to keep from laughing. Chambers got up, and we all shook hands and told each other it had been a good mission. Meszaros and Chambers left to go back to their hooch, and I went to bed.

The next morning, I was getting dressed when Proctor came into the hooch and told me that Lieutenant Jackson wanted to see me down at the officer's hooch. I slipped on my shirt and went down to see what he wanted. He and Lieutenant Williams were behind the tent, shaving, when I got there. As I walked up, Jackson looked at me and asked me what had been going on that he was hearing about last night. I told him the story, and he looked at me like I was a nut. Then, he told me that the Old Man had asked him to speak to me to confirm the story. He and Williams were both laughing as he told me that I was to go along with the Old Man at the morning formation. He said the CO was going to chew me out about going outside the wire and that he would put out the word that it had better not *ever* happen again. He felt that he needed to say something, or the new guys would be trying to do it and get their heads blown off. He also told me not to worry, the Old Man wasn't going to tip our hand about the mission.

The first sergeant called the company formation and turned it over to the CO. Captain Eklund called me out of the formation and I locked my heels at attention while he read me the riot act. He told me I had disobeyed his direct order that no unauthorized missions were allowed. He told me that I should be court-martialed, but because I had been a good team leader and was leaving for home that day, he wouldn't punish me. He also said that he knew the names of the other people who were with me, and any repeat of this type of action would get them both a visit to the Long Binh Jail. He went on to give the company a direct order that no one would ever again go outside the wire without permission. Then he presented me with the Zippo lighter the men had gotten for me and wished me a safe trip home. The formation was dismissed, and I headed for my hooch to get my bags.

I got a letter from Chambers a few months later. He told me that the mouthy new guy was still telling people that he knew Sgt. Honest John Burford, and had gone on many missions with that kill-crazed lurp. As a matter of fact, he had gone on a mission outside the wire with me one night, and we had killed two gooks. Chambers ended the letter by telling me I was a lurp legend in my own time.

I decided it was a good time for a beer, so I went to the kitchen. When I got back, my brother asked a real ringer of a question—how did I feel about killing people? I told him that a few years ago, I had been invited by Bryant Goss, my brother-in-law, to tell his fifth-grade class about the war. They had been told not to ask the big question, "Did you kill anyone?" But one boy couldn't stand not knowing, and he asked anyway. I said that I had kept a number of people from killing me, and that's how I viewed it.

I didn't have any feeling about killing. I did it as a part of my job, and I never felt any remorse or sorrow about what happened. I don't know of a person in the company who got all bent out of shape over killing someone. I told you about John Looney and the man with the wedding ring, but John wasn't upset about the killing; it was the realization that they were people just like us, in the wrong place at the wrong time.

But something about one dead person will hang with me, even if I live to be nine hundred years old. We were on a mission outside of Firebase Normandy, and we had to go down a steep path to hit a main trail we were going to patrol. Right at the junction of the trails was the body of an NVA soldier. The body had been there for months. All that was left was some hair, bones, khaki cloth, and a lot of odor. We crossed that body six or seven times on that mission, and with each crossing I got to thinking more and more about who he had been. What really got to me was the fact that a few months earlier, that pile of goo had been a man, and now he was just a pile of junk that everyone walked by. No one cared that he was there, no one cared who he was, or what he was. I wondered if he had a family and, if he did have one, did they know he was dead. Would they ever know? I found myself wondering if they would care. I knew our army would do all it could to get a body back, and even if we couldn't recover the remains, we would at least tell the family so someone knew. I doubted if the Vietnamese felt the same way about life as we did. I bet the jungle is full of bodies just like that one. A lot of theirs, and a few of ours, and they're just gone without a trace. No matter who that body on the trail was, he has someone who will always think of him and care about him, even if he was one of the enemy.

I think a lot about our MIAs who served in the Special Forces and worked on the SOG teams. I would bet a lot of them are still out there resting on the jungle floor. By now, there wouldn't even be a trace of a body. But they aren't forgotten.

CHAPTER 8

"Uncle John, you mentioned that some men in your company got killed on a mission. What happened to them?"

Company F led a charmed life from early January until 20 November 1968. Up to that time, we had three combat casualties in the unit; one in February, one in May, and one the second of June, and this was a period of light company activity. Due to other commitments during the first part of the year, the company didn't get to start pulling long-range patrols until 4 May 1968. As strange as it may seem, for the amount of action we saw, the men who got killed and wounded on 20 November 1968 were the only casualties the company had while performing long-range patrols during its first year of operation. We conducted over 124 long-range patrol missions, totaling more than 279 days in the field. We had enemy contact on fifty-four missions and killed, by actual count, sixty-two of the enemy. This is why I said the company led a charmed life. We never could field more than eight teams at any given time, and all of the missions were pulled by a core of sixty-five men who made up the operational teams.

After the Tet offensive, the NVA pulled back to the mountains of I Corps to regroup, and they got the first reinforcements that came down the trail. Our job was to go back into these mountains and find them, and we got good at our job. By the middle of October, every man who worked on a team had been in at least five contacts, if not more. I had six contacts by then, and a body count of nine for my team. We were running low on men and long on missions. All of us felt we were operating on borrowed time, and the odds were stacking against us. Our youthful exuberance kept us going back out, but we were getting numb.

On 17 November, we returned from a mission in the northern end of the A Shau Valley, and it was gook city. The eighteenth, we got the warning order for a new set of missions. We were putting two twelve-men teams into the Roung Roung area. I told Burnell, if it was put to a vote, I would rather go back to the A Shau; there would be fewer gooks. He told me that if I thought the *area* was bad, I'd love the plan. I told him to pull up a footlocker and tell me the good news.

Lieutenant Williams needed some combat time to get his CIB, so he was going to the field. He also needed some command time, and he would be the team leader on one of the two teams going out. Sergeant Burnell was going to be his ATL, and my team and Sergeant Smith's team would be cannibalized to fill the slots. Sergeant Contreros would be the team leader of the team coming from the first platoon. Burnell told me I would be going as Contreros's ATL. At that time, the company was short on people. Burnell was 2d Platoon's platoon sergeant, and the team leaders were Smith and me. The first platoon had sergeants Zoschak and Contreros as active team leaders. Many of the men who were still in the company didn't have enough time left in Vietnam to go out on missions. Zoschak had extended his tour and was going on leave. The CO had just promoted Sours and given him a team in the 1st Platoon, and Terry Clifton had been moved from the 1st Platoon and assigned to my team. It was a fruit-basket turnover. Anyway you looked at it, this mission was turning into a bag of worms, and we hadn't even left the company area.

I told Burnell that I saw some real problems with the team setup, and we needed to get it straight right now. I mentioned that the lieutenant had never been to the field and that Burnell hadn't worked with any of the men he was getting, except Don Harris, and that had been months earlier. This was supposed to be an easy mission, but the Roung Roung was a hot trip. I reminded Burnie that if it hit the fan, he would have his hands full, and he needed the regular team leaders with their men. Next, I said that I wouldn't go to the PX with Contreros, much less the field. Burnell dropped his teeth on that one, and asked me what the problem was. I laid it on him. First I outranked Contreros, and I felt I was a better team leader. Second, there was a personality clash between Contreros and me; we didn't like each other, and it would cause problems in the field. Third, I felt Contreros was a hot dog and dangerous in the field. The last thing I told Burnell was to check with Contreros, and he would see that the feeling was mutual. Burnell said he would go talk with Contreros.

Burnell came back in an hour and told me that Smith and I would go out with him and Lieutenant Williams. He was going to let Sours be Contreros's ATL, and he didn't expect any trouble on the trip. He told me that he was going to loan Looney to Contreros as his RTO. I ask Burnell if he had checked with Looney on that one. I called Looney in and told him the good news. He told me that he would be back in a few minutes and left the hooch. Thirty minutes later, Burnell came back to see me, and asked me if I knew anyone who wanted to go with Contreros. I told him I didn't know very many. I could tell Burnell's feelings were hurt; he thought the world of Contreros. The Old Man thought Contreros walked on water, but he'd never been to the field with him. Terry Clifton came in to see me and asked if I minded him trading places with James Schwartz. Clifton and Gary Linderer were good friends and had worked together for a long time. I told him I didn't see any problem with the swap. I had heard Schwartz was a good man, and I would clear it with Burnell. It took a few hours, but we got the teams set up the way we wanted.

All of the NCOs from both teams were called in for a quick preplanning briefing. We were told that the area was heavy with enemy activity, and intelligence reported that the 5th NVA Regiment was based in the area and had a sapper battalion attached to them. After the briefing, I ask Burnell why we were using heavy teams in an area that was overrun with the NVA. He didn't know, but we would cover our area and get the heck out of there. We went back to the hootch, and Williams, Burnell, Smith, and I took a look at the map. This wasn't going to be a fun trip. The only LZ in our area was on a hilltop that was an abandoned firebase called Normandy. We were going to have a radio-relay team come in, with a security team to hold the area open. The whole AO was hills, hills, and more hills, all of which were covered with triple-canopy jungle. To add to our misery, we were over twenty minutes air time from Camp Eagle, and close to the edge of the artillery fan.

Burnell and Williams made the overflight for our mission, while Snuffy and I got the team ready to go. We all drew a little extra ammo and a second round of hand grenades. I didn't care if we were the baddest SOBs in the valley of death. It was still the valley of death, and I wanted to be ready. Burnell and I had a little go-round over food for the team. Burnell was hard-core, and he only wanted to carry one meal per man per day. I sat down with him and talked over that part of the plan. I was concerned that it was November, and the weather was bad. I told him that we would have to deal with the cold as well as some steep mountains, and the men would need all of the calories they could get. This was going to be a bad trip, and there wasn't any need to add to the misery by making the men go hungry. I also pointed out that with the lack of an LZ in our AO, we could find ourselves spending an extra day, or getting in trouble and having to split up for E & E. We finally agreed on two meals per day, and each man would carry a total of fourteen meals as a safety margin. We were going for a six-day mission, and there wasn't any need to short-cut.

To add to our problems, we were having trouble getting enough chopper to make the lifts. This meant there would be three different flights going into the same general area. Our LZ was ten klicks away from Contreros's LZ, but that would still be a lot of air traffic in a very small space. The NVA would know we were coming in and could get ready for us. The absurdity of the mission was slowly sinking in, and there were a lot of somber lurps writing letters home that night.

The plans for the insertion were simple. Burnell's team would go out on the first lift, insert, and start its patrol. The ships would come back, refuel and bring out the radio-relay team with their security element. The ships would go back, refuel, the pilots would eat, and then bring out Contreros's team in the afternoon. The weather was bad when we flew out, and we couldn't make our insertion. The Hueys turned around and brought us back to Camp Eagle. We waited while they refueled, then we loaded up and headed back to the LZ. We lost over ninety minutes on the turnaround, and the lift schedule was shot. It would be late afternoon before Contreros's team got to insert.

The helicopters were heading down to the LZ when I heard a number of loud bangs towards the rear of the chopper. I looked at Burnell, who was listening on the headset, and mouthed, "What's that?" He shouted back to me that we had been hit by ground fire. I'd thought that was what the sound was, but I wanted confirmation. The ships flared out and set down on the LZ. I leaped out into the largest mud puddle I had ever seen, and fell down on my hands and knees. My M-16 disappeared under the mud, but I was doing better than Chambers who was flat on his face beside me. There we were, twelve men, slipping and sliding in mud slicker than ice. When we made it to solid ground, we decided to hold up a few minutes while some of us cleaned our weapons.

The firebase was on the highest hilltop in the area and had a commanding view of the surrounding terrain. Normandy had been abandoned a few months earlier when the 1st Cavalry had shifted south and the 101st had to spread out. The NVA had taken advantage of the move to make this a staging area for the 5th Regiment. The hilltop was a plot of naked red earth, where nothing grew. The outer edge was surrounded with abandoned bunkers and broken-down concertina wire. Even when the place had been fully functional, I could tell it hadn't been a garden spot.

We got all of the equipment cleaned and the men ready to go. Burnell had us form up in our team file, and we moved off the firebase. There was a well-worn trail down the steep side of the hill that Normandy sat on, and that was the direction Burnell had us take. We were to move down toward the valley and check the fingers and ridgelines below to find the enemy. The trail was covered with leaves, loose rocks, and mud, so the footing was treacherous. We spent as much time on our ass as we did on our feet. The steep descent tore at our leg muscles, and we were weak-kneed in no time. About halfway down, I decided that if we got hit, I would rather fight it out at the bottom than try to run back to the top. I could tell by the looks on some of the men's faces that our predicament wasn't going unnoticed: there was no way a team could fight its way back to the LZ, and there was a shortage of LZs in the AO. In this case, shortage was spelled *none*, and I was hoping that Burnell knew something I didn't.

Chambers was on point, and I was his slack. Harris, with the secondary radio, was behind me and we made up the point element for the trip. Meszaros, James Schwartz, and Lieutenant Williams were next in the file. Burnell, with Looney as the primary RTO, and Evans, were behind the lieutenant. Munoz, Saenz, with his radio tuned to the artillery frequency, and Sergeant Smith brought up the rear. Everyone was happy with the formation. We had the radios spread out, and good fire cover for every direction. Chambers was a good point man. He had good senses, and he could follow directions. Harris was covering me, and he could deal lead or the radio with equal ease. We had a team filled with experienced men, and that helped take the edge off the difficulty of the mission.

We continued down the trail for another 150 meters until we hit a junction with a larger trail that ran north and south along the ridge. Chambers pulled up when we hit the trail, to wait for new directions. In the heat, the smell of a dead body grabbed at our noses. Chambers looked around quickly, and then pointed to a pile of cloth and bones lying off the trail, right at the junction. We walked over to take a look at the body. There was some hair, goo, bones, and a little bit of khaki cloth. I guessed that the body had been there for two months. While it was a grisly sight, it was a good omen for us. The NVA did a good job of burying their dead, so this wasn't an active trail. If we had found a grave, then we'd have known the enemy was using this path. I stood there a long time, just looking at that pile of stink, and a strange feeling came over me. It was like I wanted to know who he was and where he was from. I had seen a lot of dead bodies, and made a few, but I never had a feeling like that.

Burnell decided to follow the trail to the south. We would move along the ridge on the path as far as we could, then drop down toward the valley to spend the night. The trail moved out to a long finger, and had a gentle slope, so the walking was easy. We moved for a couple of hours without seeing any signs of the enemy, and everyone was feeling better. Eventually, the team stopped and set up a defensive position to wait for Contreros's team to make its insertion. It was SOP for a team to stop and lay dog when another team was inserted in a nearby AO. With all of the assets committed to an insertion, a team on the ground getting hit could find itself with no help. For us, this was a good time to take a little longer break and relax.

We all used the same TOC frequency, so Looney and Harris monitored the insertion. I noticed a funny look on Harris's face and saw Burnell take the handset away from Looney. I asked Harris if there was a problem, and he told me the Old Man had told Contreros to abort his insertion. I asked if they had encountered ground fire, and Harris told me there wasn't any fire. Harris looked at me and said, "Contreros has gone in anyway, and the rest of the team is committed." I went over to Burnell to see what he would say. I asked him what happened, and he told me that the LZ was tall grass over a deep ravine. The choppers couldn't land, and the teams had to jump in. I asked about Contreros and the Old Man, and Burnell told me he could clearly hear the CO tell Contreros to abort. He gave the handset back to Looney and asked me if I had the point ready to move.

We left the trail and started down the hillside. We were cutting back to the north, and headed for a finger that jutted out of the hill. Burnell decided to stop on the finger for the night. On the map, it looked big enough to hold the twelve of us, and allowed us to look down into the valley. I kept Chambers on course, and we pushed to reach the knoll in thirty minutes. It was still light when we set up the night position, and we had plenty of room. Once we got settled in, Burnell told us to eat, and we could have a hot meal. I was letting my lurp soak and fixing my cocoa when the firing broke out. Twelve lurps jumped at once, and within seconds, we were ready to fight to the death. The firing stopped as suddenly as it had started, and we were sucked into the vacuum created by the silence. Burnell got on the radio to the radio-relay team on the firebase and demanded to know what they were doing firing at us. The security team leader came back to tell us they had decided to test-fire their weapons. Burnell was ready to climb back up the hill and kick some butts. We settled down for the night, and Snuffy, Burnell, and I spent some time discussing why Contreros had decided to go in after the CO told him to abort the insertion.

The next morning, we were getting ready to move out when we heard Contreros's RTO calling for a medevac helicopter. We couldn't tell who was hurt, but we did know it wasn't an injury from enemy contact. Since the ship couldn't land, they had to use the basket. I thought to myself that they were going to compromise their position with more air traffic. I hoped they were in a quiet AO. Burnell called me over and gave me the new azimuth to follow to the next ridge he wanted to hit. I looked at his map, and I looked at my map, and we were showing two different locations. I told Burnell that he had us at the wrong place, but he and Lieutenant Williams told me I had the wrong plot. We moved for an hour and still hadn't hit the ridge. While the team took a break, Burnell and I looked at the map. We shot a new azimuth from my map and started to head for the ridge. At 1030 we stopped for a break, and a few minutes later, Looney told Burnell that Contreros had popped an ambush.

Burnell decided to lay dog for a while and listen to the reports. Bacon, Contreros's RTO, reported that they had pulled the ambush at 0935 hours. I looked at my watch and saw that it was close to 1100 hours, and I remember telling Harris that it sure took them a long time to call in. I would have had gunships on station before the smoke settled. Burnell commented that they had been there too long. We heard the Old Man tell them a reaction force would be coming out. I looked at Burnell, and it was like we could read each other's minds. If the reaction force was in the air, it would take twenty minutes to get there. Where were they going to land? If the reaction force hadn't been alerted, then it would take at least thirty minutes to get them ready. No one had heard Contreros call in and alert anyone to the fact that he was in contact when the ambush was blown. I figured, at best, those men wouldn't have help for another hour. That meant they would have been at the ambush site over two and a half hours, without cover. Trouble was brewing, and it was coming up fast.

We started to move toward the ridge, and all of the men were tense. We knew the AOs were hot, and now one team was in contact. A new attitude was evident as we moved toward our objective. We had been moving for forty-five minutes when Burnell stopped us again. Harris tapped me on the shoulder and told me that the Old Man had just called Contreros to tell him there wasn't a reaction force coming out, and there weren't any helicopters to come out to extract the team. The CO did find one LOH-6 to come out to cover the team until division could scrape up some lift ships. Some cover: an LOH held five people, and didn't have any guns. What really got me was the fact that we had two twelve-men teams out in a hot AO and there wasn't one UH-1D to be had. What was going to happen if the NVA tagged us? The comment that there weren't any helicopters wasn't missed by the men. We all had friends on the other team, and we knew they were in trouble. Burnell had us set up in a defensive position while he monitored the radio.

The Old Man told Contreros to move back to the LZ and set up a defensive position. Within minutes, we heard the dreaded call, "Contact," and the request for a medevac ship. The team had not moved away from the ambush they popped over two hours ago, and the gooks had gotten around them. The CO came back on the air to tell them to hang on: two Cobras were on the way and would be on station in ten minutes. All of us were hoping the gooks couldn't tell time. Contreros came back on the radio to ask about the medevac, and report that they were being attacked by a platoon of NVA. The Cobras came in and started laying down suppression fire while the medevac pulled the wounded man out. The fighting got heavier, and we could catch bits and pieces on the radio. Things weren't sounding too good, then the Cobras ran out of ammo. Then, the Old Man told Contreros that the ships would have to go back, refuel, and rearm, because there weren't any others available. Now, the men on the ground faced another forty-five minutes alone. We heard Contreros call for artillery to take up the slack.

The CO called Burnell and told him the division didn't have any forces to send to rescue the stranded team. He ordered Burnell to move back to Normandy for extraction, so we could be inserted into Contreros's location as a reaction force. We quickly set an azimuth to the firebase and started to move. I couldn't help but think we would be a ragtag reaction force after the climb to the LZ. We had two problems, one was to get quickly to the LZ, and the other was to avoid enemy forces while doing so. All the CO needed was two teams in contact to finish off his day. I pushed Chambers to keep us moving, and we all felt the sense of urgency in this move. We hit the main trail, turned right, and quickly walked toward the uphill trail junction. We were downwind from the body, so we knew in advance that we were getting close to the trail.

We started the climb back to Normandy. Burnell had Looney call the radio relay on top of the firebase to let them know we were coming in. The climb back up the hill was a killer, and there were times when we were on all fours pulling ourselves up. We seemed to tumble over the crest, and we quickly moved across the LZ. But we were surprised that there weren't any lift ships waiting for us. Burnell got on the radio and called the Old Man to report that we were at the LZ and ready to load out. The Old Man was just bringing the second flight of gunships on station, and he told Burnell that he would have some slicks released to his control in a little while. He told us that they would try an extraction of Contreros's team first. We sat around and listened to the radios while our friends fought their battle. The reports coming from the ground weren't good; it sounded like the team was surrounded, and we didn't see how they could get to an LZ for an extraction. The battle was four hours old, and we were ready to go to the rescue, and we didn't understand the delay.

A look of anguish came over Harris's face, and he told us that Bacon was reporting an explosion. Then he shook his head in disbelief, and said, "Everyone is hit; they're all down."

We were stuck on a firebase so far from the fight that we couldn't even hear the explosions or see the choppers. Burnell was like a caged animal as he paced around the area. We could only listen as Bacon gave the casualty count—three KIAs and seven WIAs. Everyone wondered who was dead and how badly the others were hit. When Walkabout came on the radio to inquire about the medevacs, we knew there weren't any NCOs left in the fight. Five sergeants had been on that team. Sours had busted both ankles on the insertion and been medevaced early that morning. Venable had been shot early in the battle and medevaced. That left Contreros, Mike Reiff, and Frank Souza, and now none of them were able to use the radio. We knew the other men could handle any problems, but it told us that the team was hurt.

The first set of medevacs came in and picked up two of the worst wounded. The CO told the remaining team members that the medevacs would be back in forty-five minutes. He said the team should hang on. I spit on the ground and walked off; that was the second time the team had been left on its own since the battle started. We all wondered where our ships were. We were ready to go join our friends and get our wounded out of there. Where was all of that wonderful support we always heard about and had been promised over and over? The fight was well over five hours old by then, and the majority of the team was still on the ground and still in contact. The Old Man had called Burnell to tell him that the reaction force would come from Camp Eagle; it was closer, and the force could be on station faster.

The medevac choppers were on the way, along with the reaction force. We heard the CO talk to Gary Linderer, so we knew he was alive. The reaction force was made up of our short-timers, and they had been picked up from the company area, so at least we would have lurps to the rescue. The reaction force fought its way to the survivors of the team, and started to evacuate them. We could hear the radio transmissions, and they were still taking rounds from the enemy.

It was late, but we had a few hours of daylight left. We were just sitting around waiting for orders. It was starting to rain, and the ceiling was getting lower, so there wasn't an extraction in our future. Burnell and I were sitting on an abandoned fuel bladder, talking about what had happened, when Lieutenant Williams came over and told Burnell that Contreros had died from massive head wounds on the hospital ship. Burnell and Contreros had been real close friends, and Burnell started to cry. I didn't know what to do, so I just put my arm around his shoulder and sat there with him. In a few minutes, Williams came over and told me to get the team ready to move out; we were going back on patrol.

When I got Snuffy Smith and told him we were going out, he didn't believe me. I said, "No bull, it's back out," and we rounded up the men. No one was happy about going back down into the valley. We had all heard our teammates get shot to pieces, while the division sat on their butts and did nothing, and now we were headed back into the valley to find a sapper battalion. There was a lot of grumbling going on when Burnell came over. He asked me if I had the team ready to go. I said we were as ready as we were ever going to be, and he told me to get the point moving. The trip down the hill, in a pouring rain, was a disaster; everyone fell down, and we were slipping and sliding all the way. The team got strung out, so when Chambers, Harris, and I got to the junction, we had to wait for the team to get back together. I sat there looking at the NVA body, and I wondered if he was trying to tell me something. A strange bond was forming between us. When the team got back together, Burnell had me turn to the north and follow the trail. We moved until it was almost dark, and we couldn't find a spot large enough to stop for the night.

We found a large depression in the ground, near the trail, and Burnell gave an order I never thought I would hear from him—we would all sleep in the depression and build a team shelter. It was pouring, the temperature was in the low forties, and it would get lower that night. Burnell wanted us to shelter ourselves to prevent exposure casualties. With all of us sleeping together, we would be able to share our body heat.

We whipped up a shelter in a few minutes, a crude lean-to propped up on the high side of the depression. To get in, or out, we had to use the ends, and climb over the men on the outside edge. We picked out guard times and set about to fix dinner. Burnell had everyone fix a hot meal to help fortify themselves for the long, wet night ahead.

The rain kept falling, and I didn't see much chance of it letting up anytime during the night. Burnell, Snuffy, and I sat around for a while, talking about Sergeant Contreros's team and what had happened. There was a lesson to be learned somewhere in this mess, and the sooner the better. We were all worn out, so we cut the gab early, and tried to get some sleep. We decided to use only one guard at a time that night, and I got the 0300 to 0400 shift.

The hole we were sleeping in started to fill up with water, and it was up to four inches deep by the time my guard shift came around. I hadn't done much sleeping, but I was surprised that I had slept at all. I was wracked by the bone-chilling cold that comes from lying in water, and, in seven years of military service, I couldn't remember a more miserable night. I got up thirty minutes before my shift and decided I would rather sit out in the rain, on guard, then lie in the water. I relieved Schwartz and told him he could go get some sleep. He gave me a short laugh and said he would sit with me for a while. I sat there, with the rain running down my face, thinking about that dead gook. I don't know why, but I pulled out a cigarette and lit up. I just sat there and smoked on guard in the middle of the night. For some reason, the danger just didn't make any difference to me. I think the team was demoralized by the day's happenings, and everything seemed totally absurd; from the lean-to we were sleeping in, to the lack of support from the division, nothing made sense. The rain kept falling on me, and for the first time in Vietnam, I felt as if I had no control over anything that was happening to me. Schwartz sat with me until 0430, and then he decided to go lie in the water. When my shift was up, I stayed on guard and let the next man sleep.

The rain stopped around 0530, when heavy ground fog covered the ridge. I was squatting down by a tree on top of the bank by the lean-to. I had a good view of the trail for as far as I could see in the fog. At 0630, I heard a sound behind me, and I looked around. Burnell had his M-16 leveled at me, so I said good-morning and looked back down the trail. He said that he'd thought I was a gook, and he was getting ready to shoot me. I told him that I thought I'd found the best place to keep watch from. When he asked why I didn't wake him at 0500 for his guard shift, I said that I hadn't felt like sleeping and had decided to stay on guard. He was sleeping, and anyone who could sleep under these conditions didn't need to pull guard. He laughed, thanked me, and then bummed a smoke. It was getting light, and the fog was getting thicker.

We fired up some C-4 and had a hot meal before we sat down to look at the map. Burnie felt that the trail ran along the ridge and connected with a major ridgeline that was a thousand meters away. We all agreed that the big ridge would be an ideal place for a base camp. The Old Man had told us that Contreros's team had killed some headquarters-type personnel, and the 5th NVA Regiment had to be in the AO. The fact that they had a sapper battalion, which were engineers, told us they were doing some building. That meant a major base camp, and it also spelled out major trouble if we got hit. After what happened the day before, we were sure that the gooks would be on alert. They didn't like to get caught with their pants down twice. We also knew that Sergeant Contreros's men had killed some nurses, so we could expect some mad gooks. The weather was bad, and it looked like it would be overcast all day.

We got packed and picked up our team formation. I told

Chambers that we were going to stay on the trail. I would be back ten feet and staggered to the right side of the trail. We would move in a staggered formation so two people wouldn't get hit by the same bullet. There weren't any signs that the trail had been used lately, so we felt safe moving on it. I knew Chambers would be twice as alert while on the trail, and we needed to make good time. The next three hours were nerve-wracking, but quiet, and the team quickly reached the base of the next ridge. We stopped short of the ridge and set up a quick defensive position.

I could tell by the rise in the terrain that we were at the ridge. The trail started going up and turned to the left. I was holding the point, waiting for orders from Burnell. Harris came up and told me to go back to Burnell's position. When I reached them, Burnell and Williams had their map out and were looking the area over. I squatted down with Burnell just as the lieutenant got up and walked toward the point. Burnell told me that the lieutenant was going to recon the trail up to the ridgeline to see if he could find the sappers. Then Burnell looked at me and said, "You're going with him," I started to ask Burnell if he had fallen on his head during the insertion, but I saw he wasn't kidding. He told me to get a radio, so I asked for Looney. Burnell told me I could take Harris. I walked back to the point and told Harris to come with me. I told Chambers that he was to stay put and cover the trail. I also said that if he saw four people coming back in a hurry, to shoot the fourth one.

Williams, Harris, and I huddled over the map for a second and got ready to move out. I was point, Williams was walking my slack, and Harris was the tail gunner. We used a staggered formation, but stayed close together. We went a hundred meters on the trail before it started to climb up the ridge. I stopped the group and looked up the trail. The jungle was dense, but I could see the trail winding its way up the ridge. I told Williams that I could smell gooks up ahead, and Harris did too. The lieutenant said he didn't smell anything and we were going to the top of that ridge. I told him that we would leapfrog our way up the trail, two men covering the man who was moving. We hadn't seen any trail-watcher bunkers yet, so I started moving up the hill. I went a few meters and dropped down to a firing position. Williams moved next, followed by Harris. When Harris stopped, I moved again. We slowly worked our way up the trail. We were a little over halfway up the ridge when I saw the first tree stump. I waved Williams up, showed him the stump, and told him that the gooks had been cutting trees to build bunkers. I moved up the hill, and Harris came up to the lieutenant. Harris saw the stump and knew what it meant. He knew we were in a bad place.

We leapfrogged our way up the ridge for another twenty-five meters, and the stump count was getting larger. I looked to the right, and I could see the crest of the ridge. Just below the crest was a new bunker, and the gooks hadn't even had time to finish the camouflage. I waved Williams forward, pointed out the many stumps, and the bunker. Harris told Williams to sniff the air. Williams did, and he could smell cooking fires. We were able to convince the lieutenant that it was more than foolish to try to reach the crest of the ridge. I told him that we might get to the crest, but we wouldn't come back down. I also reminded him that if we got spotted, they would be all over the team, and we didn't have a close LZ for an extraction. It took a few minutes to talk him into going back, but we did. We worked our way back down the hill in a reverse leapfrog, and erased as many signs of our visit as we could. I had Harris call Burnell and tell him that we were headed back. On the return trip, I laid back to make sure we weren't followed.

When we got to the team's location, Lieutenant Williams and I sat down with Burnell and reviewed everything we had seen on the ridge. Burnell knew it was time to get our hats and leave. Looney called the radio-relay team and had them get in contact with the TOC. The weather was getting worse, and the cloud cover was affecting the radios. Sergeant Burnell decided to reverse the team. He got Snuffy Smith and told Snuffy to keep Saenz and Munoz with him as a stay-behind team. They were to set up claymores and hide. The rest of the team would start down the trail. We would move two hundred meters and wait for Smith.

Smitty was to stay put for fifteen minutes to see if the NVA were following us. If gooks were on our tail, then Snuffy was to ambush them. After he fired his claymores, his team would fire off two magazines of M-16 ammo, throw a hand grenade, and haul ass down the trail to our position. We would have a new ambush set up, and gooks in hot pursuit would get cooled off.

At Burnell's command, the team started to move out, and I became the tail gunner. I looked around for Smitty as I went by the area I thought he would be in, but I didn't see a sign of anyone. We kept moving along the trail until we had covered our two hundred meters. Burnell stopped the team, and we got down in place. While we waited for Smith, Burnell radioed the Old Man and gave him a full report to let him know we had located the sappers. The CO told Burnell that he had decided to pull the team out. There was too much enemy activity, no support available, and the weather was going sour. Burnell called me over and told me that we had our marching orders and we were to be extracted that day. All of the men were cheered by the news, but it seemed like an hour before Smitty's group rejoined the team.

I got Chambers and told him that we would be pushing it. We had to be on top of Normandy before 1700 hours to get extracted. The weather was closing in, and timing was everything. He knew I expected him to move fast, but he knew to slow down and check all likely ambush sites. Burnell passed the word that we wouldn't take any breaks, so everyone was to take a salt tablet. We were set for our race with the weather, and Burnell told me to get the point moving. We pushed off, and Chambers set a good pace. Everyone was tense; we had seen too many signs of the NVA to believe we were alone in this AO.

We kept up the pace for two and a half hours, and everybody was feeling the pain, but the terrain around me started to look familiar, and I knew we were approaching the junction. In ten more minutes, my nose told me that we were almost ready to start the hard part. Then we came to the body and made the left-hand turn to take the trail to the top.

Burnell had us stop for a five-minute break before we attempted to climb to Normandy.

I found myself looking at the body for the fourth time, and I guess I was telling him good-bye. I knew I would never be back in the spot again, and sure enough, I felt that strange feeling once more. I was glad when Burnell told me to move out. The path was wet and slippery, and we had to crawl most of the way up the hill. When we got to the top, a light rain started to fall, and the clouds were closing in fast. The lift ships called to see if we were on the LZ. The clouds were closing down, and they wouldn't have but a few minutes on the ground. I knew we were in trouble when I could see clouds above me and below me, and I couldn't figure out where the choppers were coming from. But, like ghosts, the Hueys materialized out of the clouds, and we were greeted by shouting crew chiefs. Those pilots wanted out, right now. We ran to the helicopters, scrambled aboard, and we weren't even on good when they pulled pitch and took off.

I was on the second ship, and as we flew into the clouds, I started to wonder how the pilots knew where we were. I got the answer real quick, they didn't. I had never been inside a cloud in an open ship, and it isn't like being there in an airplane. I was sitting on the edge of the door opening, and I couldn't see the tail boom. We were in a real tight spot. The pilots had to stay away from each other, and descend through the clouds into the valley and out to the coastal plains. The trick was to not hit the other ship or the numerous mountain tops in the area. Words like *vertigo* and *inverted* came to my mind, and I wished I had stayed on the mountaintop with the radio-relay team. Later, the pilots told us that if they hadn't taken off when they did, they would have had to stay on Normandy overnight. I was ready to die for a lot of things, but clean sheets wasn't one of them. The pilots were sweating every inch of the way down, and there was a collective sigh of relief when the choppers broke out of the cloud cover. The UH-1D wasn't well equipped for instrument flying, and the pilots in Vietnam didn't spend a lot of time training for that type of flying. We offered to give both crews a beer from our club, but the pilots said they needed something stronger.

Our joy at being on the ground was short-lived as the Old Man came into the club to tell us how badly the other team had been chopped up. Clifton, Contreros, Heringhausen, and Reiff were dead. Venable, Cox, and Souza were in critical condition and had been evacuated out of country. Bacon, Sours, and Czepurny would be leaving Vietnam soon, and Linderer was in the hospital in Phu Bai, getting patched up. Walkabout was back in the company area, with both hands bandaged up. Twelve men had loaded out for a mission three days ago right by this very spot, and only two would ever come back to the company. Every one of us had lost friends, and the shock was numbing.

We got the story in bits and pieces from Walkabout, the lurps on the reaction force, and some NCOs from the Air Rifle Platoon. Contreros had popped the ambush on a group of NVA. There were nurses and an officer (of unidentified rank) in the kill zone. After the ambush, the team stayed at the ambush site and didn't report the ambush for over an hour. The team had seen enemy troops at 2300 hours the night they inserted. Gary Linderer told us that the units were squad size and up, which meant nine to twenty-five men. These units came by their location two or three times and spent most of the night looking for the team. The next morning around 0900 hours, five more NVA passed the team, and thirty minutes later Contreros decided to ambush the group that they hit. The Old Man told Contreros that a reaction force would come out to secure the area, so Contreros stayed at the ambush site instead of moving back to secure the LZ. The ambush was at 0935 hours; the team reported the ambush at 1045 hours, and the CO told them that no forces were available at 1130 hours.

In the two hours that the team delayed in moving, the NVA appeared to have surrounded them. The CO ordered Contreros to move to a better spot, closer to the LZ, and when the team started to move, the trouble started. Sergeant Venable moved forward to signal the LOH and was shot in the arm, neck, and chest, and the battle started. The remaining ten men opened fire and were able to recover Venable.

Minutes later, an NVA platoon charged up the hill and was met with a wall of lead. A medevac came in and extracted Venable. The NVA kept the men under heavy fire, but the Cobra gunships were on station, helping hold the enemy at bay. When the Cobras ran out of ammo, they had to return to Camp Eagle to rearm. The team was left without cover for forty-five minutes, so Contreros called in the artillery. As the NVA put more pressure on the team, Contreros walked the artillery fire in closer to the team's location. They had the artillery firing within fifty meters of their position when the Old Man called back to tell them he was on the way with four gunships.

The team was in jungle so thick that the Old Man couldn't spot their position. When the team popped smoke to help him find them, the smoke dissipated before it could get out of the trees. Contreros had the artillery stop firing so the Cobras could start their gun runs. There was some confusion on the ground, and Contreros called for the men to tighten up the perimeter. Gary Linderer remembers the men starting to move, and then the hillside was caught in a massive explosion. In the beat of a heart, ten men were cut down. Three men died instantly, two more were critically wounded and out of the fight. Bacon, the RTO, was hit badly and going into shock, but he kept talking to the Old Man. The other four men were hit but kept up the fight. Cox fought on, despite a broken wrist and a stomach wound so large that he stuffed a towel in it. Linderer was hit in the legs, Czepurny was hit in both feet, and Walkabout was hit in both hands. For the next ten minutes these wounded men patched up their buddies, saved Frank Souza's life, and kept up a running battle with the NVA. The first two medevacs arrived, and Walkabout was able to get Contreros and Souza on the jungle penetrator and safely up to the helicopters. The Old Man called the team to tell them it would be thirty more minutes before the medevacs would be coming back. Working on guts alone, the five men left alive on the ridge held off the NVA.

The next call on the radio was the Old Man telling the team that a reaction force was on the way. More men would be on the ground in less than ten minutes. All of the guys were showing wear from their wounds, and time was running out. The reaction team was made up of short-timers who were getting ready to go home, but they hit the ground with fire in their eyes. They quickly located the downed team and set up a perimeter around them. The men had brought a couple of M-60 machine guns, and poured a deadly base of fire on the retreating NVA. The medevac ships came in, and the wounded were loaded out as fast as possible. The reaction force stayed on the ground and waited for the next set of medevacs to start loading out the dead. When the sad job was finished, the men worked their way back to the LZ and were extracted.

We hung around the club for a few minutes to drink beer, then we drifted off to clean up. The Old Man had his hands full with the after-action report, so we wouldn't be debriefed until the next day. Burnell and I helped pack some of the men's personal gear and to clean out the team hooches. When all of the work was done, we had two empty hooches. The company had suffered a heavy blow; of the twelve men who left on that mission, only two would return to the company. There was a lot of concern about how they would hold up on a mission after their ordeal. Walkabout eventually left the company, but Linderer showed what tough stuff those Missouri boys were made of and stayed with the company until the end of his tour. He also got his butt hurt again, and got his second Purple Heart.

We had a memorial service for our fallen friends, and it was a sad affair. None of the men were happy about being there. The four pairs of boots with the rifles and helmets didn't comfort any of us. The men were fidgety and uncomfortable, and glad when it was over. We had said goodbye to our friends days ago, and it was over. We didn't need some chaplain telling us how much better off they were with their Father in heaven. We didn't need anyone telling us to accept death. We were young, and we didn't accept death. We lived with death every day, and it was the enemy to be fought off with every ounce of strength we had. We didn't lightly put our friends behind us, but put them behind us, we did.

All of the men wanted to talk about the mission. We knew some mistakes had been made, and we needed to learn from those errors. Every night, groups of men would sit around to discuss what had happened and, most of all, why it happened. Every man on the team was an experienced lurp; there weren't any new guys out there. We started at the top and worked our way down. We felt that we had been let down by our leaders. Someone had to have known that the division was committed to a larger mission and that there wouldn't be enough assets left to support two heavy teams in an AO that was known to be hot. We were tipped off when there weren't enough lift ships to do a proper insertion. Why didn't the CO know we were being stuck out on a limb? Who dreamed up the mission in the first place, and why heavy teams? While hindsight is always twenty-twenty vision, everyone knew two six-man teams would have been able to do the job. The lack of good LZs dictated smaller teams; it is easier to get out a six-man unit than it is to extract a twelve-man team.

There was some talk of Contreros's team having a special mission to ambush near the headquarters of the 5th NVA Regiment, but his team didn't carry M-60 machine guns or M-79 grenade launchers, and any team deliberately going into harm's way would take some firepower. Sergeant Burnell was the most experienced team leader in the company, and the ranking NCO. If there had been a special mission, Burnell would have been the team leader. It didn't make sense to let your most experienced team leader babysit a lieutenant while a less experienced team leader was taking on the 5th NVA. I concluded that Contreros had bitten off more than he could chew. The company hadn't lost a man on patrol up to that point, and we all were getting a little too cocky, and a bit sloppy.

We hashed over the timing of the action. No one could come up with a good reason why the team didn't report the contact when it happened. The hour and fifteen minutes that were wasted sealed the death warrant for those men. The fact that they stayed at the ambush site just blew our mind. They knew enemy troops were all around; that they just sat down to finish eating breakfast was unbelievable.

Even after telling the Old Man about the contact, they sat around for another forty-five minutes, waiting for the reaction force. When the team finally decided to move, they didn't do a proper area recon. Two glaring errors were made: not putting out security after the ambush so the gooks couldn't sneak up on them; not sending out a 360-degree recon before moving. Either action could have had a great deal of positive effect on the outcome of the battle. Every team leader left made a big mental note to remember to put out security.

Once the battle was joined, every man fought as hard as he could, and the men gave a good accounting of themselves. In any battle, things get mixed up, and this one wasn't any different. After the fight, the CO stated that he had the team's location plotted three hundred meters away from what turned out to be their actual location. That error had cost the team time when the gunships were trying to come on station and when the medevac came in. No one knew how it happened, but somehow the location of the team got mixed up. The area the team was in had thick overhead cover. The smoke from the smoke grenade used to help locate the team couldn't get up through the trees, and when the jungle penetrator from the medevac was dropped, it didn't get down. The gunships are a joy to have around when the enemy is near, but there is a tendency to forget that a 2.5-inch rocket throws shrapnel in every direction, and it doesn't know friend from foe. Artillery has the same problem, and Contreros had to call the fire in close to their position. Some of the wounds suffered by the reaction force came from the aerial rocket artillery fire of the gunships that were protecting them.

After the explosion on the hilltop, the few men who were alive and able to shoot put up one of the bravest fights in the history of the 101st Airborne Division. It was two hours after the explosion before their fellow lurps were inserted and able to run up the hill to rescue them. During that time, the five wounded lurps were under fire at all times. They repulsed numerous attacks and were able to perform first aid on two critically wounded men that saved those men's lives. Walkabout found the strength to move around and drag two men over to the jungle penetrator so they could be medevacked. The efforts of that wounded man were nothing short of superhuman.

At this point, I called for a time out. "Hey, fellows, let's take a short break. I need to hit the little boy's room and get another beer." On my way back from the bathroom, I stopped in the kitchen and opened the refrigerator to grab a beer. There weren't as many as there had been. I walked back in the living room and sat down.

My brother looked over at me and said, "John, what caused the explosion on the hill?"

I almost bit the top off of the beer can at that question. Here was a gray area, and I knew it would be a tough question to answer. As a matter of fact, this one was so tough that I took a second drink of my beer before I started to talk.

No one knew what happened on the ridge other than that a large explosion cut the team down. The theory that most of the survivors hold to is that the NVA were able to slip up on their position and detonate a forty-pound Chinese claymore mine, commonly called a "forty-pound Chicom," and the shrapnel from the claymore is what hit the team.

We had talked about this mission a lot when we got back to the company area, and after rehashing the action time and time again, I decided that the team wasn't hit by a Chicom mine. Nothing about the action worked right. The claymore mine that we use is ten inches by six inches by one inch, and weighs about four pounds. A forty-pound claymore was a large dish-shaped affair with wire legs. I couldn't see how the enemy would have been able to maneuver such a large weapon into a position to use it against the team. An hour passed between the time that Venable got shot and the explosion, and in that time, the NVA had attacked the team from every direction. The lurps were able to drive back the enemy on every attempt, and the NVA never got closer than thirty meters. A claymore is, generally, a defensive weapon, and its fire pattern is directional The artillery fire that Contreras had ringing the team would have made it difficult to get the mine in position. If the NVA had gotten the mine close enough to use, then they would have had a force of men ready to follow up the blast. Just as soon as the dust from the explosion settled, they would have overrun the surviving lurps and finished them off.

A number of things made me believe that the team was hit by its own artillery fire. When the fire was brought within fifty meters of the team, they were in the danger zone. Artillery fire isn't exact, and the fall pattern of the rounds can vary up to ten meters. The correction factor for artillery is in ten-meter increments, and rarely does anyone know the exact place they are standing. I believe the team got caught in the edge of the last artillery barrage that Contreros called. The reasons I say that are simple. The team had been in dense jungle, and couldn't see the helicopters above them; after the explosion, the trees were defoliated, and the team members could see out. A claymore's blast would have been parallel to the ground, and wouldn't have defoliated the trees. The artillery was being fired with superquick fuses to get tree bursts so the blast would get the troops in the woods, and that is what took all of the leaves off the treetops. Gary Linderer's wound was another indication that there was an airburst explosion. Gary was lying down on his stomach when the blast went off. He was hit in the back of the leg above the knee, with the shrapnel going between the hamstring tendons, and the fragment came to rest against the bone.

The most telling fact was the lack of enemy action after the explosion. A claymore explosion would have been followed up with an assault. The fact was, after the explosion the enemy wasn't able to mount a serious attack, and only fired sporadically at the team. It would seem that the artillery fire had dealt the enemy a severe blow, too. No matter what caused the explosion, nothing could diminish the raw valor of the lurps on that ridge.

CHAPTER 9

"Uncle John, was every mission full of excitement and contact?"

"No, Andy, there were plenty of boring missions where we didn't have contact with enemy forces, but almost every mission had something happen that kept it exciting. Animals were one source of excitement that could pop up in the most unlikely times. Then there were times when the missions were hairy because of things we thought the enemy was doing. Let me tell about a few of those times."

My team was alerted for a mission to pull a bomb-damage-assessment patrol on a B-52 Arc Light strike on the border between Laos and Vietnam. After looking at the coordinates of the AO, I wasn't too sure how much of the AO was in Vietnam. It was a gray area, and the boundary was marked as the approximate location. The B-52s had hit the valley that held a suspected NVA base camp, and we were to go in and see how well they had done. The map showed an area of steep mountains and heavy jungle, and there weren't any LZs to be seen. I had Harris get the team together, and I told the men that we might have to rappel in and McGuire out. I got a lot of funny looks and a few grumbles. The Old Man went with me on the overflight to look for an LZ because he wasn't happy with the prospect of rappelling a team into an AO.

Captain Eklund, Proctor, and I went down into the helipad and met with Mr. Grant, who was going to fly us out for the overflight. Grant said he would have to be careful while flying in that area because it was an active area for the fighter-bombers going north. It took thirty minutes to get to the AO, and the area was a mess. The valley they had bombed was a narrow valley with steep walls, and the jungle was torn to pieces. The mountains reminded me of the mountains in Alaska—steep on both sides and four feet wide at the top. The Old Man said we could go in on the ridgeline and work our way down to the valley floor. All I could see were bomb craters and broken trees, from top to bottom.

We were swinging back over the ridge at four hundred feet and doing forty knots. The Old Man and I were looking out the side of the ship to see if we could find a hole in the jungle for us to rappel into. Suddenly we heard a high pitched squeal in the head set that burrowed right through to the brain. Mr. Grant rolled the chopper into a steep dive down the back side of the ridge. I thought I was coming out of the ship; I didn't know a Huey could pull a power dive. Grant pulled the ship level and turned back toward Camp Eagle. The CO got on the intercom and asked him what he was doing. Grant said he was headed for home, and the CO asked why. Grant told him that he had to get the ship checked to see if he had overtorqued the rotor head with the dive. When the Old Man asked him why he dove the ship, he laughed, and told us the sound we had heard in the earphones was a warning tone. The helicopter had been painted by a radar unit, and it had locked on. In the area where we were flying, the radar belonged to the NVA army in Laos and was hooked to a 37mm antiaircraft gun. They got an F-105, or an F-4, every once in a while, and he was sure they could hit a Huey.

When we got back, the Old Man went over to the Cav and told them we couldn't risk the men or equipment to go into that AO. We could have been shot down during the insertion if we had rappelled down, and once we were in, the radar guns would cause a big problem with getting us out. And the terrain was so bad that we couldn't go into the next valley and expect to get to the AO in six days. The mission got scrubbed, and all of the men gave a sigh of relief. Lurp missions we pulled right away; suicide missions, we at least liked to think over for a day or two.

On 23 November, I was alerted for a mission. The team

was tired; we had just come back from a bad mission to the Roung Roung where Contreros's team had been shot to pieces. The morale of the company was at the bottom of the scale. I guess the Old Man was trying to get us back out as quickly as he could so we wouldn't have time to dwell on the happenings of the twentieth. The area was back in the north end of the division AO, near the border, and the intelligence people told us an NVA unit was in the area. After the mess on the twentieth, I had started to have a little more faith in the G-2. After all, they told us there were plenty of NVA in our last AO, and they called that one right.

I put Harris to work on the overlay and artillery fire, while I made the overflight. When the helicopter got to the AO, we saw a pair of F-4s and an FAC spotter plane bombing the next ridge. We tuned the radio to their frequency and listened while they worked over a bunker line. We had a ringside seat for the show. The F-4s were dropping five-hundred-pound general-purpose bombs on the bunkers, and they could put the bombs on the money. Both of the aircraft were hitting the bunkers dead on. One F-4 got a bomb hung in the release on the last pass, and we heard him tell the FAC he was going to shake it loose. He pulled up and turned to dive back toward the bunkers, and on the way down he shook that plane like it was a toy. The bomb came loose and flipped out toward the jungle while the pilot kicked in the afterburner and headed for home. The FAC bid us good-bye and turned to the south.

As the chopper turned back toward our AO, we watched them fly away. We started to look for an LZ. The Old Man spotted one on the high pass, so the pilot turned the ship around, and we went down for a closer look. I almost croaked when we made the low pass over the area. The LZ was a large open area, but we could make out bunkers in the jungle that surrounded it. This wasn't the LZ for me, so we flew on to search the rest of the AO. We flew that AO from one end to the other, and there wasn't another LZ to be found. The Old Man decided that we would go in to the LZ with all of the bunkers surrounding it. We made another low pass, and we didn't draw any ground fire, so the CO said it had to be empty. I got back to the team and broke the news that we would insert into a bunker complex. The team members thought I was getting too gung ho and becoming a glory hound. I explained that the Old Man had picked the LZ and I had strongly protested the selection. I was as unhappy with the LZ as the men were, and I had let the CO know I thought it was stupid to set my team down in a known bunker complex. When the Old Man told me that was the LZ, and we would go in there, that was the end of the discussion.

We were short on people, so we only had a five-man team to go out on that mission. Just before the final mission briefing, Burnell came by to tell Harris he wouldn't be going out. Harris asked why and Burnell told him that his orders for the 51st LRRPs had come in, and he would be leaving the next day for Bien Hoa. Don helped me get the team ready for the briefing, then went to see if he could get off the orders. I couldn't find a replacement for Harris, so I would be going out with a four-man team. I went back to talk with the Old Man, and he told me the mission was still on. We had to cover that area, and we would have to make do with what we had. The team was made up of John Looney, Ken Munoz, the new medic, who was a conscientious objector, and me. This was going to be a very quiet mission. I didn't plan to shoot at anything that didn't shoot at me first.

The next morning, I felt nervous about making the insertion, and that was a new feeling for me. I just didn't feel good about inserting into a bunker complex. Harris came down to the helipad to see us off. The CO told me he had requested a second set of Cobras to be on standby in case we ran into trouble.

All the way out to the LZ, I kept thinking, What a crappy way to start the day. The Huey made the high pass and started to roll out for the descent to the LZ. I could see the bunkers, and they looked as big as houses. Looney could see them too. I looked at him and smiled while I pointed to the wood line. I kept watching for the line of green tracers that I knew would be reaching up from the jungle to greet us, but nothing happened; not a shot was fired. The ship got close to the ground, and we jumped off. We ran to the wood line and piled on top of the first bunker. I took a quick peek and saw that it was empty. We checked the next two bunkers in both directions and concluded that the complex was abandoned. I called the CO and had him release the gunships.

We spent two days on the top of the ridge, checking bunkers. Every finger had fighting bunkers on the military crest, but we couldn't find any living hooches. Trails ran from one cluster of bunkers to another, and we had looked in every direction for the sleeping hooches. I decided to move to the valley the next day to see if we could find any signs of a base camp. It was getting late, so we stopped for the night. I had the team move down from the crest; we were going to sleep on some of the bunkers. I called in the sitrep, we fixed dinner, and then picked guard times.

I was lying on top of a bunker when artillery rounds started to hit nearby. The rounds were close, and the ground shook with each impact. I told Munoz to get on his radio and call the artillery FDC to find out what they were doing firing in my AO. He told me that the FDC told him they weren't anywhere close to our AO, and they were firing a standard H & I fire mission around the buffer zone of our AO. I told Munoz to give me the handset, and as the next rounds came in I held it up and keyed the mike. After the explosions, I asked the FDC if he heard that. When he answered, "Yes," I told him to check fire, and not another round fell that night. I found out later that all of the coordinates had been plotted backward, so the FDC didn't know they were firing in the AO.

The next day, we moved down the side of the mountain and hit an area that was covered with large boulders overgrown by vines and palms. I thought we could cross the boulders, which would get us to the valley quicker. It didn't take me long to find out that I was wrong. As we went across the rocks, we found holes that were covered by the vines, and I fell in one that was over my head. There I was in this hole looking at spiders as large as my hand. Right after seeing the spiders, I thought about snakes, and how the cobra liked that type of place. I suddenly remembered, in great detail, every scary movie I ever saw where a snake popped out of the wall of the pit. Thinking about all of those snakes helped me forget about all of the spiders I had to climb over to get out of that hole. Once I got back to daylight, I found a new way down the mountain.

We patrolled the valley for two days and didn't find any sign of the NVA. As we had to move back to the LZ that we inserted into so we could make our extraction, I started to move back up the ridge. We were going to work our way around the top of the valley and back to the LZ. We stopped the fourth night on a trail that followed a finger up the hill. We were out of water, so I stopped halfway up the finger and found a place where the team could spend the night. We could tell there was a stream downhill, and I had Munoz and the medic go down to fill some canteens. Munoz and Doc got back quickly, but they had only filled four canteens. The minute Munoz got back, he told me that we needed to move. I asked him if he had seen some NVA, and he said worse than that, they had seen a hungry tiger. When I asked him how he knew the tiger was hungry, he said they had scared the tiger's dinner away. Munoz and Doc had come up to the stream and were starting to kneel to get water when they smelled a strange odor. When they looked around, a small Vietnamese deer took off through the bush by the stream. They heard a cough, and the tiger went right behind the deer. They thought they were seeing things until they walked over and saw the prints in the mud. The first set were deer prints, and the overlay set was big paw prints that were starting to fill with water. They did a quick fill on the canteens and headed back up to us. We were all concerned that the tiger might decide to follow their trail and come up for a little dinner à la lurp.

It was getting dark, and I didn't want to move, so we stayed at the same spot. No one slept on guard that night. Looney called the guys on the radio relay and told them a tiger was heading in their direction so they should keep their eyes open.

The next day, we patrolled the rest of the AO, and got to the LZ at 1500 hours for extraction. If it hadn't been for the tiger, we would have had a boring trip. Yet, five days earlier I knew we were going to get killed in that hot AO. That's what added to the stress; we never knew from one day to the next what would happen.

I was surprised at how many animals we did see. The monkeys were a problem. They would be in the trees, and they would let us get right up on them, then they would break into a loud chatter or rush off through the treetops. No matter what they did, it scared us, and their racket could alert the enemy that something was moving out there that didn't belong. A lot of large monkeys got shot by point men; there wasn't time to check out what jumped out in front of us. We fired from reflex and checked later.

I never saw a snake, and it was a good thing for both me and the snake. They had some snakes in Vietnam that could kill a person in seconds. A story was told in the 1st Cavalry about a Vietnamese who was chopping brush to clear a chopper pad for the unit when he cried out, stopped work, and sat down. He started to rock back and forth and chant while his family gathered around him, and the women started to cry. When a GI asked the interpreter what was going on, he was told that the man had been bitten by a viper, and he had sat down to die. The bitten Vietnamese keeled over dead in less than a minute. I always wore a leather glove-shell on my right hand when I was out on a mission. One reason was to make it easy to unhook wait-a-minute vines so we could move quietly through the jungle, and the other reason was to keep me from being bitten if I grabbed a snake, which would compromise the entire mission.

We came upon a small herd of elephants on one mission. There were four or five crashing around in the jungle. The bull started to make a lot of noise; I believe he could smell us. I called the Old Man to report the herd, and he told me to kill them. The NVA would capture elephants and train them as pack animals. I told him I didn't think M-16s would do the job, and it would alert the NVA that we were around. I didn't want to kill the elephants anyway. The CO sent out two gunships to do the job, but the animals got away before they got on station; I gave the pilots the wrong azimuth; it wasn't the elephant's war.

We had a close encounter one night, and it shook up the whole team. Byron was the team leader; we had two new men, Chambers, who had just come in country, and Saenz, who had transferred over from the 501st Signal. The night before, the gooks had spent most of the time looking for our team, and we hadn't gotten much sleep. Byron decided to move us away from the trail, where we could spend the night in a quiet spot so the team could get some rest. We had set up, finished a good hot dinner, picked guard times, and were settled in for the night. It was around 2130 hours, and Saenz was on guard. We were in some thick bush, and there was a heavy cloud cover. It was so dark, it was like we were in a bottle of ink. I was a light sleeper, and I would wake up every hour and spend a few minutes listening to the sounds of the jungle. I had just opened my eyes when there was a loud crashing sound, and a large bird flew through the brush right over our heads. We could hear the wings flapping as he hit every branch around. It scared me, and I bolted up to a sitting position. Saenz had been sitting up on guard, and the bird almost hit him. The bird scared Saenz so much that he hollered out, and that got the whole team in motion. I rolled over to my weapon and grabbed the claymore detonator, and I know everyone else was in the same position. Byron shouted, "Don't fire!" and everybody froze. No one heard any other sounds, so we relaxed and listened for a few minutes. We decided that there weren't any gooks around, but we couldn't figure out what had spooked the bird. We settled back down, and Byron and Chambers decided to stay up to keep watch for a while. They were both sitting cross-legged, facing each other, talking, and I had just lain down to try and get some sleep. Suddenly, a weasellike animal ran through the team circle and hit Chambers in the chest. The animal dropped into his lap and made two laps around his legs. Chambers was swatting at the weasel, and on the third lap, the weasel turned right. The animal crossed over and ran up Byron's chest and scratched off on Byron's bald forehead as he went over Byron and dashed to freedom. While Byron and Chambers flailed about, the rest of the team got ready to fight to the death with the attacking enemy. When everything settled down for the second time that night, we decided that the weasel had spooked the bird, and had been tracking it, when it ran afoul of us. After having my heart jump-started twice in one night, I was ready to go join the air force. The next morning, we all had a good laugh and confirmed that the night's adventures hadn't been a bad dream when we looked at Byron's head. Right on his forehead were two sets of long red claw marks where our intruder had made his exit. I still don't know who was the most surprised that night, Chambers or the weasel.

When John Looney told me that he saw an earthworm that was as long as his arm and two inches round, I started to take his dex tablets away, but the more I thought about it, the more likely his story seemed true. We came upon some strange things in the jungle. I saw a water leech that had to be two feet long; the land leeches were small, but they worked in gangs. We would soak our socks in bug juice before a mission, and rewet the tops of our boots every day to try and stop the leeches. I believe that the leeches started to like the bug juice as much as they liked blood. There wasn't a trip made without multiple leech wounds. I had fifteen on my leg one day in one leech-infested area. They were all around the top of my boot, so I hit them with a squirt of army insect repellent, and counted them as they dropped off. We couldn't feel them when they bit us, and they would drop off after they got their fill of blood. I always knew how bad the leeches had been by how much blood was crusted around the tops of my socks.

My favorite animal story was told by Joseph Bielesch. Bielesch was back from RECONDO school and had his own team. He had been given three cherries to train, so he was running a mission in the open area near Camp Evans. Joe had McCabe as his ATL, and Vern Kirkland was the RTO. The mission was a milk run to get the new guys ready for the field, and the team was operating close to Camp Evans. They had been out for four days, and this was their last night out. By 1700 hours, they had hit the Perfume River and decided to find a place to stop for the night. Bielesch moved the team one hundred meters back from the river and found some scrub brush to hide the team for the night. While the team was settling in for the night, Bielesch kept hearing a sound that was familiar, but he couldn't place it. Bielesch was from Philly, but soon he was able to recognize the sound of chickens. Joe took McCabe, and they crawled back toward the river to see what they could find. After working their way down the bank of the river, they hit pay dirt in the form of a stack of crates full of chickens. There were two chickens per crate, and there were fifty crates, neatly stacked, waiting for the NVA to come down the river and pick up dinner. Bielesch decided to surprise the gooks with a little C-4 for dessert.

Bielesch and McCabe went back to the team's location and started building a Joe Bielesch Special. They took four claymores and taped them together, then they taped a layer of hand grenades to the claymores. For good effect, Joe added two WP grenades, a smoke grenade, and collected the team's stash of cooking C-4 to add a little bang. Joe and McCabe took the bomb pack to the river bank, and pulled two crates out of the stack. They put the bomb inside the pile of crates and hid the detonator wire as best they could. Bielesch saw that he had a real problem with how to fire the bomb. All he had was a claymore detonator, and the wire was only fifty feet long. Bielesch wasn't one to dwell on problems, so he put it out of his mind. The plan was simple; they would take turns being at the firing device during the night, and when the gooks came to get the chickens, bang, Chicken à la Bielesch!

The team was scheduled for an early extraction, so when dawn came and the gooks didn't, Joe decided to blow up the chickens anyway. He knew this would be a good explosion, and since they were so close to Camp Evans, he called the TOC to tell them the team was getting ready to blow away one hundred chickens. He told them he was using claymores and there would be a big explosion that should kill them all. Bielesch and McCabe went up to the firing device, while Kirkland kept the cherries back a safe distance. They got down as low as they could and squeezed the firing device. It was a big explosion; the ground shook, and one hundred chickens departed this life.

Bielesch and McCabe got up and looked where the crates had been stacked. All they saw was a cloud of dust and chicken feathers hanging in the air. Both of the men were deaf from the explosion. Bielesch felt a vibration behind him and turned around. There were twenty-five Huey's on line assaulting into the open area around him. The infantrymen leaped out and charged toward them. There had to be at least two companies of men. A major, with pistol in hand, ran up to Bielesch and asked where were the one hundred chickens. McCabe pointed to the dust cloud and feathers. While the major took the infantry toward the cloud, Bielesch took his team and grabbed a chopper for the extraction.

When the team got back, Joe got everything but a warm welcome, and he couldn't understand why until the Old Man got back from a meeting with the major. It seemed the major had overheard Bielesch telling the TOC that he was going to blow away one hundred chickens, and he thought that was a lurp code word for gooks. He had rounded up a relief force to help the six lurps battle one hundred gooks. There was some talk of a court-martial, but Bielesch hadn't done anything wrong. We all felt the wrong person was being considered for the court-martial anyway.

Our teams were sent on some missions that were so screwed up, we wondered who dreamed them up. I believe there were times when the 17th Cav just didn't know what to do with us, and sent us out so they could say that the lurps were being used. Byron drew one mission like that. We were sent to patrol in the rocket belt. We inserted by helicopter, at last light, out in an open area west of Camp Eagle. The plan was to move at night and set up on the hilltops to use the Starlight Scope to spot enemy movement. During the day, we were to hide and sleep in the low scrub that covered the area. The first night we set up and kept two men on guard at all times. The guards took turns observing the terrain for signs of enemy movement, and I'm not sure we even knew how to use the Starlight Scope. The next day, we stopped in some scrub to hide and sleep. The brush wasn't high enough to give us any shade, and we lay there in the sun, and cooked. No one could sleep, and the brush stopped any breeze that might have been blowing.

We moved that night and set up on another hilltop to keep the enemy under constant observation. After another fruitless night, with our eye glued to the eyepiece of the scope, we started to move to a new hilltop that had a tree on it. The team hadn't gone fifty meters when we were spotted by the early morning pink team from the Cav. A pink team was an LOH-6 that would fly low to spot NVA movement or draw fire and a pair of Cobra gunships that flew high, and out of sight, that would attack the target spotted by the LOH. We stopped and got down hoping that the LOH hadn't seen us. We didn't know their radio frequency, and they didn't know we were working the area. We knew we were in trouble when the LOH made a quick pass over us. Byron had us take off our hats and show the flash panel we had sewed inside it. We also looked up when the LOH made a pass to mark us for the Cobras. All of us had light-colored hair, and none of us looked like Vietnamese. The LOH slowed down and came around for another pass. This time, the observer in the LOH waved to us, and the pink team flew on. Byron got on the radio and called the TOC to make sure they let the Cav know we were out there.

We got to the next hill, and there wasn't any shade to get under, so we got in the brush and put up a lean-to made with our poncho liners. We lay on that hill, and roasted, for another day. For the third night in a row, there wasn't any activity except us fighting the mosquitoes. On the fourth day, we ran out of water, but found a pond near an abandoned shrine. Barry Golden and I went down to get the team canteens filled. The water was clear, and when Golden put his hand with the canteen in the water, he got hit by two water leeches. I have never seen anything move so fast. They came out of nowhere, and in a flash, they were attached to his arm. He just laughed and kept filling the canteen. He looked over at me and told me to start filling my canteen, and to watch and make sure a water leech didn't go inside it. When we got finished filling the canteens, Barry shot the leeches with bug juice, so they would drop off. When we got back to the team, we dropped two water purification tablets in each canteen and let them sit for a few hours. Our dinner that night didn't taste so great, but it was dinner. Our fifth night was as empty as the four nights before, and we were extracted by truck the next morning. Byron and I agreed that the army could have used the 33d Mess Kit Repair Company on that mission.

Three more screwball missions stick with me. On one of them, we were inserted near Firebase Vehgel to pull a four-day mission. The gooks had been putting a lot of pressure on the area, where there had been some heavy fighting a month earlier. We were going in to see if we could find the base area where the NVA were working from. I had a good group, with Harris, Looney, Chambers, Meszaros, and Taylor. We had been lurping hard for two days, and there were plenty of signs, but no NVA were around. In the afternoon of the third day, we found a large grave near a trail. I had Looney call the Old Man on the radio to report the find. We were having trouble getting radio contact, and had to use a radio-relay team. I was killing time, waiting for the CO to get back with us, when Looney told me he had a message coming in. I heard him ask the relay to repeat the message twice, and then he walked over to me and said, "The Old Man wants us to dig it up and count the bodies."

I asked him if he was serious, and he told me he had asked the relay to repeat the message twice. I didn't know what to do; we didn't carry shovels. I looked over at the guys and they were giving me that look-what-you-got-us-into-now look. I had a rule that I would never ask the men to do anything I wouldn't do first, so I got my knife out and walked over to the grave. I looked back at the men, and they had backed away like they thought the grave would explode. I started to dig, and went down about four inches when I hit a hollow space, and the dirt caved in. The funk rushed out of that hole and knocked me to the ground. My stomach did three turns before I could get under control. I sat on the ground for a minute and looked at my fearless team; they were in tears. My stomach was still doing the flip-flop so I told Looney that it smelled like four bodies to me. John got on the radio and reported that the Tango

Llama had counted four bodies. I got the team moving out of the area fast before the Old Man could start to ask too many questions. I didn't eat any dinner that night.

Another dog mission was a two-day BDA—bomb-damage assessment—back on the border. We moved into the valley where the B-52s had hit, and it was like nothing I had ever seen before. The whole valley was churned up, and there were bomb craters lapped upon bomb craters. The little flat ground left was covered by broken tree trunks and deadfall. The explosives used in the bombs had a strong odor, and it hung over the area. We tried to make our way around the craters, but there were too many of them, and they overlapped. We had to walk down the side of the cra-ter, and then climb up the other side just to start down into another crater. Each crater was eight to twelve feet deep, and the whole team would be hidden inside the crater. The walls of the craters were sloped, but the dirt had been churned up by the explosion, and it was like walking in loose sand. I had a hard time believing the size of the hole made by the 750-pound bombs. By the end of the first day, our legs were like rubber, and I couldn't find a level spot for the team to set up on. We moved out of the valley and found a finger on the ridgeline to set up our night position. That night, I sat on the finger and looked at the valley stretched out below me. I was very thankful the NVA didn't have B-52s.

We finished the mission by walking on the ridgeline, and going down to the valley twice to check out suspicious-looking areas. We never did find any signs that the enemy was ever in the valley. I guess the Arc Light had been tar-geted on the wrong valley, but I could tell by the damage that we only had to score in every fourth valley to do a lot of damage. I found myself trying to figure out how many Arc Lights it would take to cover the A Shau Valley so we wouldn't have to go back there again.

The mission with the combat photographer was a screw-ball mission. I don't remember getting any warning that we would have a guest until the day before the mission. We were short on men and had scraped up a team to go check on some new enemy activity outside Firebase Birmingham.

No one cared if the guy went along, as long as he understood that he was to keep out of the way and be quiet. He had been out with a few line companies and had combat experience. The combat correspondent was Terry McCauley, and he came over the afternoon before the mission to meet with us. We got together and helped him put his gear in lurp order and made sure he had everything he would need for the mission.

The team was Brooks, TL; I was the ATL and had the spare radio; Harris was RTO, and Taylor was point man. McCauley spent the night with us, and we reviewed some of the special drills we used to break contact. He agreed to go on the four-day mission, and take care of his share of the load, so we gave him two extra radio batteries to carry. We got up early and made sure we were ready for the insertion. I know he had to be having some second thoughts about going with us, but he kept quiet. He started to snap pictures as soon as we left the ground. The LZ was fogged in, so we spent forty-five minutes flying around, and he got a great shot of Harris in the chopper, with the fog-shrouded jungle in the background. When the fog lifted, the insertion ship headed down, and we slipped into the LZ. The team hit the ground running, and our guest was in for the duration.

Except for the click of the camera, the mission was quiet. I have never been so frequently photographed in my life. We found an area where the gooks had set up a mortar to fire on Firebase Birmingham, and he took a lot of pictures around there. We all found it a little unnerving to be moving along, and have him go off to the flank for a picture. I wondered if he thought this was a rigged mission. We drew the line when he wanted us to cross a stream again so he could get a few more shots. Our last night, we found an area where a U.S. infantry company had been, and it was a mess. The garbage pit hadn't been burned or buried, and we dug around to see how much they left the enemy. I was shocked at the C rations we found. The men were supposed to open all cans, whether they were going to eat the food or not, so the rations wouldn't be any good to the enemy.

Before we moved on, we used our knives to damage all of the cans we found.

The last day of the mission, we heard some noise and watched a trail for a few hours to see if the NVA were in the area. At 1400 hours, we picked up and headed to the extraction point. When we got to the LZ, we set up and ran a sweep to make sure the enemy wasn't following us. When the ships were late for the pickup, it finally dawned on McCauley that this was for real. We made him an honorary lurp, and our team suffered under the tag of "Hollywood lurps." We knew all of the other men were jealous because our pictures were in the 101st Airborne *Rendezvous* magazine.

CHAPTER 10

"John, was there any special training you took to become a lurp?"

There wasn't any special training given to us before we joined the LRRP unit. We just volunteered for the unit and got on-the-job training. The guys in the company all worked with the new men to show them how to fix their gear and what they would need in the field. We had to take care of each other because there wasn't room for mistakes. We always tried to schedule a milk-run mission for the cherries so they would learn how to function in the field. It was as much for our protection as it was to break in a cherry. Not everyone was cut out to be a lurp, and we needed to find that out early in the game. In late June, we did some McGuire extraction work in the old company area, and that was the extent of our training. After mid-July, we didn't have any time to do formal training in the company. I did take my men out a few times to work on setting up ambushes, but that was all.

There was a school run by the 5th Special Forces Group, down in Nha Trang, called RECONDO School, and it was the school of the LRRP. Each LRRP unit could send men to the three-week school, but the number of slots open to a unit was limited. The school trained men from every branch in the military and from all of the allied forces as well. I was a sergeant and slated to get a team soon, so I got my orders to go to school in early September. I had been on four missions before my orders came down, and that was a big help at school. The company got to send five men down for that class, and what a crew they picked. I had David Blankinship and William Cook, who were old timers, with Ken Munoz and James Evans, who were new men, as the team that went south for school. We spent two days getting our gear together, and the Old Man let us leave a day early. When we got to Nha Trang, we had two days to goof off before our class started.

We got off the C-130 at the air base in Nha Trang and took the bus to town. We rented a hotel room and checked our weapons at the front desk. I told everyone that we would meet there at 1500 hours Sunday afternoon, so we could report in for school. Cook and I went out the door and headed toward the sound of fun. We didn't have a lot of money, but we headed for the first bar we could find. We had heard all of the stories about the girls and the Saigon tea, but we had to see it firsthand. After an hour of watching lonely GIs sitting around talking to a bunch of girls who couldn't understand what they were saying, it got very depressing. What those guys needed was some combat time to take their minds off of their problems. Most of the men in the bar hadn't ever heard a shot fired in anger. Cook and I got tired of being in a packed bar, so we headed out to find the steam baths. Our search paid off, and after a steam bath, cold shower, and complete massage, we were in much better shape. Later that night, we were walking down a side street when someone opened up with an AK-47 right down the middle of the street. We both hit a doorway and cursed the fact that we couldn't return fire.

Sunday, five worn out, broke lurps reported to RECON-DO school. We were assigned to a hooch and drew our special equipment for school. The best thing about the school was there wasn't a lot of Mickey Mouse bull going on; we were there to learn. I knew it wasn't going to be a fun school when we went out and filled a bag with thirty pounds of sand, and went over to the scales to weigh it in. From that time until the end of school, that bag was in our packs, and it could be pulled out and checked at any time. We drew two pairs of tiger-stripe uniforms and all of our classroom material. School would start at 0430 hours sharp on Monday morning.

The blast of a whistle and the call to fall out for PT came

at 0430. We did one solid hour of the army daily dozen, then went back to our hooch to get packs, weapons, and LBEs. We did a timed one-mile run the first day, and I found out that being a lurp didn't necessarily mean you were in good shape. I told Cook that was the reason I had learned to shoot a gun; I knew I couldn't outrun the gooks. The next day, after our hour of PT, we ran two miles. Wednesday, we went three miles. Thursday was our four-mile day, and Friday was the five-mile run. Saturday was the big day, and we made the seven-mile run in ninety minutes. I was smoking two packs of cigarettes a day, and I was glad to live to the end of the ninety minutes. Some wise jerk took his sandbag out of his pack and stashed it along the way. It was dark when we left, so I guess he thought he wouldn't get caught. The school cadre found it and marked it. When the run was over, we had a formation and they asked the offender to come out and own up to the fact that he had cheated on the run. No one came out, so we got to do the run Sunday morning in the light. The second week, after PT, we dropped back to running five miles a day.

The first week of school, we had our classroom work; we spent a lot of time on map reading and the compass course. The medical training was intense, and we had to pair off with another lurp to draw blood. If we had to start the serum albumin in a wounded man, it had to be into the vein or it wouldn't work. The "blood expander," as it was called, was the only thing we had to use if a man got hit and lost a lot of blood. Each of us had to draw blood and show the instructor. I was paired off with a black guy, and he had veins as big as a water hose. I put the restrictor band on him, popped his arm, and hit the vein on the first try. I drew his blood and held it up for the instructor to see. I noticed that he didn't look so good after I took the blood, but I felt he would be okay as soon as I got the band off. He took my arm and started trying to hit the vein, but he closed his eyes every time he put the needle in my arm. After the fourth try, I took the needle away from him and drew my own blood. Later he thanked me for helping him, and I told him I was helping me. We both had a good laugh.

We spent hours working with the radios. We learned more about correct radio procedure, and we had classes on jury-rigging the radio to get more range. We also learned some field tricks to use with the battery if we ran low on power. A lot of time was put in on the radio because it was our only link to help. Planning the mission was another long block of training. We learned to make out a warning order and to give the insertion briefing. We went over everything, from checking the helicopters to picking the best LZ for insertions and extractions.

Toward the end of the week, we started to spend the afternoons on the rappelling tower. Here we worked on climbing the rope ladder up the back side of the tower. Then, we would move to the wall-rappel side of the tower and rappel down a fifty-foot, vertical wood wall. After that, we had to climb a knotted rope back up to the tower. The next rappel would be from the free-rappel side, where we learned how to rappel from a chopper. We rappelled six times an afternoon. The first days' rappelling was without gear, but the next two days were with full gear. One of the students got his rifle hung up on the rope and flipped upside down on the free rappel. The instructors had to haul him back up to get him loose, and he almost choked to death before they did. After that incident, we all checked the rope clearance twice before we jumped.

On Saturday, we made the seven-mile run, had a few classes and a test. We had the afternoon off to wash our uniforms and equipment, and we had some organized-sports time to play a game of volleyball. Sunday, we made the second seven-mile run and cursed the cheater every step of the way. Sunday afternoon, the school instructors had a cookout, and everybody had a few beers and some great food. We got to eat in the Special Forces mess hall, and those guys knew how to live well. They were on TDY and got paid separate rations. This meant they bought all of their food from the locals. We had shrimp, steaks, lobster, pork, and chicken, with all of the fresh vegetables we could want. Every meal was a delight, and a few of us got to thinking about transferring to the 5th Group.

Monday of the second week, we started the field training. We did a lot of work adjusting artillery fire, and we had a live mortar crew firing for us. I thought the artillery adjustment was one of the most important parts of the training. Artillery could be our best friend; indeed there were times when it would be our only friend. But it was an unforgiving friend, one who didn't allow for mistakes. We had to know the fuse types and the bursting radius of the different rounds. It didn't do any good to have a round with a delay fuse used against troops in the jungle. We had to know to ask for the superquick fuse to get a tree burst to spread the shrapnel, and we couldn't count on the fire direction control to pick the right fuse. We worked with the illumination rounds, and figured out how to allow for wind drift with the parachute flares. The trick was to time the flares so we wouldn't have a dead space between rounds. We didn't want the light going out until we wanted it to.

We had three different live-fire ranges that we worked on. I liked the jungle trail the best because it was set up with partial silhouette targets on each side. We had to walk up the trail, watch for trip wires, and spot the targets. We only had one magazine of ammo, and we had to hit each target with two rounds. We had to fire from the hip, and we didn't have time to aim. Being a southpaw worked well for me on that range, and I ran a good score. There was a regular range that we used to zero the sights of our weapons and do target shooting. The fire-drill range was the range I had the most trouble with. On that one, we practiced breaking contact with an enemy force. The plan was simple—the point man would fire a magazine of ammo on full automatic fire, then he would turn around and run back down the trail. When he got beside the second man in the file, the second man would open up on automatic until he had fired a magazine, then he would turn and head down the trail. As each man passed the next man in the file, that man would open up. The last man in the file would fire his weapon and throw a hand grenade before he turned to go down the trail. When the fire drill was over, the team would be headed away from the enemy, and everyone would have had time to reload his weapon. The enemy would have been stopped by the wall of fire and would be delayed in getting their forces after the team. The idea was to sting them so badly they wouldn't come after us, or they'd be so cautious that we could escape.

On the fire-drill range, being left-handed worked against me. The school made us walk with our weapons on safe. For me to get my weapon from safe to fire or auto, I had to let go of the handgrip and reach around the weapon to use my thumb to flip the selector. A right-handed man's thumb rested right by the selector switch. On every run down the lane, I would be late firing, or I would only kick the weapon to semiauto and fire one round. The instructors would jump all over me, but I didn't design the M-16. I told my instructor that I didn't go out with my weapon on safe, and I always walked with it on semiauto.

We went to another range and fired a collection of old U.S. weapons and enemy weapons. We learned how to load and operate all of them. If we got in a bind, an AK-47 would work just as well for us as against us. I enjoyed firing the Swedish K-50, 9mm submachine gun and decided to try to capture one if I could. It would make a great second or backup gun. It was like old times when I got to fire the Browning automatic rifle. I had carried one of those when I was a young trooper in the 506th. Fully loaded, it weighed twenty-two pounds; my M-16, loaded, only weighed seven pounds, and I had the same firepower.

The hard work at the school was the live helicopter course, where we had to rappel from Hueys, and climb a forty-foot rope ladder into a chopper. It sounded easy in the briefing, but reality brought a new set of problems. To go up the ladder on the tower was a breeze, but to climb the ladder on a live ship was a bear. The ladder swung under the ship while the men on the ground tried to hold it still, or the ship would drift in one direction or another. Once we got up to the ship, we had to cross to the other side and climb back down another ladder. It was as hard going down as it was going up. In addition, the pilots would get tired of hovering for an hour at a time, and the drifting got worse toward the end of every shift.

Rappelling from the helicopter was even worse. Back at the tower, we were going fifty feet, with the ships we were going one-hundred feet plus. The chopper would land and pick up six men at a time. Once it got up to the proper height, we came down, two men at a time. For some reason, it just felt different coming out of a flying helicopter. Each man had to make three jumps, and by the third time, we were all hotdogging it. One man had torn his pants in the front, by the fly, and we didn't wear underwear. He was going to show everyone how it was done on his last jump. He cleared the ship and didn't brake until he was almost on the ground. When he hit the ground, he pulled fast back to clear the rope, and the very hot snap link that was attached to his harness dropped down and burned him in a very private place. Some of the men on the ground swore they heard the sizzle when the metal met flesh. The guy was in great pain, and the medic wasn't any help, as he suggested amputation to save the lurp's life. The guy had a blister the size of a dime.

The real trip was the McGuire rig training. The army still hadn't developed a harness to use on the McGuire, so we sat on a loop in the rope. The helicopter would be rigged with three 120-foot ropes. Each rope had a large loop tied in the free end, and a small loop tied beside it. The other end of the rope was tied to the floor of the chopper. One of the students asked why we put our arm through the small loop when we sat in the large loop. The instructor told him that was so if a man got shot, or fell out of the big loop, they would still have an arm to send home. The explanation wasn't met with a lot of laughter, and I don't think the instructor was kidding.

When the ship was overhead, the looped end of the rope would be dropped to us; three men would grab the loops and put them around their bodies. The two outside men would link arms with the man in the center, and all of them would hold the loop tight under their butts. The helicopter would then lift to pull the rope tight. We were practicing in an open area, so the pilots would go forward and up. If we had been in a jungle setting, the pilots would have tried to pull us straight up so we wouldn't be dragged through the trees. When we felt the rope tighten against our buttocks, we would sit on it and let the chopper lift us. The men would link their legs with the center man, and the outside men would stick out their legs to help stabilize the rope and keep us from spinning. The helicopter would climb up to ten-thousand feet to get out of range of small-arms fire, and fly away at eighty knots. In school, each ride was fifteen minutes long, and the view was spectacular if you could keep your eyes open. I know a lot of men kept their eyes closed from takeoff until they were firmly back on the ground. It was easy to spot the men who had had their eyes closed; they were the ones who fell on their faces when they landed. The only problem I had on the McGuire rig was that I always thought that the rope was slipping out from under my buttocks. Whether the rope really moved or not, I don't know, but in my mind, it kept slipping.

The week went by quickly as we rotated from the range to the artillery firing line, and on to the ropes. The school had a world-class compass course, and we ran it twice. We stayed in the field for three nights, and everyone was glad when we headed back to the school area Thursday night. Friday morning, we had classes, and after lunch we had a three-hour test. After the test was graded, we were assigned to one of the cadre to prepare for a three-day patrol in an active enemy area. The Special Forces NCO assigned to my team was called away during the planning, but we kept working on the overlay while waiting for him to come back. Then the school's first sergeant came in and told me to report to the school commandant. I went over to the field office and reported in. The major said that two of his instructors were going on emergency leave, and he didn't have anyone to go out with my team so we wouldn't be able to finish school. I asked if he could break our team down and let us go with other teams but he thought that would put too many men on a team, which might lead to trouble if we got in contact. He was right; with eight teams out, he would have a problem covering them with a normal head count. An extra man could throw off the fire drill or an extraction. The major said we couldn't be held over because our unit would be short on men, and we would be gone from our unit for seven weeks. In the end, he held one man over for the next class, and sent a letter to the Old Man telling him what happened and why we couldn't finish school. The letter didn't help my hurt feelings, but I could see there wasn't anything that could be done.

We went back to the hooch and got our gear ready to turn in. We would be on the early flight to Bien Hoa. Once we got to the 101st rear area, we'd get on a plane for Phu Bai. Blankinship, Cook, and I scraped up what money we could and went to town to get drunk. The next morning, we got our orders and left for the airfield. We spent one night in Bien Hoa at the rear base. The next morning, we were able to get a flight back to Camp Eagle, and we were home Sunday night. Two days later, we were alerted for a mission, and our two-week vacation was over.

CHAPTER 11

"Uncle John, it sounds like you had a few close calls in Vietnam. Did you ever think you were going to die?"

"No, Erik, the thought of getting killed didn't cross my mind. We just didn't dwell on death. But, there was one time when, if I'd had the time, I am sure I would have thought about it."

It was 11 December 1968, I was getting short. I didn't know the exact date I would be leaving for home, but I knew I would be leaving before the first of the year. My team was alerted for an ambush mission on the trail network in the area we called the Game Preserve. The Old Man decided to make it a twelve-man unit, so I got Snuffy Smith to join his team with mine. We had worked well together on the last ambush, and we had gotten a good body count. Snuffy said he was eager to go. We had to dig around to scrape up enough people for this mission, but we got some of the best men who were left in the company.

We would be inserting near the trail where we had killed the five gooks on 2 December. I decided to make a morning insertion out in the open area, away from the jungle. There was a lot of scrub brush near the trail, and that would give us a great place to hide and set up an ambush. I believed that the gooks would be looking for an ambush near the jungle's edge, where we hit them the last time. In the area where we were going, there were two high-speed trails within three thousand meters of each other, so the hunting should be good. I had worked both trails on prior missions, and made contact with enemy forces on every trip. I told Smith to draw a double load of claymores for the ambush and to get me some det cord and nonelectrical blasting caps. I was going to show them how to make a daisy-chain claymore ambush.

During the overflight, I found an area that was in a large depression. It was open and would make a good LZ. We would be hidden from sight by the depression, and scrub brush came right up to the rim of the bowl. We would be able to work our way through the brush right up to the ambush site. Next, we flew over the area where we had killed the gooks earlier in the month, and I saw that there were mounds near the trail. The mounds meant that the NVA had come out to bury their dead. I was sure that the gooks were still using the trail and that we could have a successful ambush. When I got back, Smith and I sat down to plan the ambush. I wanted every man to know where he was to go when we got to the trail. I also wanted to make sure we didn't leave any telltale signs that we were in the area. When we had set up the ambush on 2 December, we had left trails in the grass from the claymore mines back to our position, and I wouldn't make that mistake again.

Smith and I double-checked to make sure we had our best men in the flank positions. Since this would be a daisy-chain ambush, we had to make sure the two flank sections fired their claymores. I was going to triple the size of the ambush kill zone by using the daisy-chained claymores, and the claymore extensions would be wired to fire from their detonator. I made Smitty take the rear security again. He wasn't happy about getting stuck in the back and missing the action, but he understood the need to have a team leader back with a radio just in case something went wrong. I decided to use Larry Chambers and John Meszaros to help me set up the daisy chain. Neither one of them had any real demolitions training, but I could teach them as we went. This would also assure that there weren't too many people trampling around the ambush site.

The plan was simple. We had twelve men for the ambush, so I put Smitty and his radioman in the back. They would set up their four claymores, with wide spaces between them, to cover our rear, and those two would be the rear security. I put five two-man positions across the front kill zone, and each position had two claymores set up in front of it to fire with its own detonators. Then, I would daisy chain five claymores on det cord for each flank, and wire them into the firing device used by the flank teams. I would have a kill zone that was seven-hundred feet long, and could handle up to thirty men. The Old Man looked over the plan and gave it the final okay. We called the men together, reviewed the plan, and made sure each man understood his part in the mission.

After the team meeting, I let Smith handle the equipment issue and inspection while I preplotted some artillery fire. We had the insertion briefing at 2030 hours and cut the men loose by 2100. I went back to my hooch to get my gear ready. We would be making a midmorning insertion in order to miss any gooks that might be coming back from a visit to town.

The twelfth of December dawned clear and warm, and I was glad the weather would be working for us. We weren't going to load the ships until 1000 hours, so we ate our breakfast and took our time getting the team's equipment moved to the helipad. I made sure Chambers had all of the det cord packed, and I double-checked the box of blasting caps I had in my pocket. Caps were touchy, and I wanted to make sure I had them padded right. I could see me tripping when we inserted and blowing myself into little pieces. The RTOs worked with the radios, and everyone did what they could to pass the time. The teams weren't used to having so much time on their hands while waiting for the insertion, and we were lost for something to do. I got bored, so I went back up to the TOC to talk with Proctor. The pilots were going over the flight plans, and we were all turning into clock watchers. At 0930, the Old Man told us to get loaded up; it was time to go. I walked back down to the helipad with Mr. Grant and held his door open for him. The pilots did their preflight while we loaded our gear on the choppers. At 1000 hours, the ships lifted across the wire at Camp Eagle, and we headed west toward the Game Preserve.

The choppers came in low and dropped us right on the money in the depression. We moved to the scrub brush and got in a tight defensive position. We lay dog for ten minutes, but I was sure we wouldn't have any trouble with the insertion. I told Looney to cut the gunships loose and pass the word that we would be moving in ten minutes. I crawled over to Chambers and checked the map and compass heading that I wanted him to follow. I told him to stay in the tall brush as much as he could, and still keep on the general azimuth we had plotted. When it was time to move, I put Chambers on point and let Meszaros walk his slack. We got in a file, with Snuffy bringing up the rear, and started toward the trail. We had to go four hundred meters to reach the target, and in some places, we were on our hands and knees so we would be hidden as we worked our way over to the trail.

When we got close to the trail, I stopped the team and set up another defensive position. I told Smitty I would take Chambers and Looney and recon forward to the trail to look for an ambush site. We only had to move fifty meters to hit the trail. I got down on my hands and knees and crawled to the edge of the trail, which was covered with signs of recent foot traffic. The pattern of prints went both ways so I knew we had hit pay dirt. I got Chambers to come forward to see the trail. We had come out at a section of the trail that was straight for a couple of hundred meters, and we were on a slight rise. The terrain made a gentle slope away from my location, and the trail was worn into the side of the rise. We would be about a foot above the trail. The trail was five feet wide, and there wasn't a bit of cover on the far side. It was a clean kill zone and a great place for an ambush.

I had Chambers stand by the trail so I could see him while I went back twenty meters to make sure I had a clear fire zone. The brush was thick and went almost up to the trail. I wanted to set the claymores back a few feet to allow the blast to fan out for the best results. The team would need to be at least ten meters back from the claymore to keep from being hit by the backblast. I had to move back toward the trail until I could see Chambers, but I felt I had the safety margin I needed. I called Looney over to the position that I was lying in, and told him that he needed to set up there. Chambers and I moved toward the west flank of the ambush site to find the best location for the flank anchor team. I used engineer's tape to mark the spots where I wanted the two-man groups to set up their positions. I had Looney call Snuffy on the radio to let him know I would need a few minutes to do the site setup.

When I finished working on the layout, Chambers and I went back to Looney's position. I had Chambers go back and get the rest of the team. I told Looney to go forward and set out two claymores and arm them. He would be the security while I put the men in their positions. When Chambers got back with the team, I got with Smith and told him to pick his spot for the rear guard. I wanted him and his RTO to set out their four claymores to give me all of the rear cover he could. I told him to call Looney as soon as he was set up. I got Meszaros and Saenz and took them to the west flank position. I expected the enemy to come from that direction, and I wanted two good men to anchor that flank. I made sure that Saenz knew to keep his radio on the TOC frequency, and that I expected them to stay alert. I was counting on them to help compensate for the poor visibility we had because of the thick brush. I went back and got James Schwartz and McCain to cover the east flank. When we had finished setting up, I had five two-man positions on the ambush line, and a two-man rear security element set out. In each position, the men set out two claymores next to the trail. No one was allowed to set foot on the trail, and all of the brush was to be moved with care and returned to its original position. If the gooks came out on schedule, they would hit our area while it was still light, and I didn't want broken branches to tip our hand. I went to each man's position and checked the placement of the claymores. We were in good shape, and everyone was ready. I felt that we had a good setup.

Next, we had to set out the daisy chain to extend the kill zone. I got two claymore bags, the demo bag, my rifle, and told Chambers to get his claymores and the det cord; we were going to work. We started working on Meszaros's end of the ambush first. I set out the claymores at a twenty-five-foot interval so I would get an extra 150 feet of kill zone.

Chambers cut a fifteen-foot length of det cord and laid it with each claymore. When we laid out the five claymores, I had Chambers cut one more piece of cord, and I had Meszaros take the spool of det cord and run a double line of det cord back to his position. I reached into my pocket and pulled out a WP hand grenade. Chambers watched as I unscrewed the fuse and removed it from the grenade. I put the fuse in my pocket, and pulled out some C-4 explosive. I stuffed the C-4 in the fuse hole of the WP hand grenade, crimped a nonelectrical blasting cap on the det cord, and stuffed it in the fuse hole. I noticed that Chambers moved back when I pushed the blasting cap into the C-4. I laughed and told him if he wanted to be safe, he would need to move at least thirty meters. I tied the det cord from the grenade to the main line that Meszaros had strung out. Next, we moved back down the line to the first claymore, and I showed Chambers how to rig a blasting cap. I had him take a cap and slide it over the end of the det cord. Then I showed him where to put the crimpers on the cap so that when we crimped the cap the det cord would be held in the cap. The trick here was to crimp low enough to hold the cord without setting the cap off. I showed him how to keep the cord clear of his body so if he did set off the cap he would only lose a few fingers.

Chambers was a little slow with the caps, so I took over and let him arm the claymores and tie the firing line to the double main line. When we got back to Meszaros's location, I had Meszaros take two claymore firing devices and lay them out. I took the two caps and taped them on to the main firing line. I wanted a backup; if the first cap failed, then he could fire the second detonator. I was counting on the claymore extension to cover the kill zone, and I didn't want to leave anything to chance. I told Chambers that we could go do the other flank. He looked like he didn't want to be in the demolition business anymore, but he picked up the spool of det cord and followed me to the other end of the ambush. I finished setting up the daisy chains at 1600 hours, and we were ready for the prey. I had cut down the size of the kill zone, and placed the men closer together, so I would have better control over them.

I passed the word for everyone to eat dinner. We would have a cold meal that night, and I wanted all of the men finished eating and ready before 1730 hours. The team would be on 100 percent alert until 2100 hours, then we would go to 50 percent until 0430 hours. At 0430 hours, I would have the men back to 100 percent alert. I wouldn't let the gooks slip up on me again. This time, we would be ready and waiting. I hoped the gooks would come that evening before it got dark.

When 1730 hours came, everyone settled down and we got ready to wait for the enemy. Magazines were laid out within easy reach, and a couple of hand grenades, with the pins untaped and straightened out for easy removal, were also at hand. All of the radios were on the TOC frequency so I could check on the flank and rear elements. If we hit the gooks after dark, Smitty was to switch his radio to the artillery frequency and call in flares to illuminate the kill zone.

At 2100 hours, I stood the team down to 50 percent alert and told Looney that we would have a radio check every hour on the hour. If anyone failed to answer, he was to wake me. No sleeping beauties on this trip. The rest of the night was spent sleeping two hours and fighting the mosquitos for the two hours we were awake. At 0430 hours, I made sure we were back to 100 percent alert, and we spent a miserable four hours waiting for the NVA that never came. By 0830, I decided the gooks had taken the day off, and I let the men have a hot breakfast.

I went back to Snuffy's position, and we tried to figure out what had happened to the gooks. I checked with both flank men, and I was sure they hadn't let anyone slip by. I crawled up to the trail and looked to see if there had been any new tracks made during the night. Finally, I decided we just didn't have any visitors go by during the night. I told Smith I was going to take a recon up the trail to see if I could find out why the gooks weren't using it. Smitty said after the last chewing out he got because of me, I wasn't getting out of his sight. I laughed and told him that I would take two other men with me, and I promised to stay within sight of the trail. It took me a while to see that he was serious, so I had his radioman call the TOC and got permission to make the recon. Once the Old Man okayed the trip, Smitty was happy. I sure couldn't blame him; after all, I did get him in trouble on the other mission.

I went back to my position, told Looney that I was going to do a little recon, but that I would be back in a couple of hours. I sat down, put on my Ho Chi Minhs, and pulled out my NVA khaki shirt. I went over to Chambers and told him to get ready to go on a recon with me. Then I went to the flank position to get Meszaros. In twenty minutes, we were ready to move out. We stayed in the brush, but we moved close to the trail. I wanted to be able to stop and check the trail as we moved to the west. We had to go five hundred meters to get to the old ambush site, and we took it slow. We stopped at the stream to see if there were any signs of recent activity. As we got closer to the ambush site, I heard a strange sound, but I just couldn't place it. We finally got to the area where the ambush had been sprung, and we could see the mounds where the bodies had been buried. We moved closer, and the smell hit us like a brick. It was so bad, it brought tears to my eyes, and my breakfast did a double flip. The gooks hadn't really buried the dead, they just covered the bodies with a thin layer of dirt. The sound I heard was louder and I realized the sound was made by the buzzing flies that covered the mounds. There was a trail around the bodies where the gooks had worn a new path, so I moved on up the trail and looked in the bomb crater. The Vietnamese woman was covered with dirt, but the pig we had tossed in the hole wasn't. I gagged on that one and decided we could end the recon. I could tell the gooks had used the trail for a few days after the ambush, but I bet they weren't using it now. It would be too demoralizing to have to keep passing the bodies every day. I told Chambers and Meszaros we would start back to the new ambush site, and there wasn't any hesitation on their part. Now I was sure that we didn't have any traffic on the trail that last night, and I was sure there wouldn't be any tonight either.

All the way back to the ambush site, I was formulating a new plan. When we got back, I had Smith come up to my position. When he got there, I had the map laid out and was studying the other trail in the AO. I told Snuffy what we had seen at the old ambush site and that I didn't think the gooks would be using that trail for a while. Then I told him I was thinking about splitting the team, and making a recon over to the other trail. I would leave him with six other men to cover the ambush site. He would have one man in each position from 1600 hours until 2100 hours, then he would pull the team back to the real security area to spend the night. The next morning at 0530 hours, they would move back to the ambush site and man the claymores. If any gooks came by, it would be during those times, and I didn't expect many people would use the trail. As long as he didn't jump a large group, he would have enough firepower to cover his butt. I would take a small force over to the other trail to see if there was any activity. We would spend the night and monitor the trail. If the gooks were using that trail, we would come back over, take that ambush apart, move the whole team over to the new site, and set up a new ambush on that trail. Every claymore we owned was set up in the extended ambush, so we couldn't cover both trails. Smith liked the plan, so we got on the radio and called the TOC. I went over the problem and the solution with the CO, and he felt that it would work. As soon as I got his approval, I started to pick my men.

I would take Looney because he was my regular RTO, and I could count on him. I decided to take Meszaros and Chambers; they were both experienced and had been with me plenty of times. I wanted one more radio, and I started to take Saenz, but I changed my mind and picked McCain to go instead. Smith was happy with the split, and he had plenty of good men, just in case. I told my people to get ready to leave in thirty minutes. I decided to stay out of the jungle and to move at the edge of the tree line. There were a lot of cuts and valleys I could use to conceal the team. As long as I followed the contours and avoided ridges, we would be fine. I needed to get to the other trail as fast and as quietly as I could. Moving in the open had some risk, but I knew we would be okay. I got Chambers and showed him the path I wanted him to take. We got a general compass heading, and I told him to play it by ear but I wanted to be at the other trail by 1600 hours. I had Looney call the TOC to let them know we were moving out. When the call was completed, I signaled Chambers, and we moved across the trail and disappeared into the brush.

Chambers was moving at a fast pace, but he was following the contours as I had instructed him to. I didn't want us to be silhouetted by crossing a ridge, so we went to great lengths to work our way around those areas. I pushed the team and didn't take a break for the first two hours. When we stopped for our break, the men took up firing positions while Chambers and I worked out our location. I was pleased at our progress; we were well over halfway there, and the time was working out just fine. I told Looney to call Snuffy and let him know our location. I had John tell him we had an estimated time of arrival at the ambush site of 1500 hours. I pulled out my canteen, washed down two salt tablets, and lit up a cigarette while Chambers and I studied the map. Our trail entered the jungle from an open area. The jungle made a large L in that area, and the trail went in at the angle made by the junction of the base and the back of the letter. There was a finger with heavy woods on it that hooked out of the base on the L and made a crescent back out toward the open area. I told Chambers I wanted to hit the tip of the crescent out near the open area. There was plenty of cover, and we could see the whole trail yet be far enough away to avoid detection. We shot an azimuth to the point, and Chambers studied the terrain on the map to pick the best path. We sat for a few minutes, and I asked Chambers if he was ready to go. He looked over and said, "Waiting for you, old dude."

I got to my feet and told him to move out. We kept pushing, and I believe Chambers had some bird dog in him because we came right in on the back side of the finger out at the tip. We slipped into the wood line and set up a position to drop our gear. I told Larry that he did a great job of hitting the target and I was proud of him. I had Looney call Smith to let him know we were in position; the TOC monitored the radio, so they would also know. We sat down for a while to catch our breath. I normally didn't push that hard to get anywhere except the mess hall. I looked at my watch; it was almost 1500 hours. I told Chambers we needed to take a look at the trail for signs of foot traffic. When he asked about the gooks, I told him it was too early for them to come out. The gooks didn't get this far up the trail until late. He was going to put on his Ho Chi Minhs, but I told him we didn't have the time. McCain asked if he could go with us, and I told him I didn't see any problem with that, just as long as he stayed out of the way. We dropped our LBE and just took our rifle and one bandolier of ammo. I told Looney and Meszaros to hold the fort; we would be back in a few minutes. As soon as everyone was ready, we slipped out of the back of the wood line and headed for the trail.

We walked along the back side of the ridgeline to keep us blocked out of sight from the main woodline. Our position was on top of the ridge, and the terrain fell away down a gentle slope to the far wood line. We hit the trail out near a dead tree, and checked for footprints. I didn't see any signs of foot traffic at that point, so I decided to move closer to where the trail went into the jungle. We flanked the trail and spread out a little as we approached the junction of the wood lines. We started into the jungle on the trail, and had moved twenty feet when we spotted a grave, which I figured was for the two gooks we had killed there a few months before. I signaled McCain to hold up, and flagged Chambers forward. Larry was on the trail side of the grave, and I was on the jungle side. I was looking down at the grave as we moved forward. Chambers was two feet ahead of me, and out of my peripheral vision, I saw him stop. I looked up to ask him what the problem was, but I never got the question out. Chamber's eyes were as big as dinner plates and he was mouthing out the word "Gooks," and pointing in front of him. I looked over, and my heart stopped. Two NVA, in uniform, were squatting by the trail. One man had his back to us and was talking to the other man who, head down, was eating a bowl of rice with chopsticks. With both face and hand signs, I signaled Chambers not to fire. I could tell Chambers had it under control. I signaled him with my hand to pull back real slow. We backed out of the woods, and I bumped into McCain. He could tell something was wrong, and he didn't say a word. Once we were out of the woods, I whispered to Chambers for him and McCain to go back toward our team position. I would cover them. He was to stop by the fallen tree, halfway back, and cover me until I could link up with them. We would leapfrog back to the team's location. If the gooks came out of the woods while we were moving, the cover man would open fire to help us escape.

Looney and Meszaros noted our quick departure from the wood line and our leapfrogging movement back toward them, and took up fire positions to cover us. When Chambers and McCain stopped behind the log, it was my turn to move back. As I crossed the open ground toward the log, I could feel a gun barrel pointed at my back. I guessed it had to be at least a 155mm. It felt like it took me a week to get to the log, and we were only halfway back. We were moving through grass that was ankle deep, and didn't provide an ounce of cover. I took up a firing position behind the log and told Chambers and McCain to get to the wood line. While they ran up the slope to the woods, I kept the jungle covered. When it was my turn to go I looked at the jungle, and then I looked at the tree line. I thought this was it, and I took off with a burst of speed that would have done Jesse Owens proud. I ran all over Looney when I hit the wood line. I just collapsed, and Looney could tell by the look on my face and Chambers's face we had seen the devil. I was trying to figure out why Chambers and I were still alive when Meszaros brought me back to reality by asking us what had happened. McCain still didn't know what we had seen, and it took Chambers and me a minute to collect our thoughts.

Chambers and I were rattled. We were just lucky we weren't the only sloppy GIs in the jungle that day. I let Chambers tell the story while I thought about a course of action. I got the team settled down, then moved Chambers to a position where he could watch the wood line. I moved the rest of the team to the back side of our woods, and had Meszaros move out to a position on the right flank to keep anyone from slipping up on us from the jungle. I told Looney to call the TOC and alert the Old Man that we had found some NVA and we had them under surveillance. The CO asked if we were in contact, and John told him that we weren't. We had spotted them first, and I felt that we went undetected. I had Looney tell him that I wanted to ambush them in the morning. I decided that the thing to do was have Smith take the extended ambush apart and move to the new ambush site that night. We had enough daylight left, and I could send out guides to get Snuffy here fast. I had Looney call Smith, who wasn't happy about taking my ambush apart, and he had a right to be; he didn't know how I had it set up. He was also worried about carrying about one hundred feet of det cord with the nonelectrical blasting caps still attached. Caps are touchy, and in the heat, a slight jar could set one off. I didn't have caps for a new ambush, so he couldn't cut them off. We were talking all this over when Chambers came over and said I needed to go with him. I told Looney to help Snuffy get that ambush apart and over to the new site; we needed it to kill some gooks.

I followed Chambers back to his location, and he told me to take a peek. I looked out of the brush right at an NVA officer who was looking at me with binoculars. Three of them were standing at the trail junction of the L. The man with the binoculars had on an NVA uniform with short pants. He wore a hat, and a K-50 was hanging by his side. He was pointing at the trail we had left in the grass, and talking with the other men. I was mentally kicking myself in the butt over those trails in the grass. We couldn't have helped making them, but they were arrows right to our location. We watched the gooks for a minute or two, and tried to decide whether they had spotted us, or if they knew how fresh the trails were. I told Chambers to stay there and watch the gooks. I was going back to call the Old Man to let him know we could be in real trouble. I made sure that Chambers knew to come get me if the gooks did anything.

I walked back to Looney and told him to forget Smith; we had a problem. When Looney ended the radio conversation with Smith, I told John that the gooks had found our trail and were looking at our location. I had him call the TOC and alert the Old Man that we might be in contact, and request that the gunships be put on alert. I wasn't really sure that the gooks knew we were around, and I didn't want choppers flying around to confirm their suspicions. Looney and I were talking when Chambers came back over. When I saw him coming, I knew this day was going downhill fast. Chambers was excited and told me to, "Come here, quick." I went back to his position and took another peek.

The gooks were still at the L, and the one who was obviously the leader was pointing and making arm motions while the other two watched. I knew I was getting ready to earn my sixty-five dollars a month combat pay. Chambers asked me what they were doing, and I explained to him that the leader was deploying his men to catch us in an L-shaped firing pattern. We looked, and could see men moving in both wood lines; the woods to our front and the wood line on the left flank. I was watching the command group when Chambers said, "Look at the four men down there on the far left flank." I looked where he was pointing and saw four NVA soldiers getting ready to come out of the wood line. I told Chambers they were going to try to get behind us, start shooting, and make us move out of this cover and into the kill zone of the L. We watched as they started to put on camouflaged capes made from an American heavy-drop cargo parachute. We could tell by the fact that they had special camouflage capes that this wasn't some bush-league unit. I told Chambers we had some time, and for him to keep an eye on the recon group while I went back to talk with Looney.

I told Looney to call the CO. We were in contact, and I needed the gunships now. I showed him where the gook recon team was and how they were trying to flank us. I told McCain to go get Meszaros back in from the right flank. While McCain was gone, I told Looney that Chambers and I were going to fire up the gooks. I told John that when the firing started, he was to take the rest of the team down the back side of the ridge we were on, cross the elephant grass down in the low area, and get the team to the hilltop behind us, out in the open area. I had decided I wasn't going to stay in the woods with gooks trying to surround us. I wanted the NVA to have to cross some open ground to attack us so I could use the gunships and artillery to help even out the odds. I felt we were up against an NVA infantry company, which made it somewhere between 137 and 185 of them, and five of us. McCain and Meszaros came back, and Looney told me he understood what I wanted him to do. Looney was talking on the radio when I slipped on my rucksack and went back to Chambers' position.

When I got back to Chambers' position, he had his pack on and was ready to go. I checked my rifle. I had two magazines taped together, so when the first was empty, all I had to do was hit the release and flip the magazine for a quick reload. The first magazine in the weapon had eighteen rounds, ten rounds of tracer and then every other round was ball ammo. The magazine that was taped to it had eighteen rounds, of which every other round was a tracer. The taped magazines made reloading easy, and the tracers were good for the initial firing; they helped mark the target, and had a great psychological affect on both the enemy and us. I tapped the bottom of the magazine to make sure it was seated. I gave Chambers a quick rundown of the plan. We would step out of the wood line and kill the four gooks that were trying to flank us. I made sure he understood that I wanted him to fire from the shoulder and aim his fire. I told him that after we dropped the four gooks, we would pivot and take the wood line under fire to cover the team's withdrawal. I would fire from the L to the right and cover the front wood line. He would go from the L down the left flank to the bodies. When we finished with the wood line, we would sky up and join the team on the hill behind us. He told me he understood everything he was to do.

The four NVA had left the wood line and were moving toward us. They were still bunched together. I reached down, opened the front ammo pouch on my LBE, and pulled the string on the bottom of one magazine to make sure it would come out. I looked over at Chambers and said, "You ready?" He told me he was as ready as he would ever be, and I said, "Then, let's do it." We stepped out of the wood line, and I aimed my rifle at the approaching NVA. I started low and walked my fire right up to the cluster of troops. I could see the tracers arch toward them, and watched the camouflaged capes they were wearing flap out behind them as the rounds passed through their bodies. As they started to fall, I lowered my fire and took them all the way to the ground. Chambers and I both dumped a magazine each into the four men. With the tracers, there wasn't any doubt that we hit the target. I hit the magazine release button and flipped the new magazine into the gun. My hand went up, hit the bolt release, and I pivoted toward the wood line.

Before the firing started, Looney called the TOC, reported us in contact, and asked for the gunships. John was always cool under fire, and this time it worked against us. The charge of quarters (CQ) was a new sergeant, and he alerted the helicopter pilots. As the pilots went down to the ships, he came out of the TOC, and told them to forget it; we must be kidding. He said the radio operator was too calm to be in contact. The CO was coming out of the supply tent and heard the exchange. He blew his stack, and told the pilots to get their asses going; his men didn't kid. The CO ran up to the TOC to take charge, and ordered a UH-1D as his C & C ship. He needed to get out to our location and find out how much trouble we were in.

Looney had taken the rest of the team and was running down the hill when the Old Man called him on the radio. Looney didn't hear him calling, so the Old Man didn't have any idea of what was happening. Snuffy came up on the radio to confirm that he had heard our team report contact, and told the CO he could hear firing.

Chambers and I opened fire on the wood line, and the NVA returned the fire. I could see the muzzle flashes in the woods, and it looked like lights twinkling. The gooks at the junction of the L dove for cover as we swept the tree line with automatic-weapons fire. When my double magazine was empty, I hit the release, dropped the magazine on the ground, and slammed a new magazine into the weapon. I was working on the second magazine when a bullet from an NVA weapon hit a bush near me, and a limb flew over and hit me in the face. My brain, and the will to survive, took over from the macho side of me, and I grabbed Chambers. We spun around and showed the gooks lots of the shoe leather. We ran down the hill and caught up with the team, which was struggling to get through the elephant grass at the bottom of the hill. Chambers and I had a higher level of motivation than the rest of the men, and we passed them in the grass. I reached back and caught Looney by the pack strap and dragged him up the hill.

When we got to the top of the hill, we spread out in a semicircle around the crest and opened fire on the wood line. There wasn't a bit of cover on the hill, so we got down behind our rucksacks and made as small a target as possible. I made Looney get in the middle of the ring and told him to get on that radio and get me my gunships. Enemy rounds were zipping overhead, and Meszaros hollered that we were being flanked. Looney and Meszaros shifted fire to cover the exposed flank, while Chambers, McCain, and I worked the wood line. I heard the beat of rotor blades, and Looney shouted for me to pop a smoke for the gunships. I pulled a smoke grenade out of the pocket of my rucksack, pulled the pin, and tossed it back over my shoulder. The grenade landed right on Looney, and fell between him and the radio. I heard him holler and looked back. There was John, in a cloud of smoke, trying to drag the radio away from the smoke grenade. I heard him tell the pilots of the gunships that the smoke was us and everything else was NVA. Looney shouted up to me that the Cobras were going to take care of the flank first.

We had two Cobras on station; one ship was a heavy gunship, which meant it had four rocket pods and a 40mm grenade launcher in a nose turret. The other ship had two rocket pods and a 7.62mm minigun in the nose turret. The heavy ship made the first run, and the 2.7-inch rockets hit so close that dirt flew up and hit the team. I didn't know the gooks had gotten that close. The results of the Cobra fire were awesome. The 40mm rounds and the rockets were exploding, and the staccato fire of the minigun ripped the air. The second run was on the wood line, and the volume of enemy fire dropped. I let Looney direct the gunships, and he did a good job as the ships made pass after pass on the wood line. The Old Man joined the fray and called on the radio for a report. Looney brought me the radio, and I tried to fill the CO in on the action, but things were starting to get out of hand. I had the Old Man asking for a report on the contact; an artillery battery had come up on McCain's radio frequency to request a fire mission; the gunships were on station, and the gooks were still firing at us.

The CO asked me how I knew we were in contact with an NVA infantry unit, and that ticked me off. I wasn't some cherry, and I started to tell him to come down and see for himself. I was cursing to myself, and getting ready to answer him when Looney took the handset and asked for the Cobras to make another gun run. I think he could tell I was getting ready to get myself a court-martial. The gunships finished their run and called to tell us they were out of ammo and were heading for home. I had cooled down, so Looney handed me the handset, and I called the CO again. I told him we had seen ten enemy soldiers up close, and they all were in uniform and armed with AK-47s. I also explained that we had watched an officer deploy men on two flanks to try and trap our unit. Lastly, I told him the volume of fire that had been directed at us let me know it was more than a few porters in the woods. He rogered me back and told me an extraction ship was on the way.

The fire from the wood line had slacked off, and I had the time to give a fire mission to McCain to pass on to our artillery battery. The Old Man came back on the air, and told me that a National Guard artillery battery, new in country, wanted to fire a fire mission for us. They had a battery of 155mm guns, and it would be their first live-action fire mission. Looney looked at me and asked where I planned to fire that one. We knew we didn't want them firing close to us, so I gave them the coordinates for the steep-walled valley that I knew the trail went through. I decided that the NVA would pull back to their base camp and would have to go through that valley to get back. I also decided that the valley was far enough away to be safe.

Looney shouted to me that the extraction ship was in. I looked around and asked him, "Where's the chopper?" He told me they had landed at the bottom of the hill. When I asked him why it was way down there, he told me it was a hot LZ, and the chopper had taken fire on their approach. I told him to take the team down to the Huey, and Chambers and I would cover them. Looney, McCain, and Meszaros took off down the hill while Chambers and I fired one last magazine at the wood line. I shouted to Chambers to saddle up and grabbed my rucksack. I slung the pack on one shoulder, and Chambers and I took off down the hill. We were halfway to the ship when we saw a man jump off the helicopter and run up the hill toward us. The man was in regular jungle fatigues and carrying a CAR-15. Chambers and I grabbed the guy when he tried to get past us. It was one of the helicopter pilots we knew. I asked him where he was going, and he told me he was leaving country the next day, heard about the action, and had come out to shoot at the gooks. Chambers and I hooked him under the arms and dragged him back down the hill to the waiting chopper. We threw him in and piled on top of him until the ship cleared the ground. As the chopper climbed out, from the LZ, a line of green tracers followed us up. Our door gunner returned fire, and we sped away from the area.

I leaned back and lit a cigarette as I watched the Game Preserve fade into the horizon. My shirt was full of empty magazines, and when I checked my ammo pouches, I found I was down to my last three magazines. I tried to remember how long we had been in contact, and I didn't know. Looney told me that the Old Man had told Smith to blow the ambush and move out for extraction. We were heading in the opposite direction, so I didn't get to see my handy work, but later the Old Man told me it was a masterpiece as far as claymore ambushes went. My team went to the club and had a cold beer while we waited for Snuffy's group to come in. When the second extraction ship got back, we met them at the helipad, and the twelve of us had a welcome-home drink. It would be a few days before the closeness of our brush with disaster took hold and we realized we had cheated death once more.

The next day, I decided to write Larry Chambers and John Looney up for medals. I felt they had done great work, and should be rewarded in some way. I went to see the first sergeant to find out how it was done, because I had never put anyone in for a medal. He told me I needed to write up a recommendation for the type medal they should get, and a brief description of the action they performed to get the recommendation. I went back to my hooch and worked on the recommendation for a full day. I finally decided to put Looney in for the Army Commendation Medal with a *V* for valor. He had been so calm under fire, handled the gunships well, and took care of the flank problem quickly. I put Chambers in for a Bronze Star with *V* for valor. Chambers had handled the meeting in the wood line calmly and didn't panic. If he had opened fire on the gooks, we would never have gotten out of the woods alive. He was rock solid under fire and could be counted on to do the job he was told to do. Neither medal was a big deal, but I wanted them to know that their performance was above standard and that I appreciated their action. Chambers wrote to me after I got home and told me that both of them had been awarded their medals.

CHAPTER 12

"Well, boys, it's getting late, and I guess we had better wrap it up."

"Wait, Uncle John, I have one last question."

I looked over to my brother. "It's up to you, David."

He looked at the kids and said, "Well, it's Friday night, but only one more question, then off to bed for everyone."

I said, "Okay, but you'll have to put it on hold; I need to go to the bathroom and get another beer." I came back into the room, sat down, and told Jason to fire away with the question. "Uncle John, tell us how good it felt when you came home?"

I sat there with a funny look on my face, and David asked me if I was all right. I told him I was fine, but that this was just going to be a hard story to tell. I needed for him and the boys to understand that coming home had to be one of the worst times of my life. I thought about what to say and how to say it without getting upset. I remembered that I had made the statement that I was going to tell it like it was. This was it, put up or shut up, so I took a deep breath and started the story.

The morning of 16 December 1968, First Sergeant Fairrington called me to the orderly room. I went up expecting to get a warning order for another mission. Top called me in and told me division had called wanting to know where I was and why I hadn't showed up at Bien Hoa last week. I told him I didn't know I was supposed to be in Bien Hoa. He laughed and said that's okay because he didn't either. My 1049 request for an early out to attend college had been approved, but division rear forgot to cut the orders. I was leaving the next morning, and I needed to go get packed. I told the first sergeant I didn't want to leave. I wanted to extend my tour for six months and stay with the company. Top told me I had to go; it was too late to get anything changed. He walked around the desk, put his arm around my shoulder, and told me to go home. I had done all I could do, and my staying wouldn't change anything.

After the morning formation on the seventeenth was dismissed, everyone started to drift off to take care of their different details. I said my last round of good-byes to the men, picked up my gear, and walked up to the orderly room. First Sergeant Fairrington met me outside the door and told me to put my gear in the Old Man's jeep. Don Lynch would drive me over to the 17th Cav's orderly room to catch the truck to Phu Bai. He looked at me and said, "You're married aren't you, Burford?"

I told him that I was.

"Sarge, I'm going to tell you two things I have told married men who are going home from an overseas tour since the Korean War. First, you can't miss what you can't measure, so don't spend a lot of time worrying about what happened at home while you were away; just be glad that she is there when you get home. Second, a dime in the phone has saved many a home. Call before you go home, give your wife a chance to get ready for you to be back; if you just drop in, she may not be the only one surprised. Now, Sergeant Burford have a safe trip home." Then he went back into the orderly room.

When Don pulled up to the 17th Cav's orderly room, a young buck sergeant flagged us down and told me to get my gear on the truck; they were ready to go. I shook hands with Don, thanked him for the ride, and wished him the best for the rest of his tour. It was a dusty ride to the airfield at Phu Bai, but no one in that truck cared; we were going home. We drove parallel to the runway at the Phu Bai Air Base, and I watched as two F-4s, loaded with ordnance, blasted down the runway with their afterburners full on. I watched them lift off the strip and bank to the west, and I felt a twinge of guilt as I wondered who they were going out to rescue. We pulled up to a C-130, sitting on the loading ramp with its engines running. This was our bird back to Bien Hoa, and one hundred happy GIs lined up and marched up the open tailgate. We were packed in like sardines, but there was no gripes to be heard. We sat on the floor and held onto some cargo straps that were run across the airplane. The cargo door closed, and the plane taxied out to take off. We were held on the runway for a few minutes while a badly crippled aircraft made an emergency landing, and the temperature inside the plane just climbed on up. Then we felt the engines rev up, and we started to roll down the runway. We picked up speed, and the 130 leaped into the air. It took the air conditioner forty-five minutes to cool the cabin down. We had a cramped three-hour flight down to the 101st Division rear at Bien Hoa.

The division replacement company had been running at full steam since the first of December. The division was going through its first one-year cycle, and what was left of the old hands were going home. I was in the last batch to come out of the field, and the replacement people had out-processing down to a science. Some buses and a baggage truck pulled right up to the C-130. We walked off the airplane, threw our duffel bags on the truck, and boarded the buses. Our next stop would be the division out-process center on the other side of the air base.

The buses pulled up to a banner-draped parade field with SCREAMING EAGLES GOING HOME signs everywhere. We quickly unloaded and got into a formation. The next four hours were a whirl of activity. The first step was a roll call, and we were broken down to smaller groups. The group I was in went to the lecture first. We filled out some forms and were given a short speech about the things the army would do for us once we got home. We went back outside to pick up our duffel bags and march down to the supply area, where we turned in our field gear and moved over to the weapons cleaning area. There can be no greater torture than a trooper in a hurry having to clean a rifle good enough to turn in to a supply sergeant. My attempt at beating the system failed twice, but on the third try, the supply clerk took pity and accepted my weapon. I'm sure he saw the glint of murder in my eyes, and that helped him decide to show mercy. I walked out of the supply tent, and I felt naked. That M-16 had been a part of me; for the first time it hit me; it was over. Around 1700 hours, we had our last formation of the day, and we were assigned to hooches for the night. The replacement company commander told us that we would have a 0730-hours formation the next morning, and if we missed it, we would be held over to process with the next group coming through in four days.

We were free to go anywhere on base that night, so I hooked a ride with some MPs over to Company F, 51st LRRPs to see Don Harris. Don had transferred down to the 51st in early December, and I wanted to stop and say goodbye. The MPs took me to the company area, and I checked in at the guard post by the gate. I had to identify myself and fill out a form telling who I had come to see and why. The guard held me at the guard post until Harris could come out to identify me. The guard happened to be on Harris's team, so after he saw me and Harris hug and pound each other on the back, he signed me in.

The 51st LRRPs were attached to I Field Force, and they had an assigned strength of 250 men. In their company area, I felt like some hick relative down to visit the big city. They had barracks with concrete floors and real windows. Inside the barracks, they had regular army-issue bunks, with a mattress and sheets. Every man had a wall locker and a footlocker; it was just like the real army. We went inside the barracks and over to Harris's team section, and I got to meet his team leader and the rest of the men on his team. The real capper came when he told me the 51st LRRPs had its own helicopter unit assigned. The unit had four slicks and two of the new Cobra gunships. These guys sure did live better than their poor cousins up north, but lurps are lurps, no matter where they are, so we all sat down to have a beer and tell lies. The barracks soon filled with other troopers, and the beer flowed. We spent the night telling tales of close calls and the shared experiences that only the men who had been there could understand. I got a royal welcome and drunk as a cooter. At the end of the night, the boys of the 51st poured me in a jeep and had their duty driver take me back to the 101st Replacement Company.

O-five-thirty hours came with a vengeance reserved for those foolish people who get beer hangovers. I made it to the mess hall and choked down some army breakfast, which is the only known cure for a killer hangover. The 0730 formation was a breeze, and the rest of the morning was spent in getting our uniforms ready and our award ribbons put on straight. Many of us were told to get much needed haircuts, and no matter how we pleaded with the Vietnamese barbers, we got standard army-issue whitewalls. The formation that we had after lunch was to get assigned to buses for the trip to Long Binh for final processing and aircraft assignment. We lined up with our hand baggage and loaded the bus. The full impact of the bus ride hit me when they put an armed guard on the bus. Some of us wondered if he was there to protect us from the Vietnamese or the Vietnamese from us. None of the combat infantrymen took much comfort from the fact that our guard didn't have a Combat Infantry Badge. We just hoped he knew how to load the rifle. The trip to Long Binh was one uneventful hour, spent looking at dirt roads, rice paddies, and the passage of every type of transportation that could carry a Vietnamese.

Long Binh was another flurry of paperwork and the big shakedown. There were too many GIs bringing home the tools of the trade, and Uncle Sam was going to stop the flow of hand grenades, C-4 explosive, bombs, and bullets into the States. Souvenirs were regulated, and the weapons you could bring back had to be registered months in advance. Most of the weapons that got home were brought back by the REMFs, who traded something for them, and then had the time to get the paperwork done. We left our one khaki uniform in the barracks and took all the rest of our belongings down to the shakedown area. This place was a shed with long rows of tables, and we marched in and moved along to fill up all of the tables. Once we were in place, we were told to put all baggage up on the table and open it up. Next, the sergeant in charge gave a little speech about what was a no-no, and then announced a last-chance amnesty plan. All of the shakedown personnel would leave the shed for five minutes, and if we had any illegal items, we could place them in the no-questions-asked barrels located around the room. Upon the return of the shakedown crew, the inspection would start, and we were subject to legal action if contraband was found in our baggage. Then the NCOs left the shed, and the barrels filled up quickly. When they returned, the shakedown started. The sergeant going through my bag pulled up one lurp ration and asked me what it was for. I told him it was lunch, but he took it anyway. I believe he just wanted to get a good meal.

After the shakedown, our baggage was sealed, and we carried it out to load on the truck for the trip to the airport. Next, we headed back to the barracks to change into our khakis and get ready for the formation to get our airplane tickets. We were allowed to keep the one set of jungle fatigues and our jungle boots. Most of the REMFs threw them away, but I noticed that the infantrymen in our group kept theirs. At 1500 hours, we charged out of the barracks to load on the buses for the ride back to the Bien Hoa airfield. When we got to the airport, we unloaded and marched in a column of twos down to the loading gate. We had a one-hour wait for our freedom bird, but all 280 of us stayed there. No one would get out of line because he didn't want to lose his place.

The Northwest Orient DC-8 pulled up to the gate, and a cheer went up. I looked around and noticed that the few men who were wearing the Combat Infantrymen's Badge and infantry division patches like me, weren't cheering. Instead of cheering, we had a sad look, and a few even had misty eyes. I was feeling very guilty about leaving my men and going home before the job was done. One part of me said, "Go home," another part said, "Stay—they need you." The door to the airplane opened, and the load of new men filed down the stairway and into the gate area, pale white kids with bewildered looks on their faces. They didn't look left or right as they filed by us. The REMFs started to make catcalls and holler, "You'll be sorry." Those of us who were infantrymen just stood in silence, and while we looked at the new men, we didn't really see them; we didn't want to know them because we knew some of them would never come home.

Now it was our turn, so we headed up the steps and scrambled for seats. The stewardess got us settled in quickly while the pilot took the plane out to the runway. It was real; we were going home. The civilian flight crews didn't like to stay on the ground in Vietnam, so we had no delay in getting airborne. A low cheer went up as the plane rolled down the runway, rotated up, and gained altitude. It was an eighteen-hour flight back to the World, but no one was counting.

We made one stop in Okinawa to change the flight crew, but we weren't allowed to leave the plane. The stewardesses treated us like royalty, and they hovered over us all of the time. The whole flight home was movies and food, and every time you blinked, there was a stewardess with more food. I guess they were trying to fatten us up. I weighed 185 pounds when I left the States for Vietnam; coming home, I weighed 150 pounds.

The plane touched down at Travis Air Force Base around 1700 hours on 20 December 1968. We got off the airplane, and some of the men got down and kissed the ground. Our baggage was unloaded, and we went through a U.S. Customs inspection. I guess they felt we had been on an Asian shopping spree instead of fighting a war, but the rules were the rules. I filled out the customs forms and declared that I had nothing to declare. We processed through the regular customs inspection and loaded on the buses for the ride to the Oakland Army Terminal for our final processing.

We were supposed to go to Oakland, eat a good dinner, and get a full night's sleep, but the Christmas holidays changed that. The clerks at the terminal told us we could process that night or spend Christmas as the guest of Uncle Sam in the barracks at the terminal. We put it to a quick vote, and we set right into the processing. The first step was the complete medical checkup. It was the time to confirm service-related problems, but the medics made sure that we knew any complaint would require us to stay over until the problem was checked out. Unless it was obvious like the loss of a foot, or worse, there weren't any medical problems brought up. We were moved to a large hall and seated at desks to fill out mounds of paperwork for the administration people. The next stop was to draw winter uniforms and have them fitted. After the fitting, we headed back to the barracks area to take our showers and put on our old uniforms so we could go to the homecoming lecture. When the lecture was over, we went back and got our new uniforms, got dressed, and reported back to the lecture room to get our travel orders. After we received the orders, we were told to line up, alphabetically, by rank at the pay window.

At midnight, I got to the pay window and drew my final, $578.56, army pay. I counted my money, put the bills in my wallet, and followed the red arrows down a hallway and out a door. Outside was the gate house, and through the gate was a side street. I'll always remember that single light bulb shining over the gate. There wasn't anything out there, no bus, no cab, nothing, just an empty side street. None of us had any idea of where we were or how to get to the airport. On 13 December, my team had run into an NVA infantry company, and we almost got killed; seven days later, I am in Oakland, California, a civilian; my country is through with me, would I please go away. That blew my mind, but not as much as the shock that was waiting for me at the San Francisco airport.

Five of us walked up the street and finally flagged a cab for the trip to the airport. There was nothing the U.S. Army could have done to get us ready for the airport. The place was full of people. It was Saturday, December 21, about 2:00 A.M., and the holiday travelers were everywhere. I wasn't used to large crowds, and I felt crushed by all the people. The most overwhelming thing was the size of the antiwar feeling that blasted me from every direction. Peace signs and antiwar slogans were everywhere, and there was every size, shape, and description of hippy and some scummy-looking people hanging around. It looked like a world upside down. I knew that Alice would be by at any time.

I made my way toward the Delta Airlines counter, and I

passed a well-dressed young mother holding the hands of her two small children. She looked at my uniform, gave me a look of utter contempt, and spit right at my feet. It's a good thing she missed my boots or there would have been two orphans standing there. I don't believe those people understood some of us had short fuses; killing had lost its taboo, and we had no sense of humor. All the way to the ticket counter, I was the subject of hard looks and snide remarks.

I got to the Delta ticket counter and told the agent I'd like to get a flight to Atlanta. He shook his head and told me that all flights to Atlanta were booked up full through 26 December, due to the holidays. He told me that he could sell me a ticket now, and I would be able to go on military standby. He felt there was a good chance I could get out sooner than the twenty-sixth because there were always people who overbooked flights. While he wrote up my ticket, I noticed the other agent working the counter got some paper and started writing down a list of flight numbers. I paid the agent, and he handed me my ticket and a short list of all the flights to Atlanta. Beside each flight number was the gate number and the departure time. They told me I had to be at the gate at least one hour in advance of the flight and to turn my ticket into the gate agent. I would be put in the standby line, and if there were any "no-shows," we would be given their seat in the order we turned in our ticket. I thanked them; I could tell that both of the agents were really trying to help me get home.

It was a little after three in the morning in San Francisco, so it was only after 6:00 A.M. in Georgia. Even so, I decided to call home and tell my wife, Sandra, that I was back in the States, but that I was having trouble getting a flight home. I gave her the list of all the flights going to Atlanta and the flight I was booked on for the twenty-seventh. I explained to her how standby worked and told her that I would try to call and let her know if I got on an earlier flight. I looked at my list and saw the first flight was leaving at 0730 hours. I had three hours to kill before I had to be at the gate. I knew I couldn't sit down and sleep. I hadn't been in a bed in over forty-eight hours, and I would never wake up in time to get to the gate. Delta was using the gate for another flight, so there wasn't any room, and I knew they wouldn't like me to sleep in the gate area. I ended up walking around the airport for three hours, killing time until I could turn in my ticket.

I got to the gate at 0600, and five people were already in line for standby. When the agent got to the gate, fourteen people were waiting for standby. The airplane started boarding at 0700, and two standbys got seats. I looked at my list to see when and from which gate the next flight was leaving. I got to the gate one and a half hours early, and I was number eleven in the line. I spent the rest of Saturday and most of Sunday playing the standby gate shuffle. I got six hours of sleep in a chair in the main lobby of the airport. On Sunday, the twenty-second, I was number five in the line for the 1730-hours flight to Atlanta. The plane loaded, and the first four people in line got seats. I was getting up to leave, then they called my name. They had one more seat, and it was mine. I looked around for a phone but the stewardess was waving for me to come on, so I just dashed up the ramp. I was on a Delta DC-8 headed to Atlanta. The stewardess took me to a row with an empty center seat. I could tell by the dirty looks I got from the young lady by the window and the man with the end seat that they didn't want any company. I sat down and fastened my seat belt, and neither the man or the woman said one word to me for the whole trip. I was so wired, I couldn't go to sleep, so I just sat there in silence for the five-hour flight home.

The plane landed in Atlanta at 10:30 P.M. Sunday, and it seemed like it took a lifetime for the plane to taxi to the gate. The airplane came to a stop, and everyone started to get ready to get off, but for some reason, I didn't feel like getting up. I was one of the last people to come down the ramp, and the waiting area was almost empty. I stopped at the doorway to the waiting area, and I looked all around. I don't know why I did, but I guess I expected to see a banner saying WELCOME HOME, JOHN BURFORD, or my wife, or mother, or brother. God, I wished someone, anyone, had been there to welcome me home. I walked on down to the baggage claim in the main terminal, got my duffel bag, and went looking for a phone.

I called home and woke Sandra up. I told her that I was at the Atlanta airport and asked her to come pick me up. We lived in Marietta, and it was about an hour-and-a-half drive from the house to the airport. It was a Sunday night in Atlanta, Georgia, during 1968, and the bars in the airport were closed. I was feeling down and couldn't even get a drink. I walked around the main terminal to kill time for an hour or so, and then I went to the passenger pickup area to wait for Sandra.

I stood there in the waiting area, just looking out the glass doors, and I let my mind wander. I stood there for a while, and I was watching a stewardess walk out of the building when a woman walked up to me. I looked right at the woman a full minute before I recognized her. My wife, Sandra, had walked up to me, and I didn't even know her. She had contact lenses, and a different hair style, and she just didn't look the way I expected. I believe all of the men in Vietnam let their thoughts of home drift off to a fantasy world as a defense mechanism to help us through the war. Everything would be so great when we got home. All wrongs would be righted, and everyone would live happily ever after in a world that worked just the way we dreamed it would every day we were in Vietnam. The strange sound I heard when I saw Sandra was the bubble popping. It was a very cool meeting, and I could sense something was wrong. She ask me if I had enjoyed watching that girl walk out the door. I just picked up my bags and said, "Let's go home." We walked to the car, and I asked her to drive back to the house because it had been a while for me, and I didn't feel like driving home. The trip was very quiet, and there was very little talk. I was hoping there would be some kind of a homecoming for me at the house. I thought Sandra might have called my family and told them to come over. I was somewhat let down when we pulled up to a dark house.

I got my bags out of the car while Sandra opened the door to let me in. I walked in the front door and was surprised to find a coffee table in the middle of the entrance way, with a lamp sitting on it. The lamp was on, and lying on the table was an eight-by-ten, glossy, black-and-white picture of a girl from Fort Campbell, Kentucky. Fort Campbell had been my last duty station before going to Vietnam.

This was a professional picture that had been done by a studio photographer, and the girl was in a long evening dress. The picture was signed, "Good luck in Vietnam, and I wish you a safe return." The girl in the picture was a car hop at a burger joint outside gate number four at Fort Campbell, and she'd had the pictures made to give to her customers. She had worked there since 1965 and had seen more GIs off to war then most any other person in America. She had over thirty pen pals at any given time, and wrote them all. She passed out hundreds of pictures over the years. I went out there a lot for lunch, and she gave me a picture.

The picture had been mixed in with some papers that I had put in a footlocker in the basement when I left for Vietnam. I had been in my house less than five minutes, and there was my wife demanding to know who that "whore" was and why I had her picture. I didn't say a word, I just picked up the picture and walked down the stairs to the basement. The footlocker had been pulled out to the middle of the floor. I opened the locker, and it was in shambles; my papers were scattered, packages were open, and everything had been searched. I remembered a letter from Sandra in which she had asked about the locker, and I had written back that it was full of personal papers. I told her we would look at it when I got home. I sat in the basement for a half hour then went upstairs and asked Sandra why she had opened the locker. She said her mother had found it and asked her what was in it, that they'd eventually looked in it to see if there were any papers she would need for the insurance in case I didn't get back. I just looked at her and walked back to the bedroom and went to bed. The next day things between Sandra and me weren't any better; I had never felt so betrayed in my life.

Christmas was a mess; I didn't get to shop, so there weren't any gifts. My mother came by, and David and

Debbie stopped in, but no one talked much, and everyone seemed in a big hurry to get away from me. I didn't know what to do. What do you say to someone who just came home from the TV war. I missed my men, and I missed the war. Slowly, I began to understand the saying "When you're there, you want to be home; and when your're home you want to be back there." I got depressed, and the guilty feeling I had about leaving my team, my men, and my life, just got stronger.

The week between Christmas and New Year's, Sandra was off from work, and it was a very strained week, filled with more surprises. I had gotten a two-month early out from the army to go back to college. As part of the deal, I had to attend at least the first quarter full-time. I had figured it down real close. I had ninety days from the time I got out of the army to reclaim my job at Lockheed. As long as I reported for work in ninety days, they had to give me my old job back. I decided I could go the first quarter without having to go back to work. It would be close, but I needed the time to regain my study habits, and I had to pass all of the courses. I had sent money home, and Sandra had worked at Lockheed while I was gone, so the finances should have worked out.

As I looked at the bills, I started to realize that the plan was out the window. Even though I had sent six hundred dollars a month home, there wasn't any money in the bank. I now had all of the credit cards you could get—Penny's, Rich's, Davison's, Bank Americard, and Master Charge, and they were all up to the limit. I looked at Sandra's Lockheed pay stubs, and I found very few that showed a full forty-hour work week; I found some pay stubs for fourteen hours out of a forty-hour week. The biggest blow was the two bills, marked paid, that I found, one for a nine-hundred-dollar living-room suite and one for an eleven-hundred-dollar dining-room suite.

The whole reason I had left my men in Vietnam early was to come home and go to school to try and build a good life for Sandra and me. Now all of that was gone. Just to survive, I'd have to go to school full-time, and go back to work at Lockheed full-time.

New Year's Eve came, and Sandra wanted to go out. I tried to explain that I didn't feel like going out, that my world was coming unglued; I felt betrayed at home, guilty for leaving my men in Vietnam, and I had only been out of combat seventeen days. Sandra and her two girlfriends, Pat and Dot, kept saying, "Let's go out," so I gave in and said okay. When I asked where we were going, Sandra said we would go to the NCO club at Dobbins Air Force Base.

As the night wore on, the drinks, noise, and the crowd were getting to me. I felt trapped, and everything was closing in around me. I had a strange feeling that I couldn't shake. I hadn't had very many drinks, but I didn't feel right. At the stroke of midnight, Sandra and I were dancing; the noise picked up, and some dumb jerk lit a string of fire crackers. The fire crackers went off, and so did I. I took out three tables getting to the floor; drinks went everywhere, and the band stopped. I was lying on the floor, soaked with the drinks I had knocked over, and a lot of people were standing around me. A few of the people were mad about their drinks, but most of those standing around were laughing at me. I just lay there on the floor, wishing I had my M-16! The master at arms came over, helped me up, and said I was too drunk to stay in the club. He asked me to leave. I didn't try to explain to him what had happened because I was ready to go anyway. Sandra and her friends were mad at me because we had to leave the club, and we didn't speak for the rest of the night. The next day I got up, took two aspirin, and I told Sandra we would be getting a divorce as soon as I could get enough money to rent an apartment.

I started school at Kennesaw Junior College on the sixth of January. Everyone I knew when I had been there two years earlier had graduated and moved on while I was in the army. The school was small, and it was only a two-year school, so there wasn't much antiwar fervor on campus. I could feel a lot of uneasiness in the people around me, but no one bothered me. There were a few other vets in school, but we didn't hang around together.

I started back to work at Lockheed on 14 January, and I went back on the night shift in a new department. All of my friends were in the old department in a building three miles away. I didn't know anyone in the new department, and it was depressing going to work that night. Two men I knew from my old job came by to see me. They had been in the Korean War, so they spent thirty minutes telling me how easy I had it in Vietnam. They had seen it all on TV, and we had it made. When I started to tell them about my unit in Vietnam, they had to leave. I was so alone it hurt, and I felt like I had a big hole in me; I was empty. I wished I was back in Vietnam with the people who wanted me and needed me. I missed the rush of combat, the responsibility, the honor. Now everything was gone. We got our lunch break at 7:30. I got my lunch bag, walked over to some crates, sat down, and pulled out a sandwich. It hit me all at once. This was it, this was all there was—WELCOME HOME, JOHN BURFORD, WELCOME HOME.

WHERE ARE THEY NOW

1. John Looney and his wife, Gail, live in Wheeling, WV. John works for the VA as a counselor.
2. Larry Chambers is a freelance writer and financial consultant living in Ojai, CA, with his daughter and son. He is the author of a book for the first time investor and another on his experiences in Vietnam (*Recondo*).
3. Don Harris, his wife, Jeannie, and their two sons live in Maryville, TN. Don is with the U.S. Postal Service.
4. Gordon "Snuffy" Smith and his wife, Eileen, live in Chandler, AZ. Gordy is a cardiovascular intensive care RN and is still serving in the Army reserve. Snuffy and his wife have four children, with number five on the way. Their oldest son is serving with the 82nd Airborne division.
5. R. C. Burnell is working in the Mid-East after retiring from the U.S. Army as Command Sergeant Major of the 18th Airborne Corp.
6. Ken Eklund is a self-employed insurance agent and freelance writer living in California.
7. John Meszaros lives with his wife and two sons in Tecumseh, MI. John is a computer instructor. He also teaches anthropology classes at Jackson Community College.
8. Kenn Miller lives in Los Angeles with his wife and two children. Kenn works as a translator and is the author of *Tiger the LURP Dog*. He is collaborating on a company history with Reynel Martinez and Gary Linderer.
9. Gary Linderer lives with his wife, Barbara, and their four sons in Festus, MO. Gary works in the field of in-

vestment and is a freelance author with two successful books on the subject of his time as a LRRP in Vietnam, *Eyes of the Eagle* and *Eyes Behind the Lines*, both from Ivy.

10. William T. Grant and his wife, Jackie, live in Virginia. WO5 Grant still drives a Huey for the army. There are rumors that it is the same one he flew in Vietnam. *Wings of the Eagle*, Mr. Grant's autobiographical account of his service in Vietnam, has just appeared from Ivy Books.

11. Larry Saenz lives in Sterling Heights, MI. Larry has his masters degree in education and is teaching special education. He is also a professional artist.

12. Don Lynch lives with his wife, Ann, and his two children Joshua and Marie in New Hope, MN. Don has been married for 23 years and has been working as a mechanical designer for the last eight years.

13. Joe Bielesch has his own heating and air business in Philadelphia, PA. He still has a great fondness for beer and life and will tell a war story on call.

GLOSSARY

A

Air burst—The above-ground explosion of an artillery round or bomb to increase shrapnel range to inflict maximum damage to exposed troops.

AK-47—Communist-made 7.62mm assault rifle. Primary individual weapon of the NVA.

AO—Area of operation. A geographically defined area where military operations are conducted.

ARA—Aerial rocket artillery. A term used for the helicopter gunships.

Arc light—A B-52 Bombing mission, using 750-pound bombs in a carpet bombing run.

Artillery fan—Area that is within range of supporting artillery.

ATL—Assistant team leader. The second in command on a combat team.

B

BDA—Bomb damage assessment. A mission to check the results of a bomb mission.

Berm—A high earthen levee surrounding most permanent U.S. military installations as part of their defense system.

Blasting cap—The device that initiates the actual detonation of an explosive charge.

Bush—Slang term for the jungle.

C
CAR-15—Short version of the M-16.

C-4—Plastique explosive.

CIB—Combat Infantryman Badge.

CID—Criminal investigation.

CO—Commanding officer.

Cammo stick—Dual-colored camouflage greasepaint in a metal tube.

Cav—Short term for cavalry.

Cherry—A new man in country.

Chicom—A term for Chinese Communist or an item of Chinese Communist manufacture.

Chopper—Slang term for a helicopter.

Claymore mine—A command-detonated antipersonnel mine that used C-4 to scatter 750 steel balls in a fifty-foot arc, five feet high.

Compromise—To be discovered by the enemy forces.

Concertina—Coiled barbed wire used to build perimeter defense fence.

Contact—Finding the enemy force.

D

Daisy chain—Using detonator cord to link explosive devices together for simultaneous detonation.

Det cord—Detonator cord. Fast-burning cord used to tie explosive devices together has a burn rate of 36,000 feet per second.

Dex tablet—Dextroamphetamine tablet used to prevent sleep, and could cause hallucinations.

E

Early out—Termination of military service prior to normal separation time.

E & E—Escape and evasion to avoid capture.

Extending—To prolong one's tour past the normal rotation time.

Extraction—The removal of troops from the field.

F

F-4 (Phantom)—The workhorse fighter-bomber of the Vietnam war.

FAC—Forward air controller. Directed air attacks on ground targets.

Firefight—A small-arms battle with enemy forces.

Fire mission—A directed firing of an artillery battery.

Free-fire zone—An area that was considered enemy held and could be fired on at any time.

G

G-2—A unit's intelligence section.

Gook—A derogatory name for a person of Oriental descent.

Gunship—Any armed aircraft used for close support of ground troops.

H

HE—High explosive. HE rounds were used against troops and light structures.

H & I fire—Harassment and interdiction fire. Preplotted artillery fire that was fired at random intervals to keep enemy on edge.

Halazone tablets—Used to purify water.

Heavy team—A LRRP team of more than six men.

Ho Chi Minhs—A sandal made from a used tire.

Hooch—A slang term for any small building in Vietnam.

Hot—Term used to describe an area where there is enemy contact.

Huey—A slang term for the UH-1 family of helicopters.

I

I Corps—Northernmost military district in Vietnam.

Insertion—A term used to denote the placement of a team in an AO.

J

Jungle penetrator—A metal cylinder with fold-out legs that was lowered from a hovering helicopter to extract wounded men in thick jungle.

K

KIA—Killed in action.

Kill zone—The target area of an ambush.

Klick—A kilometer, one thousand meters.

L
LBE—Load bearing equipment: pistol belt and harness.

LOH—Light observation helicopter.

LRRP—Long-range reconnaissance patrol.

LZ—Helicopter landing zone.

Lay dog—Holding your position after insertion, to wait and listen for signs of enemy activity.

Lock 'n' load—To chamber a round in a weapon.

M
M-16—Standard infantry weapon during the Vietnam war: 5.56mm light automatic weapon.

M-60—Standard platoon machine gun, 7.62mm, belt fed.

M-79—Shoulder-fired 40mm grenade launcher that loaded like a single-barrel shotgun.

MIA—Missing in action.

MPC—Military payment certificate issued to American forces.

McGuire rig—120-foot rope dropped to extract men in thick jungle.

Medevac—The medical evacuation of wounded men.

N
NVA—North Vietnamese Army.

O

Overflight—Aerial scouting of an AO to pick the landing zone and extraction point.

P

Prc-25—Man-portable backpack radio used by troops in Vietnam.

Pink team—Hunter-killer team of one LOH-6 and two Cobra gunships that scouted free-fire zones.

Point man—The first man in a file, who scouts ahead.

Pull pitch—Helicopter term meaning to take off.

Push—A slang term for the radio frequency used by the team.

R

RPG—Communist-made rocket launcher that fired a 3.5-inch B-40 rocket. Effective against armor and fortifications.

R & R—Rest and recreation leave given to men in combat zones.

RTO—Radiotelephone operator, or the radioman.

Rappel—The use of a rope to make a controlled descent from a high place.

Reaction force—A unit established to respond quickly to a request for help.

Recondo School—A training program used to teach small-unit reconnaissance skills.

Rock 'n' roll—Slang term for automatic fire with M-16.

S

SERTS—Screaming Eagle Replacement Training School.

SOI—Signal operating instructions: the book of call signs and radio frequencies.

Sapper—Specially trained enemy who could be used as an engineer, or for special missions.

Selector switch—Three-position device that set the M-16 on safe, semiautomatic, or automatic fire. Not designed for southpaws.

Short-timer—A person with less than sixty days left in country.

Sitrep—Situation report made by field unit to the command group on a regular schedule.

Six—Radio call sign for unit leader.

Slack—The second position in the file. The man who covers an exposed man like the point man.

Slick—Slang term for UH-1 that is unarmed.

Stand down—Return to a base camp to rest and rearm.

T

TL—Team leader.

TOC—Tactical operations center.

Tracer—Ammunition containing a chemical composition to mark the flight of the round by a trail of fire.

W

WIA—Wounded in action.

WP—White phosphorus ammunition used to mark a location or start a fire.

Wait-a-minute vine—Very strong vine with curved thorns that caught clothing and made movement difficult.

Warning order—The first alert that a team was to prepare for a mission.